Florida's Other Courts

Florida Government and Politics

UNIVERSITY PRESS OF FLORIDA

Florida A&M University, Tallahassee
Florida Atlantic University, Boca Raton
Florida Gulf Coast University, Ft. Myers
Florida International University, Miami
Florida State University, Tallahassee
New College of Florida, Sarasota
University of Central Florida, Orlando
University of Florida, Gainesville
University of North Florida, Jacksonville
University of South Florida, Tampa
University of West Florida, Pensacola

FLORIDA'S OTHER COURTS

Unconventional Justice in the Sunshine State

Edited by Robert M. Jarvis

Foreword by David R. Colburn and Susan A. MacManus

UNIVERSITY PRESS OF FLORIDA

Gainesville / Tallahassee / Tampa / Boca Raton

Pensacola / Orlando / Miami / Jacksonville / Ft. Myers / Sarasota

Printed in the United States of America on acid-free paper

This book may be available in an electronic edition.

23 22 21 20 19 18 6 5 4 3 2 1

Library of Congress Cataloging-in-Publication Data
Names: Jarvis, Robert M., 1959– editor. | Colburn, David R., author of foreword. | MacManus, Susan A., author of foreword.
Title: Florida's other courts : unconventional justice in the Sunshine State / edited by Robert M. Jarvis ; foreword by David R. Colburn and Susan A. MacManus.
Other titles: Florida government and politics.
Description: Gainesville : University Press of Florida, 2018. | Series: Florida government and politics | Includes index.
Identifiers: LCCN 2017032245 | ISBN 9780813056685 (cloth : alk. paper)
Subjects: LCSH: Courts—Florida—History. | Courts of special jurisdiction—Florida—History.
Classification: LCC KFF510 .F576 2018 | DDC 347.759/01—dc23
LC record available at https://lccn.loc.gov/2017032245

The University Press of Florida is the scholarly publishing agency for the State University System of Florida, comprising Florida A&M University, Florida Atlantic University, Florida Gulf Coast University, Florida International University, Florida State University, New College of Florida, University of Central Florida, University of Florida, University of North Florida, University of South Florida, and University of West Florida.

University Press of Florida
15 Northwest 15th Street
Gainesville, FL 32611-2079
http://upress.ufl.edu

Contents

List of Figures vii
Foreword ix
Preface xiii

Introduction 1
James M. Denham

PART I. GENERAL JURISDICTION COURTS

1. Spanish Courts 9
M.C. Mirow
2. British Courts 28
Robert M. Jarvis
3. Territorial Courts 43
Christopher A. Vallandingham
4. Confederate Courts 77
Robert W. Lee

PART II. SPECIAL JURISDICTION COURTS

5. Military Courts 89
David J.R. Frakt
6. Religious Courts 110
Donna Litman
7. Black Courts 143
Ernesto A. Longa
8. Indian Courts 166
Tonya Kowalski and Robert M. Jarvis

About the Contributors 199
Index of Cases 201
General Index 205

Figures

1. Pedro Menéndez de Avilés 10
2. James Grant and George Johnstone 31
3. William P. DuVal 52
4. Jesse J. Finley 79
5. U.S. Court of Appeals for the Armed Forces 101
6. Reverend Monsignor Gregory C. Wielunski 113
7. Lawson E. Thomas with black police officers 143
8. Seminole Tribe of Florida Chairman James E. Billie swearing in Willie Johns as Chief Justice 177

Foreword

Florida has held a unique place in the American mind for over six decades. For many retirees, its environment has been like a healthy elixir that allowed them to live longer and more active lives; for others, it served as a place of renewal where all things were possible; and for immigrants, it offered political freedom and access to the American dream. Historian Gary Mormino described Florida as a "powerful symbol of renewal and regeneration." Others have suggested that, if Florida had not been accessible to Americans after World War II, they would have been much poorer for it. Those who have followed Florida politics and watched the 2000 presidential election unfold, however, wondered if that were in fact so.

During World War II, Americans from all walks of life discovered Florida through military service, and it opened their eyes to the postwar possibilities. With the end of the war in August 1945, Florida veterans returned home, where they were soon joined by hundreds and then thousands of Americans who were ready to pursue a new life in the Sunshine State. In the sixty years between 1945 and 2013, 18 million people moved to Florida, increasing the state's population to 19.5 million people in 2013 and making it the fourth largest state in the nation.

Florida's population growth, the settlement patterns of new residents, and their diversity had a profound effect on the state's place in the nation as well as the image Floridians had of themselves. Prior to 1940, Florida was the smallest state in the South and one of the poorest in the nation. Its society and economy were rural and agricultural, biracial and segregated. Most residents resided within forty miles of the Georgia border, and their culture and politics were consequently southern in orientation. Like its southern neighbors, Florida was a one-party state with the Democratic Party dominating politics from the end of Reconstruction in 1876 to 1970.

All that changed in the fifty years following World War II. In less than an average life span today, Florida became by 2013 the largest state in the region, soon to become the nation's third largest, a haven for seniors and foreign residents, and a dynamic multiracial and multiethnic state. Most Floridians now reside closer to the Caribbean than they do to Georgia, and, for most of them, their image of themselves and their state has changed dramatically to reflect this new geographic orientation.

As Florida changed, so too did its politics. Voters threw out the Constitution of 1885 in favor of a new document that would speak to the needs of a new state in 1968. They then gradually abandoned the Democratic Party in favor of a dynamic two-party system. By the 1990s, Republicans took their expanding constituency and their control of the redistricting process following the 1990 census to secure majorities in the state legislature and the congressional delegation. These were remarkable political developments and reflected the transformative changes in the state's population. However, in statewide races for governor, U.S. senator, and elected cabinet positions, as well as in presidential contests, Democrats remained competitive with their Republican counterparts, in large part because they held a 6 percent lead in registered voters (42 percent to 36 percent for Republicans).

Such a politically and demographically complex and diverse population has made Florida today something other than a unified whole. The political maxim that "All politics is local" is truer of Florida than most other states. For example, those who reside in north Florida share little in common with those living in central or south Florida and vice versa. While those residing in southeast Florida see themselves as part of the "new America," those in north Florida view Miami as a foreign country. Ask a resident what it means to be a Floridian and few, if any, can answer the question. Ask a Floridian about the state's history, and even fewer can tell you that it has operated under five different flags, or that its colonial period began much earlier than that of New England or Virginia. Perhaps one in ten or twenty can tell you who Democrat LeRoy Collins was, despite Republican Jeb Bush's acknowledgement of Collins as the model for all governors who followed him. It is literally a state unknown and indefinable to its people. Such historical ignorance and regional division become major obstacles when state leaders try to find consensus among voters and solutions that address the needs of the entire state.

An essential purpose of this series is to put Floridians in touch with their rich and diverse history and to enhance their understanding of the political developments that have reshaped their state, region, and nation. This series focuses on the Sunshine State's unique and fascinating political history and on public policy issues that have influenced the state and nation. The University Press of Florida is dedicated to producing high-quality books on these subjects. It is also committed to publishing shorter essays of twenty-five to fifty pages in this series that address some of the immediately pressing public policy issues confronting Florida. As part of this series, the University Press of Florida also welcomes book manuscripts on the region that examine critical political and policy developments that impacted Florida.

This edited volume, *Florida's Other Courts: Unconventional Justice in the Sunshine State*, compiled by Robert M. Jarvis of Nova Southeastern University, gives readers a fresh and engaging view of the evolution of the state's judicial system from pre-statehood days to the present. It focuses on the dispensation of justice by both general jurisdiction courts (Spanish, British, territorial, and Confederate) and special jurisdiction courts (military, religious, black, and Indian). The book's introduction by historian James M. Denham notes "the paucity of scholarship addressing courts lying outside the normal federal-state paradigm" prior to Jarvis's volume.

Individual chapters, written by legal experts, detail how the various courts emerged and transitioned over time. In-depth discussions of the "trials and tribulations" of minorities are a common thread tying the chapters together, as are struggles over court jurisdiction, qualifications and selection of judges and juries, and the age-old debate over punishment vs. rehabilitation. Difficulties plaguing the judicial system today were evident in the early courts—problems with ensuring speedy trials, securing the requisite number of jurors, insufficient jail space leading to limited sentencing options, and the forms of corporal and capital punishment. Land disputes were preeminent and commonplace in Florida's early history as were controversies over the separation of church and state. They remain so today.

Part 1, "General Jurisdiction Courts," chronologically traces the formation of legal entities charged with defining the principles of good and bad behavior and the dispensation of punishment from the 1500s through the Confederacy. For example, during the time Florida was a Spanish province (1513–1763, 1783–1821), M.C. Mirow describes a judicial system with no separation of powers. It was "a single government official, addressed as 'judge' by those coming before him, and sitting as a 'tribunal' during deliberations, [who] dispensed justice." Most often the territory's governor, a military man with no legal training, was the judge. Punishment ranged from "banishment, fines, and corporal punishment to imprisonment and involuntary servitude" and was often more severe for "blacks, Indians, and forced laborers." There was, however, some evidence of the existence of an early code of judicial conduct. Governors were subject to inquiries from higher authorities regarding alleged improper conduct.

The volume also highlights the state's history of regional divides and patronage battles. During the brief time of British control (1763–1783), Jarvis details the splitting of the territory into East Florida (capital St. Augustine) and West Florida (capital Pensacola). Each had its own governor and an independent judicial system, replicating that found in England—complete with appointed legal officers and a jury system, with petit and grand juries. The whole judicial system was tossed out when the Spanish again took control in 1783. But the regional divide continued to characterize the state's demographic and political makeup.

Another common theme is the preeminence of land disputes throughout Florida's history, along with perennial intergovernmental tensions between the federal government and the state—both well-documented in Christopher A. Vallandingham's chapter on territorial courts beginning in 1819 with the signing of the treaty transferring Florida to the U.S. Congress. The treaty authorized President Monroe to take possession of East and West Florida, but established no court system, leaving the territory's governor Andrew Jackson to assume "judicial powers previously vested in the Spanish officials in both East and West Florida." It was a long journey to purge the old from the new, replete with jurisdictional battles between Congress and local territorial leaders. Unfunded mandates were "a perpetual source of frustration for local officials"—as they still are today. Federal vs. state court jurisdictional authority battles were also evident during Florida's days as a Confederate state, as detailed by Robert W. Lee in his chapter, although the state's "legal philosophy remained closely tied to the United States."

The authors of the chapters in part 2, "Special Jurisdiction Courts," provide significant insights into judicial bodies holding authority, either historically or presently, over sizable and important subsets of Florida's population—members of the military (David J.R. Frakt), religious groups (Donna Litman), blacks—Miami's now defunct Negro Municipal Court (Ernesto A. Longa), and Native Americans, specifically the Seminole and Miccosukee Indian tribes (Tonya Kowalski and Jarvis). As noted by Denham, "These little-known entities reflect the needs and ethos of the communities that produced them . . . [yet] few outsiders know anything about them." Each chapter reflects the struggles to ensure justice for individuals, following the dictates of unique cultures with differing views of crime, punishment, and governance. These chapters are highly engaging and informative and likely to be used in classrooms throughout the state.

Florida's Other Courts is also an invaluable resource for legal scholars. It is a treasure trove of ideas for future research and places to go for primary source materials that have largely been untapped. Many of these are located in Cuba and are now more accessible to scholars. Others are in collections at the University of Florida, the Library of Congress, the St. Augustine Historical Society, and the State Archives. The notes section of each chapter is rich in detail and is as interesting to read as the text itself. It is a book that offers something for everyone interested in the interface between Florida's diverse peoples and its evolving judicial system.

David R. Colburn and Susan A. MacManus
Series Editors

Preface

During my Fall 2014 American Legal History seminar, a student brought to my attention Professor Ernesto A. Longa's article on the Miami Negro Municipal Court (published at 18 St. Thomas Law Review 125 [2005]). That happy discovery soon was joined by two others: Professor M.C. Mirow's essay on Florida's Spanish courts (55 American Journal of Legal History 89 [2015]) and Judge Robert W. Lee's study of Florida's confederate courts (15 St. Thomas Law Review 485 [2003]). Collectively, they became the impetus for this book.

Substantial praise is due to the University Press of Florida, particularly senior editor Sian Hunter and acquisitions assistant Ali N. Sundook. Their continuing support and interest has been most gratifying.

The research for this book closed on December 31, 2016. Because this is a work by lawyers, the endnotes follow *The Bluebook: A Uniform System of Citation* (20th ed. 2015) (https://www.legalbluebook.com/). Occasionally, we have deviated from it to improve readability.

Lastly, additional author information can be found in the section "About the Contributors."

Robert M. Jarvis

Introduction

JAMES M. DENHAM

This collection of essays profiles courts that adjudicated disputes in Florida during its time as a Spanish province (1513–1763, 1783–1821); as two British colonies (1763–83); as a U.S. territory (1821–45); and as a Confederate state (1861–65). It also examines the use of special jurisdiction tribunals by Florida's military, religious, black, and Indian communities.

Professor Robert M. Jarvis conceived this study due to the paucity of scholarship addressing courts lying outside the normal federal-state paradigm. As readers undoubtedly will agree, the contributors have done their work exceedingly well and have set a high standard for those who decide to undertake similar studies in their own jurisdictions.

Professor M.C. Mirow's lead-off essay points out that while Spain devoted considerable resources to its New World possessions, Florida almost always was considered a region of minor, albeit strategic, outposts. Thus, its system of justice never fully developed into the standard structures of Spanish colonial government. Military governors, occasionally assisted by legally trained advisors known as *asesores*, acted as judges. The question of whether local municipal officers—known as *alcaldes*—served as magistrates remains an open one.

Regardless, there were numerous tribunals in Spanish Florida. Litigants and officials recognized jurisdictional divisions and utilized distinct procedures for different kinds of cases, and criminal and civil matters were handled in ways consistent with Florida's membership in the colonial Spanish world.

In their administration of Florida, Spanish officials generated numerous documents. As Mirow notes, many of these have yet to be explored and remain waiting for researchers in archives in Cuba and Spain (and, increasingly, on the web).

When Great Britain obtained control of Florida in 1763, it divided Florida into two colonies (East and West) with capitals, respectively, at St. Augustine and Pensacola. As Jarvis notes in his chapter, British authorities empowered

Florida's governors to create tribunals styled after those in England, with all such arrangements being forwarded to the Board of Trade in London for approval.

Accordingly, courts of common pleas and general sessions were formed in both colonies, with a right to appeal (in most cases) to the Privy Council. During their short time in Florida, the British also introduced the jury system and the positions of chief justice and attorney general.

By the time the United States purchased Florida from Spain in 1821, the practice of substituting Anglo-American legal traditions for French or Spanish ones had become commonplace. Nevertheless, as Professor Christopher A. Vallandingham reports in his contribution, until Congress enacted legislation establishing the territorial government of Florida the area continued to operate under Spanish legal precedents. The opposition of Anglo settlers, coupled with Governor Andrew Jackson's arbitrary behavior, often caused disorder and uncertainty.

In an effort to place its new acquisition on a more stable legal footing, Congress passed the Florida Territorial Act (1822), specified the duties and responsibilities of local officials, and authorized two judicial districts (Eastern and Western). As time went on, three other districts were added (the Middle in 1824, Southern in 1828, and Apalachicola in 1838).

Superior court judges, selected by the president, served four-year terms. In addition to federal disputes, they heard criminal offenses under territorial law and civil matters in excess of $100. In 1823, Congress passed legislation setting up a court of appeals comprising the superior court judges, who sat together once a year.

Below the superior courts were the county courts. These entities had jurisdiction in matters involving $20-$100; they also handled various administrative tasks in their counties. To cope with this workload, governors were permitted to name up to three judges per county.

Until 1845, when it became elective, the territory's legislative council appointed multiple justices of the peace for each county. These officials adjudicated small disputes and could take evidence for use in trials throughout the territory. As the officials closest to the people, nearly every criminal act or disturbance was brought to them to determine whether the offending individual should be bound over for criminal prosecution. Justices of the peace also had the power to order arrests and set bail.

One of the most vexing problems facing the Florida territory was land ownership. Early on, Congress set up a board of three commissioners to settle Spanish title claims arising before January 24, 1818. This work eventually fell to the superior courts, with many cases being appealed to the U.S. Supreme Court. Because of the absence of documentary records, the complicated nature of the disputes, and accusations of fraud, the adjudication of these disputes took decades.

No less complex was the task of resolving wrecking disputes in the Florida Keys. In 1828, Congress addressed the situation by establishing the Southern Judicial District of Florida and providing it with special admiralty powers, thereby replacing the short-lived wreckers' courts (which, despite their name, were actually arbitration panels).

In his piece, Judge Robert W. Lee recalls that when Florida seceded from the Union and joined the Confederate States of America in 1861, justice functioned in much the same way as it had before, except that the Confederate government created its own federal court system that proved inconsequential. This should come as no surprise, given that the Confederacy was founded on the principle of "states' rights" and therefore was skeptical of federal power. Other difficulties included the lack of a Confederate Supreme Court and the fact that Confederate district courts shared jurisdiction with the state courts.

Having almost nothing to do, Florida's chief Confederate judge resigned his post and joined the army. And with Key West remaining in Union hands throughout the war, the Confederate appointee to its court was unable to take up his post. To fill these breaches, state circuit courts assumed ever more authority, although many of their sessions had to be suspended because of the war. As the conflict escalated, Florida's patrol system (used to control slaves) broke down due to a lack of available white men. As a result, the Florida legislature authorized citizens to hold so-called slave courts as needed.

Since the end of the Civil War, Florida's judiciary has operated along now-standard lines, with state courts handling the bulk of the docket and federal courts hearing claims implicating subjects of national concern. But as part 2 of this book reveals, Florida also has (or has had) courts that exist outside this model. These little-known entities reflect the needs and ethos of the communities that produced them. Being insular in both design and practice, few outsiders know anything about them.

Colonel David J.R. Frakt's essay on military courts advises readers that Florida's 57,000 active duty military personnel are subject to the courts of the armed forces. These tribunals adhere to laws and procedures that differ in key respects from what is found in civilian courts. After a look at Florida's numerous military installations, Frakt briefly summarizes four of the state's most famous military trials: the nineteenth-century Alexander Arbuthnot-Robert Ambrister (espionage) and Samuel Mudd (assassination) cases and the twentieth-century Wallace Wheeler (murder) and Walter Perkins (treason) cases. Frakt then skillfully sketches out the military justice system as practiced under the Uniform

Code of Military Justice. Among its proceedings are summary courts-martial, special courts-martial, general courts-martial, and Article 32 investigations (the equivalent of grand juries). Finally, Frakt contrasts the role of judge advocates with those of prosecutors and public defenders.

Shifting gears, Professor Donna Litman focuses her attention on religious courts in Florida. As she demonstrates, many religions have their own courts, both to settle internal operational disagreements and to adjudicate differences between individual members. Alternate dispute resolution methods also are becoming increasingly popular due to their ability to blend law and faith.

Litman outlines the court procedures of the Roman Catholic and Presbyterian churches, both of which rely on hierarchical governance. As in other jurisdictions, Florida's Catholic courts adhere to the international Code of Canon Law, handle a wide variety of cases (but most often focus on marital matters), and have an appellate process. The Presbyterian judiciary is governed by the national Book of Order, which establishes permanent judicial commissions and provides detailed rules for the trial and appeal of disciplinary and remedial cases. While independent, Jewish courts address both religious issues (such as conversion, marriage, and divorce) and business matters and can be convened in the same manner as Florida arbitration panels.

As a general rule, Florida's secular courts lack jurisdiction over ecclesiastic disputes (due to the First Amendment). Occasionally, however, they will hear such controversies. When they do, they rely on neutral principles of law. As Litman points out, this often occurs in cases involving the property rights of a locally governed congregation, such as a Baptist church.

In his chapter, Professor Ernesto A. Longa discusses Miami's Negro Municipal Court ("NMC"), the only black court to ever exist in the United States. The City of Miami created the NMC in 1950 at the urging of black businessmen and professionals, who felt that the existing courts were failing to pay enough attention to the problem of black-on-black crime. These proponents also believed that black defendants were not being accorded the same respect as white defendants.

The NMC heard cases involving black defendants, arrested by black police officers in black neighborhoods, accused of committing crimes against other blacks. White defendants, as well as cases involving criminal acts by blacks against whites, were excluded from the NMC's jurisdiction.

To preside over this new court, Miami tapped Lawson E. Thomas, one of Florida's most respected black lawyers. A native Floridian, Thomas had earned a law degree from the University of Michigan in 1923 and then spent years practicing in Miami's white courts. His reputation, as well as his calm demeanor, elicited respect from everyone who came before him, including white lawyers who found themselves handling an NMC case.

From the beginning, the NAACP and the national black press railed against the NMC. Others, however, argued it was the one forum in which blacks were assured of receiving justice; they also held the NMC up as proof that the black community could govern itself. By 1960, however, progressive forces in Miami were actively campaigning to end all forms of segregation. In their view, the NMC was just another example of the South's "Jim Crow" mentality.

The dawning of the national civil rights movement, together with the loss of its black judge, meant that the NMC's days were numbered. The end finally came in 1963, when Miami's city manager ordered all municipal facilities to be integrated. Today, following a meticulous renovation, the NMC's building has been turned into a museum.

Professor Tonya Kowalski's concluding piece on Indian courts, co-authored with Jarvis, describes the courts run by the Miccosukee Indian tribe of Florida and the Seminole tribe of Florida. The modern-day Miccosukees and Seminoles are the descendants of those Florida Indians who refused to obey President Andrew Jackson's order to relocate to Oklahoma. Although small in size, the Miccosukees (600 members) and Seminoles (4,000 members) have in recent years played an outsized role in Florida due to their highly lucrative gambling enterprises.

In accordance with their respective histories and points of views, the Miccosukee and Seminole courts could not be more different. Whereas the Miccosukees run their court (established in 1981) in relative secrecy and rely heavily on unwritten tribal customary law, the Seminoles have gone to great lengths to be transparent and have consciously modeled their court (opened in 2015) after Florida's courts.

At the same time, the Miccosukees and Seminoles increasingly have found themselves being sued in federal and state courts due to their gambling enterprises. Quite often they have been able to get such lawsuits dismissed on the basis of tribal sovereign immunity.

While the first four essays in this book deepen our understanding of Florida's early legal evolution, those in the second half demonstrate that one of the consequences of Florida's cultural diversity has been a perceived inability of the mainstream courts to provide justice to all citizens. By bringing these stories to light and collecting them in a single place, the editor and his fellow contributors have provided an invaluable service to everyone who works in, studies, or simply wants to better understand Florida's legal system.

PART I

General Jurisdiction Courts

1

Spanish Courts

M.C. MIROW

From 1513 to 1763, and then again from 1783 to 1821, Florida was a Spanish possession (*La Florida*), part of both the Viceroyalty of New Spain (*Virreinato de Nueva España*) and the Captaincy General of Cuba.[1] For a variety of reasons, however, we have only a rudimentary understanding of how legal disputes were handled by the Spanish during their time in Florida.[2]

Institutions

Other Spanish colonies had institutions that were predominantly or exclusively judicial.[3] In Florida, however, no such entities existed.[4] Instead, a single government official, addressed as "judge" by those coming before him, and sitting as a "tribunal" during deliberations, dispensed justice.

In most instances, the judge was the territory's governor. As Professor John Jay TePaske has commented, "Florida was too poor and too meagerly populated to support a court system, [which meant that] the governor was also the chief colonial judicial officer."[5]

Most of the Spanish governors who were sent to Florida were military men[6] who had neither a law background nor a legally trained advisor to guide them.[7] Despite these handicaps, they heard a wide assortment of civil and criminal cases; they also settled competing land claims, ensured the proper distribution of testamentary property, and resolved complex trade issues.[8] As part of the incidents of his office, each governor was given a staff of justice (*vara de justicia*), which he was expected to publicly display and that served as a symbol of his judicial authority.[9]

Law in the First Spanish Period

Early Colonization

Ordered government and defined jurisdiction were integral to colonization from the earliest moments of Spanish contact. Negotiated charters for new lands incorporated aspects of juridical jurisdiction, and as the Crown established permanent settlements, each fort or town would develop its own apparatus for resolving civil and criminal disputes.[10]

As has been noted elsewhere, Spanish occupation was a highly legalistic process.[11] Early Florida adventurers, such as Lucas Vázquez de Ayllón (originally a royal judge stationed in Hispaniola), Pánfilo de Narváez, and Pedro Menéndez de Avilés, were granted the titles of "adelantado, captain general, and governor."[12] The last of these designations was closely associated with the power to adjudicate legal matters.

Figure 1. Pedro Menéndez de Avilés, Spanish Florida Adelantado, Captain General, and Governor. Courtesy of the State Library and Archives of Florida.

Spanish life in the Americas sought to reproduce peninsular hierarchies, institutions, and structures, particularly those of Castile. As Professor Eugene Lyon has observed, Menéndez, the founder of St. Augustine, "kept court like a viceroy, with noble retainers and liveried servants."[13] It is quite likely that he served as a judge in civil and criminal matters in the same manner.

Following Menéndez's death in 1574, Florida shifted from a proprietary colony led by an *adelantado* ("advance man") appointed by the monarch to a Crown colony with a governor answerable to the Council of the Indies (*Real y Supremo Consejo de Indias*), the body created in 1524 to oversee Spain's possessions in the new world. In 1577, Pedro Menéndez Marqués became Florida's first governor under the council system.[14] There also were broader changes taking place in Spanish colonial administration during this time that affected Florida; for example, in 1573 and 1574, King Philip II issued ordinances dealing with, respectively, pacification, patronage, and populating.[15] These three pieces of royal legislation prescribed Spanish relations with native populations, carefully defined the respective roles of the church and the government in the colonies, and set precise rules for physical construction and governmental institutions in any areas that were settled.[16]

Prior to departing from Florida in the mid-1560s, Menéndez de Avilés issued municipal regulations creating a city council (*cabildo*) with the power to tax and distribute land.[17] Because local judges (*alcaldes*) were part of the typical colonial *cabildo*, the existence and nature of this institution in Florida must be examined.[18]

Municipal Government in St. Augustine

As explained above, royal legislation set out the arrangements for local governments and courts. This theoretical model was not followed closely in Florida, but it did provide a framework from which local modifications emanated. City councils outside Florida usually were composed of two local judges (*alcaldes ordinarios* or *alcaldes*) and from four to six town councilors (*regidores*).[19] The royal provisions for the office of *alcalde ordinario* contemplated judges who exercised, through delegation, the civil and criminal jurisdiction of the governor.[20] Because *alcaldes* were given a vote in city councils, they were viewed as members of such bodies.[21]

Throughout the Spanish Empire, *alcaldes* usually handled first-instance civil and criminal matters. A legally trained *fiscal* and *procurador* might represent the Crown in criminal cases and supply legal opinions. Similarly, an *asesor* might provide advice related to civil, criminal, and military law. Other officials served papers on parties, collected fines, and maintained a written record of the proceedings.[22]

Scholars have debated whether St. Augustine had a city council during the first Spanish period. If the existence of such a body is linked to the provision of local judges, this question would take on great importance as we search for local courts outside the purview of the governor. Professor TePaske has argued that city councils disappeared from Florida when the first Spanish inhabitants left in 1570.[23] Professor Amy Turner Bushnell has challenged this assertion:

> It has often been written that there was no cabildo in Florida after the departure of Pedro Menéndez. It is true that there was no municipal government house, no complement of municipal bailiffs and justices after the first twenty years or so, and perhaps no separate chest for municipal revenues, but a cabildo did exist, serving as both the council for the "noble and loyal city of St. Augustine," and the "assembly of the republic" (*ayuntamiento de la república*).[24]

Professor Bushnell provides several examples of how the St. Augustine city council continued to operate and be recognized in government and ceremony after 1570, but it must be stressed that none of her examples suggest that there were local judges elected as part of it.[25] Thus, a fully functioning city council was not present in St. Augustine during the first Spanish period.

The lack of a complete city council has been attributed to St. Augustine's small population, military purpose, and, perhaps, the desire of governors to single-handedly control municipal affairs. Without local judges supplied through a city council, the governor stepped in to fill various roles related to the administration of justice and the courts.[26] As Professor Christopher A. Vallandingham has pointed out:

> During the first Spanish period, the governor often had to fulfill many functions that were delegated to other officials in larger Spanish settlements in the New World. Spanish colonial Florida did not have the resources to support a court system, so the governor usually fulfilled the role of both judge and *procurator*. Other court functions were handled by soldiers.[27]

Thus, the governor often acted under the title of "judge," and his deliberative institution was referred to by litigants as a "court" or "tribunal."

Governors as Judges

It appears that Florida never developed the local courts contemplated in municipal legislation for Spanish colonies. Nevertheless, there were plenty of legal disputes, legal arguments, and legal records produced. As a result, governors sat as judges while complaining about their lack of legal training and the absence of legally trained assistants (*asesores*) to aid them in their duties.[28]

In criminal matters, the governor was authorized to punish petty offenders and impose penalties, which ranged from banishment, fines, and corporal punishment to imprisonment and involuntary servitude. Included in this jurisdiction was the authority to hear cases involving blacks, Indians, and forced laborers. Professor TePaske has observed that this led to excessive discretion and the sometimes cruel administration of justice. For example, one governor ordered that the head and hands of a forced laborer, who had been executed for killing his Spanish overseer, be displayed at both the murder site and at Fort San Marcos de Apalache (a military garrison located just south of present-day Tallahassee).[29]

Most historical commentary focuses on criminal cases in Spanish Florida. However, there also must have been a significant number of civil cases, as there were in Spain itself.[30] Lawsuits also likely varied according to activity and population. For example, St. Augustine started with more than a thousand inhabitants, but most of these individuals quickly returned to Spain; as a result, by 1570 the number of Spanish subjects had dwindled to around 300.[31] The city had a Hispanicized population of approximately 700 in the 1590s; 1,500 in the 1680s; 2,000 in the 1730s and 1740s; and 3,000 at the end of the first Spanish period in 1763.[32]

Appeals

In legal matters, Florida was subject to the *Audiencia* of Santo Domingo, which was supposed to hear appeals from decisions made in St. Augustine. In practice, however, many cases were sent directly to the Council of the Indies in Spain.[33] For general matters, the governor of Florida was directly subordinate to the Council of the Indies but was required to follow the commands of the Viceroy of New Spain (Mexico).[34] Criminal cases involving soldiers from Cuba, such as those serving in the Castillo de San Marcos at St. Augustine, were subject to review by the governor of Havana.[35]

Audits

Further information about a governor's tribunals can be obtained from the official audits of that governor's performance at the end of his term, called *residencias*, or intermittent investigations, known as *visitas*.[36] One *visita* led to judicial reform. In 1720 Antonio Ponce de Léon was ordered to leave Cuba to investigate Florida governor Antonio de Benavides. On Ponce's arrival in St. Augustine, he was beseeched by Bernardo Nieto de Carvajal, who feared that Ponce's investigation would stir up past accusations against him.

Benavides had coerced a confession for embezzlement from Nieto and then shipped him off to Spain for sentencing. Instead of praising Benavides for his swift and resolute action against Nieto, the Council of the Indies expressed concern over Benavides's failure to follow procedural formalities, his use of a paid informer, and the quality of Nieto's defense. Noting that Benavides's poor performance was the result of his lack of familiarity with the empire's laws, the Council of the Indies ordered all future cases to be reviewed by legally trained individuals in Havana.[37] We do not know if this requirement was followed (and if it was, whether it was later abandoned). However, this may help to explain why the reports of certain Florida legal proceedings appear in Cuban archives and records.

According to Professor TePaske, from 1700 to 1763 only two of Florida's ten colonial governors were subjected to a *residencia*, an official investigation based on written questions to individuals under the governor's jurisdiction.[38] During these reviews the governor's "administration of justice" usually was a topic of enquiry.[39] Witnesses and those examining the effectiveness and honesty of the governor addressed the question with examples of proper and improper conduct, particularly in the making of arbitrary arrests and the meting out of punishment for criminal activities.[40] *Residencias* prior to the period studied by Professor TePaske may provide additional information regarding not only legal cases but also where officials felt particular governors had strayed. For example, Professor Lyon notes that the *residencia* of Pedro Menéndez contains references to several civil and criminal cases.[41]

Other Sources of Law

Even less is known about the many other means by which law was effectuated in Spanish Florida. For example, when naval and trading hostilities in the 1740s made it difficult to obtain supplies, Governor Manuel de Montiano established a court of admiralty to license privateers to seize British ships and cargo.[42] A similar judicial function was carried out by the royal officials charged with administering the goods of persons who died without wills. These goods (*bienes de difuntos*, or assets of the deceased) were dealt with in Florida by the *tenedor* (holder or keeper) *de bienes de difuntos*.[43] The church also served as a locus for lawmaking, particularly regarding marriage, and the records of St. Augustine's Roman Catholic parish contain a trove of legal data that has yet to be analyzed.[44]

Documentation

That so little is known about the judicial and quasi-judicial institutions of the first Spanish period is due mainly to the fact that their files have not been preserved in one location. As Professor Susan Richbourg Parker has pointed out:

> The departure of Florida's Spanish residents between June 1763 and late January 1764 meant the departure of the documentation of their lives as well. . . . Departing Spanish officials transferred the military and civil records, some of which went to the Office of the Exchequer in Havana. Some of the documents were stored in other government buildings in Cuba. Official correspondence also rested in other locations, as copies of reports and letters sent from Florida were often sent to administrators in Spain, Cuba, Santo Domingo (now the Dominican Republic), and New Spain (now Mexico).[45]

It is possible here to mention only a few of the methods available for locating these records. In writing about lawsuits from the sixteenth century, Professor Lyon refers to documents found in the *Archivo General de Indias* in Seville.[46] Some of these materials may be culled from the John Batterson Stetson Collection.[47] This repository originally was curated by the University of Florida and contains approximately 150,000 copies taken from the *Archivo General de Indias*. It covers all aspects of Spanish activity in the southeastern region from 1518 to 1783. Organized by date, the items have been "calendared" by the University of Florida, the Library of Congress, and the St. Augustine Historical Society. There is a microfilm version of the calendar, consisting of approximately 14,000 cards, available on three reels.[48] The image of each card provides provenance, the document's salutation, date, a brief abstract, and a reference to the reel in the collection. Calendar entries from 1512 to 1651 are available online;[49] cards from 1651 to the end of the collection must be examined on microfilm. A very cursory viewing of this calendar indicates that a variety of legal cases are included among these documents from the first Spanish period.

Another useful source for legal cases from the first Spanish period is a website known as the *Portal de Archivos Españoles* (PARES).[50] A search in this database under "Florida *tribunales*" leads to three collections ("*Contaduría*," "*Escribanía de Cámara de Justicia*," and the "*Audiencia de Santo Domingo*") in the *Archivo General de Indias*. A search for "Florida *causas civiles*" leads to "*Papeles de Cuba*," "*Escribanía de Cámara de Justicia*," and "*Audiencia de Santo Domingo*." And a search for "Florida *pleitos*" leads to three subdivisions in the *Archivo General de Indias*, one in the *Archivo Histórico Nacional*, and another in the *Real Audiencia y Chancellería de Valladolid*.

As these examples make clear, there are numerous cases available for exploration and analysis from the first Spanish period. Future research in these and other archives will help us better understand the courts of the first Spanish period.

Law in the Second Spanish Period

Records

During their brief control of Florida (1763–83), the British had used the Apalachicola River as the dividing line between the colonies of East and West Florida. Upon reassuming control in 1783, Spain kept this division. As a result, St. Augustine served as the capital of East Florida and Pensacola served as the capital of West Florida.[51]

Our knowledge of legal institutions and practices is substantially different for East Florida and West Florida. This is the result of the divergent fates of each province. Many of the East Florida records from 1783 to 1821 survive in the Library of Congress and have been microfilmed.[52] In contrast, when the West Florida archives were being transferred from Pensacola to Havana, the ship carrying them was captured and the papers were tossed overboard.[53]

Furthermore, the papers from West Florida were not kept together and were moved from place to place under less security than those of East Florida. A fire (of unknown date) destroyed additional West Florida documents after its transfer to the United States.[54]

Despite these calamities, some records have survived to the present day. For example, historian Irene A. Wright has traced the migration of a significant number of manuscripts related to property titles in West Florida from 1781 to 1821. Although it is probable that most of these documents contain only surveys and grants, they have not been examined for legal cases and court records.[55] Likewise, Professor H. Glenn Boggs has described the six diplomatic efforts to recover land records from Cuba and concluded that a significant number of legal papers from both East Florida and West Florida are still in Cuba or were moved to Spain in 1888 and 1889.[56]

Jurisdictional Oversight

Even in the absence of complete records, we can say with confidence that during the second Spanish period both East Florida and West Florida were under the jurisdiction of a single individual, who either was the captain general of Cuba or the viceroy of New Spain (Mexico).[57] For example, in 1781, after Bernardo de

Gálvez defeated the British in battles for the control of Mobile and Pensacola, he was granted a captaincy general over the Floridas and Louisiana.

Following Gálvez's death in 1786,[58] oversight of the Floridas was transferred from New Spain (Mexico) to Cuba for reasons of administrative ease and as a reward to the new captain general, José de Espeleta.[59] Regardless of the political subdivision given supervision over the Floridas, it was common practice for their governors to communicate directly with Spain while providing copies of correspondence to other officials. This also was the practice elsewhere in the empire.[60]

Constitution of Cádiz

The late eighteenth and early nineteenth centuries were particularly unsettled times for West Florida due to the level of oversight and jurisdictional control exercised by captains general, intendants, and viceroys situated in Cuba, Louisiana, or Mexico.[61] The Constitution of Cádiz, sporadically in effect in the 1810s and 1820s, caused even greater disturbances to the place of the Floridas in the political hierarchy of the constitutional empire.[62]

While the constitution had rather broad application in East Florida, its use in West Florida was limited largely to Mobile, Pensacola, and St. Marks.[63] City councils (*cabildos*) were established under the constitution, but it appears that *alcaldes* did not exercise a judicial function. Nevertheless, after the constitution's re-promulgation in 1820, questions arose during the last few months of the year regarding whether Pensacola should have an *alcalde* and the extent of his authority. A negative decision from the authorities in Havana was not enforced because of the province's cession to the United States. The *alcalde*, unaware of his lack of authority, was present when the city was turned over to U.S. forces, and he continued to argue for his power under the constitution even as Spain relinquished control of the territory.[64]

Judicial Proceedings

In the second Spanish period, governors were sometimes assisted by an *asesor*, a legally trained advisor who delivered written legal opinions (*dictamenes*) regarding pending petitions. The governor usually incorporated by reference the advisor's reasoning and suggested result into his ruling or decree (*decreto*).[65] For example, in the 1790s Juan Nepomuceno de Quesada, the governor of East Florida, was assisted by *Licenciado* José de Ortega, whose official title was "*Abogado de los Reales Consejos, Teniente de Governador, Auditor de Guerra, y Asesor General de esta ciudad*."[66] When the Intendancy of Louisiana was moved to

Pensacola in 1806, an *asesor* was added to the staff to provide legal advice.[67] According to Professor Duvon Clough Corbitt, the assignment of an *asesor* to the region was probably the result of replacing the military government with a civil one:

> Until the cession of Louisiana [in 1803,] there were no civil officers in West Florida. Financial and judicial, as well as administrative affairs were carried on by the post commanders assisted by their lieutenants and other employees, usually from the military forces. . . . Judicial and administrative decisions were appealable to the governor in Louisiana, and beyond him to the king by way of Havana or Santo Domingo according to the *fuero*, or charter of privileges that might be involved; the judicial powers of the governor of Pensacola himself were practically limited to conciliation and evidence collecting. Minor cases were handled after the manner of a police court, or as by a referee or friend. Major suits, along with the evidence collected, were referred to New Orleans for review by the governor and his *asesor* as long as Louisiana belonged to Spain.[68]

As Professor Seán Patrick Donlan found while studying the period after 1803, various secondary sources describe the duties of *alcaldes* within the Spanish colonial legal system and give us some understanding of the theoretical hopes for such officials. For example, the description of the duties of judicial officers in the 1804 regulations of West Florida governor Juan Vincente Folch contemplated functioning local judges.[69] But Professor Donlan is quite right when he sounds a note of caution: "It is a more complex question, of course, whether these principles—and in this form they are little more than principles—were applied in practice."[70] Careful study of the primary sources is necessary before one can conclusively speak of *alcaldes* exercising judicial functions and settling legal disputes on a local level in West Florida during the second Spanish period.

The situation in East Florida appears to have been very much the same. For example, although East Florida returned to Spanish rule in 1783, it was not until 1791 that permanent regulations for its government were established. Judges and courts are not mentioned in these directives, although many other government functions, officials, and staff are provided for—especially with respect to the region's church, hospital, and treasury, as well as to a school and a fleet of gunboats to guard the port.[71] Only later was a legal advisor—the *Auditor de Guerra and Asesor*—added to the list.[72]

There were, however, significant differences in the authority granted to the governors of East Florida and West Florida. As Professor Corbitt has mentioned, "Through the entire period, the governor of East Florida, unlike his brother officer in West Florida, directed the financial, political, judicial, military, and even ecclesiastical branches, except during the two short constitutional periods."[73]

At the beginning of the nineteenth century, within the context of the East Florida governor's broad powers, Governor Sebastian Kindelán appointed *capitanes de partido* (regional captains) and *jueces pedáneos* (local magistrates), officials also found in Cuba.[74] These rural legal officials encouraged conciliation and heard small civil and criminal cases, with their decisions appealable to the governor.[75] The individuals chosen for these positions were both prosperous and well-known in their communities: "Philip Robert Yonge was selected to rule the Fernandina district, Francisco Facio [also Fatio or Fattio] that of the Upper St. Johns, and Farquahar Bethune the Lower St. Johns."[76] This system continued along the St. Johns River until the cession of the territory to the United States but was modified following a proposal from George J.F. Clarke, who suggested that the magistrates be popularly elected. Clarke's democratic idea was not used in Fernandina on Amelia Island, ostensibly because the appointed officials had sufficient time to hear and resolve disputes.[77]

Civil cases often dealt with property rights, usually enslaved humans and land. As to the former, individuals disputed numerous legal aspects of slavery, including *coartación* (the ability of a slave to purchase his or her freedom), leases, manumission, status, and transfers of ownership.[78] As to the latter, extensive records relating to land holding, such as grants, surveys, and occasionally litigation, also exist.[79]

East Florida Papers

Researchers studying Florida courts in the second Spanish period are fortunate to have a large collection of documents called the *East Florida Papers*. This assemblage has served as the source for several initial studies related to legal decision making and courts during this period.[80] Consisting of approximately 65,000 folios microfilmed onto 175 reels, these papers cover almost all aspects of colonial administration including, for example, city council proceedings, indigenous communities, notarized instruments, slave titles, and taxation.[81] The *East Florida Papers* offer a particularly rich and relatively unexplored array of legal materials, including series related to civil cases, criminal cases, courts-martial, notarial instruments, slaves, state prisoners, treasury accounts, and miscellaneous legal instruments and proceedings.[82]

For example, twenty-one bundles of documents in the *East Florida Papers* are labeled as dealing with civil causes, and there are over 500 entries under this topic from 1785 to 1821.[83] A brief survey of these cases makes it clear that they contain a wealth of information related to civil disputes between individuals,[84] including business transactions, debts, houses and land, shipping, and slaves. Commercial cases and cases dealing with slaves frequently crossed political and linguistic borders, and the tribunals used official translators for English documents and employed Indian interpreters.[85] Likewise, required oaths were adjusted for Protestant witnesses.[86] Importantly for present purposes, some cases went to arbitration, either because of the administrative complexity of the matter involved (such as insolvency), or because the parties requested this procedure.[87]

For the period 1783 to 1821, the *East Florida Papers* contain 370 testamentary proceedings corresponding to 166 decedents. The governor, serving as an ordinary or probate judge, appointed executors, ordered inventories, proved testaments, enforced the payment of claims, and distributed decedents' property.[88] In such proceedings the governor would be styled the "tribunal" (*tribunal*) and may have had the assistance of his legal advisor (the *asesor*).[89] As in civil cases, the testamentary documents reveal a rather scrupulous attention to detail despite the governor's lack of formal legal training. Much of this must have been due to the *asesor* (when he was available). Judicial decisions by the governor could be appealed to the *audiencia* in Puerto Príncipe (now Camagüey), Cuba.[90]

These examples of civil and testamentary proceedings indicate the depth of the material that has yet to be explored for Florida's courts in the second Spanish period. In addition to the topics mentioned above, the *East Florida Papers* contain numerous other entries that will tell us much more about the governors and their courts. These include twelve bundles of criminal cases (1785–1821); one bundle related to cases at the *audiencia* (1800–1821); thirteen bundles intriguingly labelled "miscellaneous legal documents" (1784–1821); three bundles of courts-marital (1785–1821); two bundles of criminal proceedings arising from the failed East Florida Rebellion of 1795; seventeen bundles of notarial documents; numerous bound volumes of notarial documents from Fernandina; and slave registers.[91] In other words, we have only scratched the surface of the available material related to Florida's courts in the second Spanish period.

Claims Commissions

While not Florida courts, there were several other institutions and settings in which Spanish court decisions and Spanish colonial law were applied to settle the claims of individuals. These usually were the result of treaties that provided for the restitution of lost property from those who suffered the economic effects of war or changes in sovereignty. Treaties dealing with the transfer of Florida from Spain to Britain, Britain to Spain, and Spain to the United States all provided for the recognition of rights in land that might depend on Spanish rulings or law.[92] Professors Parker and William S. Coker, for example, mention a manuscript collection of materials on Patriot War claims at the St. Augustine Historical Society and the Spanish Land Grant Claims at the State Archives of Florida.[93] Little is known about the workings of such commissions and particularly the way Spanish records were used and interpreted to establish claims and titles.[94]

One important institution was the commission created to settle land claims after Florida became a territory of the United States. Based on the 1819 Adams-Onís Treaty transferring Florida to the United States, a U.S. commission to determine claims to titles to land in the territory of Florida held its first session in 1823.[95] Alexander Hamilton Jr., the second son of the Federalist leader, served as one of its three commissioners.[96] The commissioners of the East Florida Land Commission debated at length the construction of rules related to claims, the various sources to be consulted, and the advisability of recognizing titles perfected through improvement or possession.[97] Frustrated by the lack of clear rules in Spanish law and practice, Hamilton withdrew from the commission and offered to resign.[98] Eventually, the U.S. Supreme Court stepped in and settled several large disputes.[99] Once again, these materials await further study.

Conclusion

During Spain's centuries-long ownership of Florida, a range of officials handled a variety of legal disputes. Many judicial functions were carried out by the governor, who was styled a judge and the head of a tribunal. Although usually not legally trained, the governor was at times assisted by a legally trained *asesor*, a practice that appears to have been more common in the second Spanish period than in the first Spanish period. Collections of legal documents reveal that colonial administrators, legal officials, and litigants had a clear understanding of the different jurisdictions available to them (i.e., civil, criminal, and testamentary).

Significant archival work remains to be done to remove the tentative quality of what one can say about Florida courts in the Spanish colonial periods. One cannot write definitively about the existence or absence of local judges (*alcaldes*) in Florida during the Spanish colonial periods, although studies based on archival materials indicate that they did not exist as judicial officers hearing cases even under the Constitution of Cádiz (when city councils were greatly empowered). Likewise, little is understood about the appeal of cases from Florida to *audiencias* or higher royal officials and how these cases were handled.

Despite the present limitations, scholarship on the colonial administration of justice already has effectively refuted earlier claims that Spanish justice was completely corrupt and biased—assumptions that followed from an older school of "Anglophone historiography that painted Spanish colonialism as inherently tyrannical, corrupt, and inefficient."[100] Jettisoning these facile conclusions, legal historians now are faced with complex questions concerning the hybrid, plural, and rather sophisticated legal world of the Spanish Empire in Florida. Fuller descriptions and analyses of the Spanish courts and their functions in Floridian colonial legal culture will come only from careful work in the archives. In this regard, researchers are fortunate to have many available resources, and more and more materials relating to Florida's Spanish courts are being added almost daily in readily accessible and easily searchable digital formats.

Notes

1. From 1763 to 1783, Florida was a British colony. *See infra* Chapter 2 of this book. In 1821, Florida became a U.S. territory. *See infra* Chapter 3 of this book.

2. *See generally* Christopher A. Vallandingham, *Tracking Down Legal Sources on Prestatehood Florida, in* 1 Prestatehood Legal Materials: A Fifty-state Research Guide, including New York City and the District of Columbia 249 (Michael Chiorazzi & Marguerite Most eds. 2005).

3. *See* M.C. Mirow, Latin American Law: A History of Private Law and Institutions in Spanish America 19–33 (2004).

4. John Jay TePaske, The Governorship of Spanish Florida 1700–1763, at 20 (1964).

5. *Id.*

6. *Id.* at 16. For a list of Florida governors from 1565 to 1706, see Amy Bushnell, The King's Coffer: Proprietors of the Spanish Florida Treasury 1565–1702, at 141–42 (1981). For a list of Florida governors from 1699 to 1764, see TePaske, *supra* note 4, at 231.

7. *Id.* at 20.

8. For the origin and nature of the governor's office, see id. at 7–9. The scope of the governor's powers was set out by his individual grant and royal law. *Id.* at 20, 23. *See further* Recopilación de Leyes de los Reynos de las Indias, Lib. 5, Tít. 2, LL. 1–52 (1791) [hereinafter "R.I." followed by "book," "title," and "law"].

9. R.I., Lib. 5, Tít. 2, L. 11.

10. Michael Gannon, *First European Contacts, in* The History of Florida 18 (Michael Gannon ed. 2013). *See also* Enrique Sánchez Goyanes, *Cómo y de la Mano de Quién se fundó por España el Derecho en Norteamérica hace hoy 500 años*, Diario La Ley, No. 8387, Sección Doctrina, 29 de Septiembre de 2014, Año XXXV, Editorial La Ley, 6291/2014 (2014), at 1–21 (focusing on the ordinances related to Ponce de León's voyages and attempted settlements, including, id. at 6, a grant of civil and criminal jurisdiction to him in 1512).

11. *See* Amy Turner Bushnell, *Republic of Spaniards, Republic of Indians, in* The History of Florida 76, 77 (Michael Gannon ed. 2013); Mirow, Latin American Law, *supra* note 3, at 11–18.

12. Gannon, *First European Contacts, supra* note 10, at 26; Eugene Lyon, *Settlement and Survival, in* The History of Florida 55, 58 (Michael Gannon ed. 2013); TePaske, *supra* note 4, at 9–10.

13. Lyon, *Settlement and Survival, supra* note 12, at 67.

14. *Id.* at 72.

15. Bushnell, *Republic of Spaniards, supra* note 11, at 76.

16. Mirow, Latin American Law, *supra* note 3, at 12, 26, 62, 64. *See also* Axel I. Mundigo & Dora P. Crouch, *The City Planning Ordinances of the Law of the Indies Revisited (Part I)*, 48 Town Planning Rev. 247 (1977).

17. Amy Bushnell, *The Noble and Loyal City, 1565–1668, in* The Oldest City: St. Augustine, Saga of Survival 27, 33 (Jean Parker Waterbury ed. 1983). *See also* Pedro Menéndez, *Ordinances which Pedro Menéndez . . . Instituted in these Provinces of Florida, in* Pedro Menéndez de Avilés 274 (Eugene Lyon ed. and trans. 1995).

18. For general aspects of the *cabildo*, see R.I., Lib. 4, Tít. 9, LL. 1–23.

19. TePaske, *supra* note 4, at 26. Orders issued in 1761 to establish a town council in St. Augustine became moot when the territory was transferred to England in 1763. *Id.* at 27.

20. These judges were charged to "hear in first instance all business, causes, and things that the governor or his lieutenant may hear regarding civil and criminal" matters. *See* R.I., Lib. 5, Tít. 3, L. 1.

21. R.I., Lib. 5, Tít. 3, L. 15.

22. TePaske, *supra* note 4, at 59.

23. *Id.* at 27.

24. Bushnell, The King's Coffer, *supra* note 6, at 107.

25. *Id.* at 107–13.

26. If local judges (*alcaldes ordinarios*) were available, the governor was prohibited from hearing the civil and criminal causes under their jurisdiction. *See* R.I., Lib. 5, Tít. 2, L. 14.

27. Vallandingham, *supra* note 2, at 252.

28. TePaske, *supra* note 4, at 59–60. If they were not legally trained, governors of other, larger cities were provided with legal advisors. *See* R.I., Lib. 5, Tít. 2, LL. 37–40.

29. TePaske, *supra* note 4, at 61–64.

30. *See generally* Richard L. Kagan, Lawsuits and Litigants in Castile, 1500–1700 (1981).

31. TePaske, *supra* note 4, at 5.

32. Juan Ignacio Arnaud Rabinal, Alberto Bernárdez Alvarez, Pedro Miguel Martín Escudero & Felipe del Pozo Redondo, *Estructura de la Población de una Sociedad de Frontera: la Florida Española, 1600–1763*, 17 Revista Complutense de Historia de América 95, 98, 100, 106, 108, 117 (1991). *See also* John R. Dunkle, *Population Change as an Element in the Historical Geography of St. Augustine*, 37 Fla. Hist. Q. 3 (1958).

33. TePaske, *supra* note 4, at 58.

34. R.I., Lib. 5, Tít. 2, L. 1.

35. R.I., Lib. 5. Tít. 10, L. 15.

36. TePaske, *supra* note 4, at 33–57, 68–69.

37. *Id.* at 35–36 (citing AGI, Escribanía de Cámara, Legajo 153A, Papel del fiscal, Nov. 28, 1721, and AGI, Santo Domingo, Legajo 833, Consulta del Consejo de las Indias, Nov. 28, 1721).

38. TePaske, *supra* note 4, at 40.

39. *Id.* at 41, 42, 53.

40. *Id.* at 43, 47–48.

41. Eugene Lyon, *Spain's Sixteenth-Century North American Settlement Attempts: A Neglected Aspect*, 59 Fla. Hist. Q. 275, 286 n.37 (1981).

42. Daniel L. Schafer, *Raids, Sieges, and International Wars*, *in* The History of Florida 112, 124 (Michael Gannon ed. 2013).

43. Bushnell, The King's Coffer, *supra* note 6, at 114.

44. These are the cathedral parish records at the Archives of the Diocese of St. Augustine. *See* Susan Richbourg Parker, *In My Mother's House: Dowry Property and Female Inheritance Patterns in Spanish Florida*, *in* Signposts: New Directions in Southern Legal History 19, 24, 41 n.8, 42 n.15 (Sally E. Hadden & Patricia Hagler Minter eds. 2013).

45. *Id.* at 23–24.

46. *See* Lyon, *Settlement and Survival*, *supra* note 12, at 74 nn.6 & 8 (referring to "AGI Escribanía de Cámara"). The *escribanos de cámara* (scribes) were charged with maintaining the records of the *audiencias* (regional royal courts). *See* R.I., Lib. 2, Tít. 23, LL. 1–63.

47. The author thanks Dra. Marisol Floren, FIU College of Law Library, for her assistance with information on the Stetson Collection, P.K. Yonge Library of Florida History, University of Florida, Gainesville, Florida. *See* http://web.uflib.ufl.edu/spec/pkyonge/stetsonp.html. The collection now is held at the St. Augustine Historical Society. In addition to copies from the classification "*Escribanía de Cámara*," the Stetson Collection contains copies of records from the classification "*Justicia*," a promising place to start when looking for Florida legal records. *See* Paul E. Hoffman, *New Numbers for the Stetson Collection*, 55 Fla. Hist. Q. 347 (1977).

48. P.K. Yonge Library of Florida History, Stetson Collection, 1512–1783 [microform]: Spanish Florida Borderlands Calendar of the P.K. Yonge Library of Florida History (1980) (call number 975.9 P111s Fla MF).

49. University of Florida Digital Collections, *Unearthing St. Augustine's Colonial Heritage, Calendar Cards Descriptive by Year of Manuscript—Documents Drawn from the Archivo General de Indias in Seville*, *at* http://ufdc.ufl.edu/USACH00595/.

50. Portal de Archivos Españoles, *at* http://pares.mcu.es/.

51. *See* Susan Richbourg Parker & William S. Coker, *The Second Spanish Period in the Two Floridas*, *in* The History of Florida 162 (Michael Gannon ed. 2013).

52. *See* M.C. Mirow, *Law in East Florida, 1783–1821*, 55 Am. J. Legal Hist. 89 (2015). *See also* Mabel M. Manning, *The East Florida Papers in the Library of Congress*, 10 Hispanic Am. Hist. Rev. 392 (1930) (discussing the migration of the East Florida Papers); Irene A. Wright, *The Odyssey of the Spanish Archives of Florida*, *in* Hispanic American Essays: A Memorial to James Alexander Robertson 169 (A. Curtis Wilgus ed. 1942) (a detailed account of the migration of the Spanish papers from East and West Florida).

53. Parker & Coker, *supra* note 51, at 172. It appears that many records also were lost in a fire on October 24, 1810. *See* Duvon Clough Corbitt, *The Administrative System in the Floridas, 1781–1821*, 2 Tequesta 41, 52 (Aug. 1942).

54. Wright, *supra* note 52, at 183–85, 188, 190–207.

55. *Id.* at 169–71, 202–07.

56. *See* Glenn Boggs, *The Case of Florida's Missing Real Estate Records*, 77 Fla. B.J. 10 (Oct. 2003).

57. Corbitt, *Administrative System*, *supra* note 53, at 41.

58. *Id.* at 42–43.

59. *Id.* at 43.

60. *Id.* at 44.

61. The legal and jurisdictional complexity of West Florida in the second period is analyzed in Seán Patrick Donlan, *Entangled up in Red, White, and Blue: Spanish West Florida and the American Territory of Orleans, 1803–1810, in* Entanglements in Legal History: Conceptual Approaches 213 (Thomas Duve ed. 2014).

62. Corbitt, *Administrative System, supra* note 53, at 45–46, 49. For the text of the Constitution of Cádiz, see M.C. Mirow, Florida's First Constitution: The Constitution of Cádiz—Introduction, Translation, and Text (2012). *See also* M.C. Mirow, *The Constitution of Cádiz in Florida*, 24 Fla. J. Int'l L. 271 (2012).

63. Corbitt, *Administrative System, supra* note 53, at 59.

64. *Id.* at 61–62.

65. *See, e.g.*, Petition, 17 July 1802, East Florida Papers (Manuscript Div., Library of Cong.) [hereinafter "E.F.P."], Reel 157, Part I, ff. 5v–12; *Dictamen*, 23 Aug. 1802, E.F.P., Reel 157, Part I, ff. 18–49; *Decreto*, 26 Aug. 1802, E.F.P., Reel 157, ff. 49–49v.

66. E.F.P., Reel 152, Apr. 4, 1794, No. 18, Item 1794–10, f. 18.

67. Corbitt, *Administrative System, supra* note 53, at 50.

68. *Id.* at 57. Concerning the manner in which a personal *fuero* might interfere with standard judicial procedures, Professor Corbitt has written:

> The Spanish administration of justice was a confusing jumble because so many persons enjoyed *fueros*, or the right to be tried in the special courts of their class, rank, order or organization. Suits in the Floridas involving *fueros* reached Spain by way of Havana, where the captain general ordinarily presided over the special courts of appeal. Ordinary suits went to the *audiencia* in Santo Domingo (in Puerto Príncipe, Cuba after 1800) before going to Spain.

Id. at 57 n.10. It appears that *foral* rights were recognized from the earliest days of Spanish contact. *See* Sánchez Goyanes, *supra* note 10, at 8.

69. *See* Donlan, *supra* note 61, at 232.

70. *Id.*

71. *See* Duvon Clough Corbitt, *The Administrative System in the Floridas II, 1781–1821*, 3 Tequesta 57, 59 (July 1943).

72. *Id.* at 60.

73. *Id.*

74. *Id.* at 62.

75. *Id.*

76. *Id.*

77. *Id.* at 63.

78. Manning, *supra* note 52, at 393–94.

79. Both primary and secondary materials dealing with land grants can be found at https://www.floridamemory.com/collections/spanishlandgrants/related.php#p.

80. *See, e.g.*, M.C. Mirow, *Causas civiles en la Florida Oriental, 1785–1821, in* Estudios en Homenaje al Profesor Doctor Don Abelardo Levaggi (Ricardo Rabinovich-Berkman & Agustín Parise eds.) (forthcoming); M.C. Mirow, *Testamentary Proceedings in Spanish East Florida, 1783–1821, in* Studies in Canon Law and Common Law in Honor of R.H. Helmholz 281 (Troy L. Harris ed. 2015); Nancy O. Gallman, *Reconstituting Power in an American Borderland: Political Change in Colonial East Florida*, 94 Fla. Hist. Q. 169 (2015); Mirow, *Law in*

East Florida, *supra* note 52; Alejandro Quiroga Fernández de Soto, *Military Liberalism on the East Florida "Frontier": Implementation of the 1812 Constitution*, 79 Fla. Hist. Q. 441 (2001).

81. *See* Laura J. Kells, *East Florida Records: A Finding Aid to the Collection in the Library of Congress* (rev. 2011), *at* http://rs5.loc.gov/service/mss/eadxmlmss/eadpdfmss/2005/ms005002.pdf. Digital images of the *East Florida Papers* are available in the Gale database *Slavery and Anti-Slavery: A Transnational Archive, at* http://gdc.gale.com/products/slavery-and-anti-slavery-a-transnational-archive/.

82. Kells, *supra* note 81.

83. Library of Congress, Handbook of Manuscripts in the Library of Congress 121–22 (1918); Library of Congress, Report of the Librarian of Congress 59 (1905).

84. Mirow, *Causas civiles*, *supra* note 80.

85. Mirow, *Law in East Florida*, *supra* note 52, at 97–103.

86. E.F.P., Reel 151, July 13, 1790, Item 1790–2.

87. Mirow, *Law in East Florida*, *supra* note 52, at 99, 103.

88. Mirow, *Testamentary Proceedings*, *supra* note 80.

89. *Id.* at 297–300.

90. Corbitt, *Administrative System*, *supra* note 53, at 47.

91. Kells, *supra* note 81.

92. For U.S. confirmations of Spanish land grants in Florida, see https://www.floridamemory.com/collections/spanishlandgrants/. See also a detailed list of materials concerning U.S. confirmations of grants in *American State Papers* in Vallandingham, *supra* note 2, at 274 n.104. The real estate bar in Florida has a special interest in these materials. *See* Boggs, *The Case*, *supra* note 56; Glenn Boggs, *Florida Land Titles and British, Not Just Spanish, Origins*, 81 Fla. B.J. 23 (July/Aug. 2007).

93. *See* Parker & Coker, *The Second Spanish Period*, *supra* note 51, at 178. The Patriot War (1812–14) is examined in James Cusick, The Other War of 1812: The Patriot War and the American Invasion of Spanish East Florida (U. Ga. Press 2007) (2003). As he explains:

> If you want a three-sentence summary of a very complicated story, it runs like this: In March 1812 an agent for the U.S. government used American forces to seize a border town in Florida, an action that severely embarrassed the administration of President James Madison. However, when war broke out with Great Britain a few months later, the Madison administration decided to leave American troops in Florida, and the state of Georgia used its militia to reinforce them. As a result, for the next two years angry American citizens in Georgia and angry Spanish subjects in Florida slugged it out in a kind of no man's land at the edge of a bigger conflict.

Id. at x.

94. Similar work on Spanish documents and Spanish colonial law was undertaken after the 1848 Treaty of Guadalupe Hidalgo, which ended the Mexican-American War. *See, e.g.*, U.S. General Accounting Office, *The Treaty of Guadalupe Hidalgo: Findings and Possible Options Regarding Longstanding Community Land Grant Claims in New Mexico* 33–34 (June 2004) (GAO-04-59), *at* http://www.gao.gov/new.items/d0459.pdf. *See also* Guadalupe T. Luna, *En el Nombre de Dios Todo-poderoso: The Treaty of Guadalupe Hidalgo and Narrativos Legales*, 5 Sw. J.L. & Trade Am. 45 (1998); Guadalupe T. Luna, *Legal Realism and the Treaty of Guadalupe Hidalgo: A Fractionalized Legal Template*, 2005 Wis. L. Rev. 519.

95. *See* George C. Whatley & Sylvia Cook, *The East Florida Land Commission: A Study in Frustration*, 50 Fla. Hist. Q. 39 (1971); Wright, *supra* note 52, at 179.

96. Whatley & Cook, *supra* note 95, at 41. Courts and land commissioners during the Territorial period (1821–45) were overwhelmed with cases concerning land, many of which depended on Spanish titles. *See* Boggs, *The Case*, *supra* note 56, at 13–14. *See also infra* Chapter 3 of this book.

97. Whatley & Cook, *supra* note 95, at 43–52.

98. *Id.* at 45.

99. *Id.* at 52. *See, e.g.*, United States v. Arredondo, 31 U.S. (6 Pet.) 691 (1832); United States v. Percheman, 32 U.S. (7 Pet.) 51 (1833); United States v. Clarke, 33 U.S. (8 Pet.) 436 (1834); United States v. Wiggins, 39 U.S. (14 Pet.) 334 (1840). A list of fifty similar cases can be found in Boggs, *Florida Land Titles*, *supra* note 92, at 31.

100. Donlan, *supra* note 61, at 231.

2 ~

British Courts

ROBERT M. JARVIS

During the long occupation of Florida by Spain (1513–1821), there was a brief period when Florida functioned as two British colonies (1763–83). This interruption began with the ninth Treaty of Paris, which settled the Seven Years' War, and ended with the tenth Treaty of Paris, which concluded the American Revolutionary War.[1]

Upon taking control of Florida, the British divided the territory into two halves, known respectively as East Florida (with St. Augustine as its capital) and West Florida (with Pensacola as its capital).[2] Much scholarly attention has been paid to these entities, although the primary focus has been on their economic systems, political loyalties, and relations with neighboring Indian tribes.[3]

Despite holding sway in Florida for only two decades, the British, following their usual overseas practice, set up courts in both colonies that replicated, as nearly as possible, the forms and processes of justice found in England. Because these courts were dismantled when the Spanish regained control of Florida, and their records have all but disappeared,[4] few modern lawyers (or historians) know anything about this fascinating aspect of Florida's legal culture.[5] Yet as has been noted elsewhere, "The English introduced an independent judicial system, with Chief Justices for both East and West Florida. They also established a Court of Common Pleas, a Court of General Sessions and a Vice-Admiralty Court."[6]

Royal Directions

In October 1763, King George III, then in the third year of his star-crossed rule, issued a proclamation concerning the new colonies.[7] As in other royal provinces, the proclamation commanded the governors of East Florida and West Florida

> to erect and constitute . . . courts of judicature and publick justice . . . for the hearing and determining [of] all causes, as well criminal as civil, according to law and equity, and, as near as may be, agreeable to the laws of *England*, with liberty to all persons who may think themselves aggrieved by the sentence of such courts, in all civil cases to appeal under the usual limitations and restrictions to us, in our privy council.[8]

Following British protocol, the proclamation was augmented by commissions (which were intended to be made public) and instructions (which were for the governors' eyes only).[9] Thus, for example, the governor of West Florida was told

> to establish, with the advice of his council, courts patterned after those already in operation in the other colonies, and more particularly in Georgia. Judges and justices of the peace were to be appointed [by the governor] with the advice of [his] council to serve during pleasure; but neither they nor any other officers were to be removed except for good and sufficient reasons, which should be immediately transmitted to the Board of Trade [the body in England that oversaw all of the royal provinces]. The governor was forbidden to exercise any of the judicial offices either directly or through [a] deputy. Appeals from the provincial courts, in civil causes, to the governor in council and thence to the Privy Council were to be allowed, with the procedure in such cases governed as nearly as possible by the regulations prescribed for such processes in the instructions to the governor of Georgia. Copies of all commissions establishing courts and jurisdictions were to be submitted to the Board of Trade for royal approval. The governor was reminded of the frequent complaints that had come from other plantations of delays and undue proceedings in the courts. He was admonished to see that justice was promptly and impartially administered in the province under his care.[10]

Creation of the Courts

In East Florida, James Grant, a law-trained Scotsman who had commanded troops at the Siege of Havana during the Seven Years' War, was inaugurated as the colony's first governor in October 1764.[11] On the same day, six men (their numbers subsequently increased to twelve) were sworn in as "His Majesty's Council for East Florida."[12] This body had many functions, including serving as the upper chamber of the colony's yet-to-be-formed legislature and, as discussed below, hearing judicial appeals.

Establishment of the courts followed in stages:

> [I]n November [1764] the Court of Common Pleas and the Court of General Sessions of the Peace, Oyer and Terminer, Assize and General Goal Delivery were constituted by commissions of the governor. . . . The other courts of the province were all created later. The Court of Chancery [presided over by the governor] was constituted in October, 1768 [and] the Court of Vice Admiralty . . . was created in April, 1771. . . . [Although the] governor's ecclesiastical powers gave him the right to hold an Ordinary's Court [for probate matters] . . . it is not clear whether it was ever held. . . . [13]

In West Florida, George Johnstone, a fellow Scotsman who had been a naval commander during the Seven Years' War, became governor in November 1764.[14] He, too, was joined by a provincial council that had the same duties as its East Florida counterpart.

Johnstone organized a General Court of Pleas in January 1765 and a Court of Vice Admiralty in February 1765.[15] Later tribunals included a small claims court ("court of requests") and a criminal court ("court of oyer and terminer").[16]

From 1772 onward, the courts in East Florida met in the "old Spanish hospital in the center of the town," which had been "reconstructed as a courthouse and jail."[17] In West Florida, plans were made at an early date for the building of a courthouse at Pensacola,[18] but such a structure was not erected. As a result, beginning in 1769 court was held in the former home of General Frederick Haldimand, the province's military leader.[19] Although perpetually short of money, the authorities in West Florida did manage to "purchase . . . six sets of Burn's *Justice [of the Peace and Parish Officer]*, an appropriate reference work for the province's part-time judicial officers, and a set of the *Statutes at Large* for the chief justice."[20]

Jurisdiction of the Courts

In East Florida, the Court of Common Pleas was directed to meet in St. Augustine four times a year on the second Tuesday of January, April, July, and October.[21] Possessing the jurisdiction that in England was exercised by the King's Bench, Common Pleas, and the Exchequer, the new court was empowered to hear civil cases in which the amount in controversy exceeded 40 shillings,[22] the current equivalent of $276.[23]

In contrast, the colony's Court of General Sessions was directed to meet in St. Augustine twice a year on the third Wednesday of June and December.[24] Mirroring the King's Bench, the Justices of Assize, and the General and Quarter Sessions of the Peace, its jurisdiction extended to all serious criminal matters.[25]

Figure 2. *A*, James Grant, British East Florida Governor. *B*, George Johnstone, British West Florida Governor. Courtesy of the State Library and Archives of Florida.

Minor offenses, however, were made the responsibility of the Commission of the Peace, which was staffed by the provincial council "and four others as justices of the peace."[26]

Similar arrangements were made in West Florida. A Court of General Pleas, possessing both civil and criminal jurisdiction, was directed to meet in Pensacola four times a year on the second Tuesday of January, April, July, and October.[27] Minor criminal matters were left to the provincial council and nineteen others acting as justices of the peace.[28]

Curiously, courts in both East and West Florida were prohibited from hearing piracy cases. Instead, such defendants had to be sent to the "governor of Georgia to be tried and punished under the authority of the commission established for those parts."[29]

Juries

Following English practice, petit and grand juries were empanelled in both East Florida and West Florida.[30] As time went by, however, grand juries increasingly focused on political matters. Thus, for example, in June 1770 an East Florida grand jury sitting at the Court of General Sessions "presented as a great grievance the lack of an assembly [i.e., legislature] and the resulting insecurity of property through the lack of proper laws."[31] Similarly, in February 1778 a West Florida grand jury "requested [Governor Peter] Chester to inform the home government of the defenseless state of this section of the province and to make clear the need of militia for protection from a slave insurrection and for defense in case of a rupture with Spain."[32]

Appeals

In both colonies, appeals in civil cases went first to the provincial council and then to the Privy Council in England.[33] Appeals to the provincial council were permitted only in cases where the judgment was for at least £300 ($41,400); this figure rose to £500 ($69,000) for appeals to the Privy Council.[34] An appeal to the Privy Council additionally required permission from either the provincial council or the Privy Council itself, the posting of security, and compliance with strict filing deadlines.[35]

Asking the Privy Council for relief was expensive and time-consuming.[36] Nevertheless, some litigants did pursue such redress, and records have survived from several appeals taken from the West Florida vice admiralty court.

In 1772, for example, a trader named Evan Jones complained that the court had refused to give him clear title to a vessel he had purchased at a prize auction. After investigating the matter, the Privy Council declined to intervene.[37]

In 1773 John Campbell sued Samuel Thomas and Phillips Comyn, the owners of the brig *Africa*, after a trunk Campbell had shipped from London to Pensacola failed to arrive. The vice admiralty court found for Campbell and the defendants appealed to the Privy Council. In the meantime, a question arose regarding the vice admiralty court's jurisdiction, leading to the issuance of a writ of prohibition by the General Court of Pleas. In 1775, the Privy Council affirmed Campbell's judgment.[38]

Lastly, in 1781, John Buttermire, the master of the *Nelly*, captured the Spanish schooner *El Poder de Dios*. Because Buttermire lacked a letter of marque, the authorities seized the *El Poder de Dios* when Buttermire towed her into Pensacola harbor. Buttermire subsequently asserted a prize lien, but the vice admiralty court refused to recognize his claim. Although Buttermire appealed, the British lost control of Pensacola before the Privy Council could issue a ruling.[39]

In both East Florida and West Florida, criminal cases followed essentially the same procedure as civil cases.[40] Technically, it was not possible to appeal a criminal verdict to the Privy Council, but this difficulty could be overcome by filing a "writ of error."[41]

Chief Justices of East Florida

Even before taking office, Governor Grant tapped James Moultrie, South Carolina's former attorney general, to be the colony's first chief justice.[42] The position came with an annual salary of £500 ($69,000).[43]

Moultrie's tenure as chief justice lasted less than a year, for he died in August 1765.[44] In 1766, William Grover, a former chief justice of Georgia, was appointed to succeed Moultrie, but he perished aboard the sloop *Mary* when she sank en route to St. Augustine.[45] As a result, in 1767 William Drayton, who had been filling in since Moultrie's death, was made chief justice.[46] Drayton, originally from South Carolina, had studied law in London at the Middle Temple. Possessing a quarrelsome nature, Drayton's stormy tenure (he was suspended twice, first in 1776 and then again in 1777) came to an end in 1778 when he resigned.[47]

During Drayton's first suspension, Reverend John Forbes, a graduate of Aberdeen University, stepped in as temporary chief justice. He did so again during Drayton's second suspension and was nominated for the position by Governor Tonyn after Drayton resigned.[48] However, the job went to James Hume, the former acting attorney general of Georgia.[49] Hume served from 1779 until the colony's demise,[50] at which time he relocated to the Bahamas.[51]

It appears that no serious study has been made of any of these men, with the notable exception of Drayton.[52] However, a short profile of Forbes does exist.[53] It explains that while he had no legal training, he was one of the few educated men in East Florida and therefore was pressed into judicial service.[54]

Chief Justices of West Florida

Unlike East Florida, West Florida had only one chief justice: William Clifton. Because there is no published biography of him,[55] much about his life is uncertain.[56] We do know that he was the second son of Sir Gervase Clifton, the fourth baronet of Nottinghamshire, and that he joined Gray's Inn on February 8, 1721.[57] This last fact suggests he was born about 1700.

Of his career in England we have no information, for the trail goes cold until November 1754, when Clifton arrived in Savannah to become the first attorney general of Georgia.[58] Among his other achievements, Clifton designed the colony's judicial system, which he modeled after the high courts of London.[59]

Clifton remained attorney general until 1764, when he was appointed chief justice of West Florida.[60] Upon his departure, the lower house of the Georgia Assembly passed a resolution thanking him "for his upright conduct in his office."[61] In his new post, Clifton was given a salary of £500 ($69,000).[62]

Once in Pensacola, Clifton quickly found himself embroiled in a feud between Governor Johnstone and Lieutenant Colonel Ralph Walsh regarding the province's military affairs. When Johnstone had Walsh arrested, Clifton signed a writ of *habeas corpus* freeing Walsh. In response, Johnstone suspended Clifton for dishonesty, ignorance of the law, and neglect of duty.[63] The standoff ended when Johnstone, having managed to make enemies out of just about everyone, was recalled by the Crown.[64]

Clifton's battle with Johnstone was a harbinger of things to come. In 1769, for example, Montfort Browne, the colony's lieutenant governor, shot and nearly killed Evan Jones during a duel. After Browne voluntarily turned himself in, he asked to be released on bail. When Clifton refused, Browne sought out Alexander Moore, a justice of the peace, who issued the requested order. Although Clifton complained about Moore to the provincial council, it declined to remand Browne to jail.[65]

In 1779, as Spanish forces were making plans to attack, Governor Chester raised the possibility of declaring martial law. While the military members of the provincial council supported the idea, Clifton opposed such a move on constitutional grounds.[66]

Judges of the Vice Admiralty Courts

As noted above, both East Florida and West Florida had their own vice admiralty courts with their own judges. In East Florida, the first judge was Reverend John Forbes, who was appointed in 1771 and served until 1776, when he resigned to become acting chief justice during William Drayton's first suspension from office.[67]

Forbes was succeeded by Dr. Robert Catherwood, who originally came to St. Augustine to run its military hospital.[68] Catherwood served as vice admiralty judge until 1783, when he was suspended for malfeasance.[69] Because no official financial support was given to the vice admiralty courts, they funded their operations (and paid their judges) out of the monies collected from guilty parties.[70] This led to a variety of abuses, with Catherwood, who presided over a very busy court, one of the prime offenders.[71]

Upon Catherwood's suspension, Lieutenant Colonel William Brown, the commissioner of embarkation at St. Augustine, became the acting vice admiralty judge, but shortly after his appointment the colony reverted to Spanish control.[72]

In West Florida, Edmund Rush Wegg, the colony's attorney general,[73] was simultaneously vice admiralty judge from 1765 until 1768, when a barrister named

> Alexander McPherson appeared in the province bearing a deputation from Alexander Duncan, who had been commissioned judge of the West Florida vice-admiralty court by the High Court of Admiralty. . . . He acted as judge and register until his death in 1774 when Governor Chester appointed Elihu Hall Bay [to take his place].[74]

Bay, who was from Maryland and later became a judge of some renown in South Carolina, was the colony's last vice admiralty judge.[75]

Conclusion

The work of the judges in both East Florida and West Florida was supported by a number of other officials. Professor Charles L. Mowat has compiled a list of these individuals, whose titles included "assistant judge," "clerk of the crown," "clerk of the pleas," "provost marshal," "coroner," "public vendue master," "master in chancery," "examiner and register of court of chancery," "register of court of [vice] admiralty," "marshal of court of [vice] admiralty," and "advocate general of court of [vice] admiralty."[76]

Nevertheless, when the last British citizens left Florida in 1783, the courts they had built ceased to exist. As Professor Cecil Johnson has explained, this was because "there was little in the English system of administering a royal province which . . . conform[ed] to the Spanish ideal of colonial government."[77]

Notes

1. *See* David J. Weber, The Spanish Frontier in North America (1992), and J.H. Elliott, Empires of the Atlantic World: Britain and Spain in America, 1492–1830 (2006). The loss of Florida did not sit well with Spain, as witnessed by its decision to enter the Revolutionary War on the American side. *See further* Mark F. Boyd & José Navarro Latorre, *Spanish Interest in British Florida, and in the Progress of the American Revolution*, 32 Fla. Hist. Q. 92 (1953).

2. As has been noted elsewhere: "East Florida [was] roughly equivalent to the present-day state of Florida [while] West Florida [consisted of] the Gulf Coastal strip that forms portions of present-day Florida, Alabama, Mississippi, and Louisiana. . . . The British used the Apalachicola River to mark the boundary between the Floridas." Junius P. Rodriguez, *West Florida, in* The Louisiana Purchase: A Historical and Geographical Encyclopedia 350 (Junius P. Rodriguez ed. 2002).

3. The two leading works on the colonies, coincidentally published in the same year, are Charles Loch Mowat, East Florida as a British Province, 1763–1784 (1943), and Cecil Johnson, British West Florida, 1763–1783 (1943). Each man was unaware of the other's work until shortly before their respective books were published. Mowat, *supra*, at vi–vii. A succinct summary of their findings appears in *Resources for the History of the British Floridas*, 24 Fla. Hist. Q. 218 (1946). For other commentary, see, e.g., Bernard Romans, A Concise Natural History of East and West Florida (Kathryn E. Holland Braund ed., University of Alabama Press 1999) (1775); Richard L. Campbell, Historical Sketches of Colonial Florida (1892); Charlton W. Tebeau, A History of Florida 71–87 (1971); Robin F.A. Fabel & Daniel L. Schafer, *British Rule in the Floridas, in* The History of Florida 144 (Michael Gannon ed. 2013); Andrew Jackson Forney, *"An uninhabited country": Empire and Ecology in British East Florida, 1763–1774* (unpublished M.A. dissertation, Texas Christian University, 2011); Wilford O'Neal Simmons, *The Divergent Colony: British West Florida, 1763–1783* (unpublished M.A. dissertation, Southeastern Louisiana University, 2004).

4. Much of what does still exist can be found in the P.K. Yonge Library of Florida History at the University of Florida. *See further* http://www.library.ufl.edu/spec/pkyonge/index.html.

5. *See, e.g.*, Glenn Boggs, *Florida Land Titles and British, Not Just Spanish, Origins*, 81 Fla. B.J. 23, 23 (July/Aug. 2007) ("All Florida lawyers should know that the state traces its colonial heritage back to Spain, and many, particularly real estate practitioners, are aware that some Florida land titles begin with a grant from the Crown of Spain. Relatively few, however, know that title to a smaller number of parcels began with a grant from Great Britain.").

6. *The Evolution of Justice in Florida: Historical Documents, Photographs and Images*, at 4, *available at* http://www.floridasupremecourt.org/library/evolution_of_justice.pdf [hereinafter Evolution].

7. *See Proclamation of George III, R. (Upon the Acquisition of East and West Florida)*, 3 Fla. Hist. Q. 36 (1925) [hereinafter Proclamation]. Along with East Florida and West Florida, Britain acquired Grenada and Quebec. As a result, the proclamation also applied to these jurisdictions. For a further discussion, see Colin G. Calloway, The Scratch of a Pen: 1763 and the Transformation of North America (2006).

8. Proclamation, *supra* note 7, at 37–38 (italics in original).

9. *See* Royal Instructions to British Colonial Governors, 1670–1776, at 5 (East Florida) and 14 (West Florida) (Leonard Woods Labaree ed. 1935).

10. Johnson, *supra* note 3, at 18. For a look at Georgia's colonial courts, see Scott D. Gerber, *The Origins of the Georgia Judiciary*, 93 Ga. Hist. Q. 55 (2009).

11. For a biography of Grant, who served as governor until 1771, see Paul David Nelson, General James Grant, Scottish Soldier and Royal Governor of East Florida (1993).

12. Mowat, *supra* note 3, at 14.

13. *Id.* at 15–16 (footnote omitted). A district court was added in 1782. *See id.* at 138.

Grant's order establishing the Court of Common Pleas read as follows:

> George the Third by the Grace of God of Great Britain, France and Ireland King, Defender of the Faith, and so forth—
>
> To all to whom these our present letters shall come Greeting, know ye, That we tendering the state and condition of our province of East Florida and being desirous that Right and Justice according to Law be duly administered therein, have thought fit to erect and constitute, and, by these presents do erect and constitute a Court of Record by the name and stile of the Court of Common Pleas to be holden yearly at St. Augustine in our said province on the second Tuesday in [January] on the second Tuesday in [April] on the second Tuesday in [July], and on the second Tuesday in [October] before our Chief Justice of our said province for the time being, and in his absence or sickness before the Senior Justice of our said Court for the time being and his Associates or either of them, and we do hereby Give and Grant unto our said Justices of our said court for the time being, Full power Jurisdiction and Authority to hold pleas in all manner of causes suits and actions whatsoever as well civil as real personal and mixed, arising happening or being within our said province, where the Sum or thing demanded shall exceed the value of Forty Shillings Sterling, except only where the Title to any Freehold shall come in question, and to proceed in such pleas, suits and actions, by such ways means and process as may with the greatest safety dispatch and justice bring the same to a final determination, and also to hear and determine all such pleas, suits, and actions, and judgment thereupon to give, and execution thereof to award/ and issue, and this as fully and amply as can or may be done by our courts of King's Bench, Common Pleas, and Exchequer in England, doing therein what of Right and Justice ought to be done.
>
> In Testimony whereof we have caused these our Letters to be made patent, and the Seal of our said province to be affixed thereto. Witness our Trusty and well beloved James Grant Esq., Captain General Governor and Commander in Chief in and over our said province this third day of November, in the Fifth year of our Reign.
>
> Signed James Grant
> By his Excellency's command
> Signed John Dunnett

FSU Special Collections & Archives, *Photocopies of British Documents, East Florida* (Box 138, Item 3). Grant's order establishing the Court of General Sessions of the Peace, Oyer and Terminer, Assize and General Goal Delivery was similar:

> George the Third by the Grace of God of Great Britain, France and Ireland King, Defender of the Faith and so forth—
>
> To all to whom these present Letters shall come Greeting, know ye that we being

willing and desirous as much as may be to prevent long imprisonments within our province of East Florida, and that all offenders against us and our laws, may as speedily as possible be brought to their tryals, have thought fit to erect and constitute, and by these presents do erect and constitute a Court of General Sessions of the Peace, Oyer and Terminer, Assize and General Goal Delivery to be held yearly at St. Augustine in our said province on the third Wednesday in [June] and the third Wednesday in [December] before our Chief Justice of our said province for the time being, and in his absence or sickness before the Senior Justice of our said court for the time being, and his Associates or either of them. And we do hereby accordingly give and grant unto such our said Chief Justice and Justices, full power and authority to enquire by the oaths of good and lawful men of our said province, and by other ways means and methods which they shall know [of] and have in their power by whom the truth of the matter may be better known and enquired into of all treasons, misprision of treason, insurrections, rebellions, counterfeitings, clippings, washings, false coinings, and other falsities of money of Great Britain and other kingdoms and dominions whatsoever. And of all murders, felonies, manslaughter, killings, burglaries, rapes of women, unlawful meetings and conventicles, unlawful uttering of words, assemblies, misprisions, confederacies, false allegations, trespasses, riots, routs, retentions, escapes, contempts, falsities, negligences, concealments/maintenance, oppression, champerty, deceit and all other evil doings, offences, and injuries whatsoever, and also the accessories of them within our said province, by whomsoever and in what manner soever, done committed or perpetrated, and of all other articles and circumstances concerning the premises and every of them or any one or more of them in any manner whatsoever in as full and ample manner to all intents and purposes whatsoever as any Judges or Justices of the Court of King's Bench, Justices of Assize, Justices of Oyer and Terminer and Goal Delivery, or any Court of General or Quarter Sessions of the Peace, do, can or lawfully may have, hold, use, exercise and enjoy in the Kingdom of Great Britain[.]

In the Govr's Letter of 22 Nov. 1764.

Read Oct. 29, 1765.

Id. (Item 4).

14. For a biography of Johnstone, who remained governor until 1767, see Robin F.A. Fabel, Bombast and Broadsides: The Lives of George Johnstone (1987). Because the new governors of Grenada and Quebec also were Scotsmen, allegations of cronyism permeated London. *See further* Calloway, *supra* note 7, at 156.

15. Johnson, *supra* note 3, at 27.

16. Willam S. Coker & Jerrell H. Shofner, Florida: From the Beginning to 1992, at 43 (1991). *See also* Johnson, *supra* note 3, at 143.

17. Mowat, *supra* note 3, at 17.

18. *See* Clinton N. Howard, *Colonial Pensacola: The British Period—Part I*, 19 Fla. Hist. Q. 109, 125 (1940) (reporting that in November 1765 the West Florida provincial council passed a resolution calling on the crown to provide funds for the construction of various government buildings, including "courts . . . and a jail.").

19. Clinton N. Howard, *Colonial Pensacola: The British Period—Part II*, 19 Fla. Hist. Q. 246, 260 (1941).

20. Julius Groner & Robert R. Rea, *John Ellis, King's Agent, and West Florida*, 66 Fla. Hist. Q. 385, 397 (1988).

21. Mowat, *supra* note 3, at 15.

22. *Id.*

23. All of the currency conversions appearing in this chapter come from http://www.measuringworth.com.

24. Mowat, *supra* note 3, at 15.

25. *Id.*

26. *Id.*

27. Johnson, *supra* note 3, at 27.

28. *Id.* at 26–27.

29. Labaree, *supra* note 9, at 452. For a further discussion, see Erwin C. Surrency, *The Procedure for the Trial of a Pirate*, 1 Am. J. Legal Hist. 251 (1957).

30. *See, e.g.*, Evolution, *supra* note 6, at 5 (reproducing the first page of the *East Florida Gazette* from Saturday, April 26, 1783, which carried "an announcement by the District Court of fines of 20 shillings [$138] to five individuals who failed to answer summons as jurors.").

31. Mowat, *supra* note 3, at 45. A later grand jury, meeting at the June 1778 Sessions of the Peace, had the same complaint. *Id.* at 92. In March 1781, Governor Patrick Tonyn finally gave in to these demands and convened a provincial legislature. *Id.* at 127–28.

32. Johnson, *supra* note 3, at 207.

33. In addition to hearing appeals from colonial courts, the Privy Council reviewed colonial legislation. On at least two occasions, it struck down recently passed West Florida laws. *See id.* at 48–49 (discussing the rejection of, respectively, an election law and an immigration law).

34. Clarence E. Carter, *The Beginnings of British West Florida*, 4 Miss. Valley Hist. Rev. 314, 329 n.61 (1917). The £500 requirement was waived in ecclesiastical disputes, property seizures, and suits in which the Crown was a party. *See further* Arthur Meier Schlesinger, *Colonial Appeals to the Privy Council—Part I*, 28 Pol. Sci. Q. 279, 284–86 (1913).

35. Johnson, *supra* note 3, at 18 n.43.

36. Sharon Hamby O'Connor & Mary Sarah Bilder, *Appeals to the Privy Council Before American Independence: An Annotated Digital Catalogue*, 104 Law Lib. J. 83, 86–87 (2012).

37. Johnson, *supra* note 3, at 230. Additional background regarding this case can be found in Interim Appointment: W.C.C. Claiborne Letter Book, 1804–1805, at 377–78 (Jared William Bradley ed. 2002).

38. Johnson, *supra* note 3, at 230–31.

39. *Id.* at 231.

40. Joseph H. Smith, Appeals to the Privy Council from the American Plantations 240 (1950).

41. For a further discussion, see David Rossman, *"Were There No Appeal": The History of Review in American Criminal Courts*, 81 J. Crim. L. & Criminology 518, 537–38 (1990).

42. Mowat, *supra* note 3, at 15. Moultrie was joined in East Florida by his brother John, who was appointed lieutenant governor. *Id. See further The Moultries*, 5 S.C. Hist. & Genealogical Mag. 229 (1904).

43. Mowat, *supra* note 3, at 37. Moultrie also was provided with two unpaid assistant judges (a common practice in colonial courts). *Id.* at 15.

44. *Id.* at 44.

45. *Id. See also Obituary of William Grover, at* http://files.usgwarchives.net/ga/chatham/obits/g/grover7876gob.txt.

46. Mowat, *supra* note 3, at 44.

47. *Id.* at 105.

48. *Id.* at 126, 162.

49. *Id.* at 126.

50. *Id.* at 162.

51. *See* Carole Watterson Troxler, *Uses of the Bahamas by Southern Loyalist Exiles, in* The Loyal Atlantic: Remaking the British Atlantic in the Revolutionary Era 185, 190 (2012).

52. *See* Charles L. Mowat, *The Enigma of William Drayton*, 22 Fla. Hist. Q. 3 (1943). Mowat suggests that Drayton's troubles as chief justice stemmed largely from the fact that he was "a champion of the American cause in a loyalist colony." *Id.* at 4. In 1772, for example, the St. Augustine customs collector requested a general writ of assistance, which would have given him unfettered power to search for goods that had not paid customs. Although the failure to pay import duties had become a serious threat to the Crown's finances, Drayton refused to issue the writ on the ground that it would "injur[e] . . . the rights of His Majesty's other loyal subjects." Mowat, *supra* note 3, at 73–74. For a further look at Drayton's life, see Roger C. Smith, *The Façade of Unity: British East Florida's War for Dependence* (unpublished M.A. dissertation, University of Florida, 2008).

53. *See* Edgar Legare Pennington, *John Forbes (d. 1783)*, 8 Fla. Hist. Q. 164 (1930).

54. *Id.* at 166 (quoting Forbes as saying that after his appointment to the bench, he began to pay "particular attention to the elements and principles of law.").

55. Lamenting this fact, one commentator has written: "Clifton merits study as a colonial chief justice. The [judicial independence] ideas attributed to him by Governor Johnstone must have been unusual for a man in his position." *Colonial Pensacola—Part I, supra* note 18, at 119 n.41.

56. We can say with confidence that he was a slaveholder, and there are numerous references to an incident in which one of his African American servants discovered a flower that later was named for Clifton. *See, e.g.*, A.B. Rendle, *Notes on Myricaceae*, 41 J. Botany 82, 87 (1903).

57. Joseph Foster, The Register of Admissions to Gray's Inn, 1521–1889, at 364 (1889).

58. Joseph R. Lamar, The Bench and Bar of Georgia During the Eighteenth Century 15 (1913).

59. *Id.* at 14–15.

60. *Id.* at 15.

61. *Id.* at 16.

62. Johnson, *supra* note 3, at 21.

63. *Id.* at 55–56.

64. *Id.* at 60.

65. *Id.* at 72–73.

66. *Id.* at 214.

67. Mowat, *supra* note 3, at 165.

68. *Id.* at 15.

69. *Id.* at 165.

70. In January 1779, John H. Haley, the marshal of the East Florida Court of Vice Admi-

ralty, was directed by Catherwood to arrest as suspected prize the schooner *Grace*. Catherwood's order has survived and reads as follows:

> George the Third by the Grace of God of Great Britain, France, and Ireland King, Defender of the Faith and so forth—
>
> To the Marshal of our Court of Vice Admiralty, Greeting:
>
> Whereas a certain libel on information has been preferred, exhibited, and duly admitted in our said Court at the instance and promotion of Dominica Martinico, [the] lieutenant commanding the private schooner of war called the RECOVERY, on behalf of himself, the Owners, other officers, and crew of the said private vessel of war, and all others interested therein, against a certain schooner or vessel called the GRACE, of the burthen of about twenty tons, her tackle, apparel, furniture, and cargo, consisting as it is said of rice and other produce of the American rebellious colony of South Carolina, and four slaves called Andrew, Peter, Jack and Bob, now lying in the harbour of St. Augustine, and was found coming from trading and going to trade to and with some of the inhabitants of the rebellious colony of South Carolina contrary to the form of the statute in such case lately made and provided.
>
> And we rightfully and duly proceeding thereupon and willing that what of justice is required may be done therein we therefore command you that you forthwith [] cite and admonish or cause to be cited and admonished all and every person and persons whomsoever in our said province whom it may concern, or who may have or pretend to have any claim, right, title, or interest of, in, or to the said schooner or vessel called the GRACE, her tackle, apparel, furniture, and cargo, and the four slaves as aforesaid, that they be and appear in our said Court to be holden at St. Augustine on the fourth day of this present month of January, then and there to come in and answer [] to the said libel and defend the said schooner, her tackle, furniture, apparel, and cargo, and the four slaves as aforesaid, and to do and perform thereupon what of right may be required and by the said Court directed.
>
> And likewise that you do intimate or cause to be intimated unto all and every such person or persons the effect of this our monition and that in case there is not any person to appear, claim, or defend the said schooner, her tackle, apparel, furniture, and cargo, and the four slaves as aforesaid, in our said Court at the time and place aforesaid that for want thereof judgment will [issue] according to the prayer of the libel above mentioned, and that you make known to our said Court then and there to be holden what you have done herein and have then there this Writ.
>
> Witness the Honorable Robert Catherwood, Sole Judge of our said Court at St. Augustine aforesaid, the first day of January in the year of his Lord one thousand seven hundred and seventy nine and in the nineteenth year of [the King's] reign.

FSU Special Collections & Archives, *British East, West and Territorial Florida, Georgia, South Carolina, Tennessee and Mississippi Miscellaneous documents, letters, etc., 1773–1868* (Box 138, Item 4). Haley subsequently sent back the following reply: "Pursuant to the written Writ to me directed I have cited and admonished all and every person and persons whomsoever who had or pretended to have any claim, right, title, or interest to the within mentioned schooner by fixing up at the most publick place in St. Augustine a copy of the written Writ as thereby it is to me commanded." *Id.*

71. Mowat, *supra* note 3, at 127. By the time of the Revolutionary War, the corrupt nature of the vice admiralty courts had become one of the colonists' chief complaints. *See further* Carl Ubbelholde, The Vice-Admiralty Courts and the American Revolution (1960).

72. Mowat, *supra* note 3, at 165.

73. Wegg served as attorney general throughout West Florida's existence, although in 1766 he briefly was suspended on a trumped-up charge of incompetency stemming from his decision to request a postponement in a criminal trial. Johnson, *supra* note 3, at 55. *See also* 1 Mississippi Provincial Archives, 1763–1766: English Dominion 293–96 (Dunbar Rowland ed. 1911) (reproducing a letter from Governor Johnstone discussing his decision to replace Wegg). After the colony's fall, Wegg became the attorney general of the Bahamas. *See* Sandra Riley, Homeward Bound: A History of the Bahama Islands to 1850, at 168 (1983). In contrast, East Florida had four attorneys general: James Box (1764–70), a Savannah lawyer; William Owen (1770), a Dublin solicitor; Arthur Gordon (1771–78), of whom almost nothing is known; and Henry Yonge (1779–83), a London barrister. Mowat, *supra* note 3, at 162. In both colonies, the attorney general's annual salary was £150 ($20,700). *See id.* at 37; Johnson, *supra* note 3, at 21.

74. Johnson, *supra* note 3, at 229.

75. *Id.* at 230. An exhaustive recounting of Bay's life appears in 1 John Belton O'Neall, Biographical Sketches of the Bench and Bar of South Carolina 53–65 (1859).

76. Mowat, *supra* note 3, at 164–65. Similar positions existed in West Florida. *See* Johnson, *supra* note 3, at *passim*.

77. *Id.* at 234.

3

Territorial Courts

CHRISTOPHER A. VALLANDINGHAM

On March 3, 1845, Florida became a state after more than twenty years as a U.S. territory. The path to statehood had been difficult. Florida was an impoverished, thinly populated outpost on the fringe of the Spanish Empire at the time (1821) of its transfer to the United States. Much of the richest agricultural and pastoral land was undeveloped, burdened by unresolved title claims, or inhabited by Native Americans. There was Pensacola to the west and St. Augustine to the east and not much between the two. To the far south was the desolate island of Key West, where piracy, the slave trade, and general lawlessness abounded.

After the United States took possession of Florida, local officials quickly purged all traces of Spanish law and practice. At the same time, they sought to forge an identity separate from the federal government, whose policies and lack of financial support soon became sources of ongoing tension.

The chief problems of territorial Florida were economic, political, and security related. The purpose of this chapter, however, is to give readers a glimpse into the workings of the territorial courts, the disputes that came before them, and the varied personalities of their staffs.

Creation of the Transitional Government

Due to the complexity of the underlying issues, the negotiations between the United States and Spain over the future of Florida dragged on for years.[1] Spain wanted assurances that the United States would not recognize the independence of Spain's rebellious colonies elsewhere in the Americas, while the United States wanted a clear set of boundaries to end the problems caused by the vague wording of the Louisiana Purchase (1803).[2]

On February 22, 1819, the treaty transferring Florida to the United States was signed.[3] Both parties were given six months for ratification.[4] While Congress acted almost immediately, Spain did not do so until October 24, 1820.[5] Due to this long delay, Congress ratified the treaty a second time on February 19, 1821.

On March 3, 1821, just before adjourning, Congress passed legislation authorizing President James Monroe to take possession of Florida.[6] Congress directed that "all the military, civil, and judicial[] powers, exercised by the officers of the existing government of the same territories, shall be vested in such person and persons, and shall be exercised in such manner, as the President of the United States shall direct."[7] This arrangement was intended to be temporary and to continue until, at the latest, the end of the first session of the next Congress (May 8, 1822).[8]

Congress left it to Monroe to create and fill the offices of the transitional government. Accordingly, in the months prior to the official transfer of Florida, he established the positions of governor, judge, commissioner, secretary, marshal, and U.S. attorney.[9] With the division between East and West Florida still in place—a holdover from the brief period when Great Britain controlled Florida (1763–83)—the offices created for East Florida mirrored those created for West Florida.[10] As a result, only the governor had authority over the entire territory.

Spanish laws remained in force during the transition; the only U.S. laws extended to the territory were those dealing with revenue collection and slave importation.[11] As to the former, Monroe was authorized to create tax districts and could appoint officers to do the collecting.[12] The commissions of these officers were to lapse as soon as Congress established a territorial government.[13]

Governor Andrew Jackson

One week after the passage of the Act of March 3, 1821, Monroe tapped Andrew Jackson to be the territory's military governor and granted him the powers previously exercised by the governor and captain-general of Cuba, the intendant, and the governors of East and West Florida.[14] Jackson's authority, however, was not complete. Monroe withheld from him the power to impose new taxes and to confirm land titles[15] and also made it clear that he could not suspend officials appointed by Monroe.[16] In all other respects, however, Monroe gave Jackson the freedom to administer the territory "in the best manner in your power."[17] Secretary of State John Quincy Adams assured Jackson that these terms were "conformable" with those applied to the governor of the Territory of Louisiana.[18]

In many respects, Jackson was the natural choice to become Florida's territorial governor. A former Tennessee congressman, senator, and superior court judge, as well as the former commander of the U.S. Army's southern division, Jackson seemed to possess the ideal credentials to lead a provisional government on the American frontier. But Jackson had an explosive temper that frequently got him into trouble with peers, higher-ranking officials, and foreigners. When

Monroe earlier had mentioned to Thomas Jefferson that he was considering making Jackson his minister to Czar Alexander I, Jefferson replied, "My God! He would breed you a quarrel in Russia in less than a month."[19]

When Jackson arrived in Pensacola, he assumed the powers of the governor and captain-general of Cuba. This meant, as one writer put it, that his position was "a very anomalous one[:] an American Governor under Spanish law, of an American territory not yet under the Constitution and laws of the United States."[20]

Florida's Judicial System: 1821–1822

In the act authorizing President Monroe to take possession of East Florida and West Florida, Congress made no provision for the establishment of courts. Instead, for the time being, all the military, civil, and judicial powers exercised by Florida's Spanish government were to remain in place. As Attorney General William Wirt later would write to Monroe, the "government then which *congress* adopted for the Floridas, is the spanish [*sic*] form of government *as it existed in actual operation* on the 3 March 1821."[21] Whether the administrative machinery in place in the two Florida provinces actually complied with Spanish law was largely beside the point.[22]

On July 10, 1821, the date East Florida officially was transferred to the United States,[23] Jackson issued a proclamation stating that "all the laws and municipal regulations which were in existence at the cessation of the late government, remain in full force[,] and all civil officers, charged with their execution, except those whose powers have been specially vested in me, and except, also, such officers as have been entrusted with the collection of the revenue, are continued in their functions during the pleasure of the governor for the time being or until provision shall otherwise be made."[24]

Upon the transfer of West Florida a week later, Jackson did not find much of a government in existence at Pensacola. In a letter to John Quincy Adams, Jackson wrote that "[i]n this province, the Government, like everything else, was in a state of dismemberment and neglect. The circumstance of being on the eve of a transfer to the United States occasioned a total indifference and carelessness in the administration of all its branches."[25] He added that "[a]ccording to the Spanish scheme of municipal administration, there ought to have been an *Alcalde* [judge] . . . a *Fiscal* [prosecutor], a *Cabildo* or Corporation [city council], and *Alguazils* [sheriffs.]"[26] Instead, only the position of *alcalde* was filled, and its occupant did not know the exact nature of his duties.[27] In St. Augustine, Colonel Robert Butler reported a slightly better situation, with the city having both an *alcalde* and a *cabildo*.[28]

Henry Marie Brackenridge, a lawyer from Pennsylvania who Jackson appointed *alcalde* in Pensacola, submitted a report to him in which he provided more details regarding Spain's administration of the city.[29] According to Brackenridge, the *alcalde* in Pensacola had very limited authority, acting as a mediator in cases in which mediation was required by the Spanish constitution and handling cases for liquidated damages in which the amount of the debt was admitted. If the mediation failed, or a question of law arose during the proceedings, the *alcalde* would render a decision, which could be appealed to a higher tribunal (the *Real Audiencia*). Although Brackenridge could not ascertain the precise nature of the *alcalde*'s criminal jurisdiction, in major criminal cases he was limited to deposing witnesses.

By supplementing existing methods, Brackenridge believed that a judicial system could be created that would approximate the Spanish one, and therefore not deviate too drastically from Congress' mandate to continue the existing form of government.[30] Unsurprisingly, Jackson did not hesitate to eschew Spanish law and practice, explaining in a letter to John Quincy Adams that "[t]o limp along with this maimed and imperfect state, seemed to me intolerable."[31]

During Jackson's brief tenure, many residents of the territory believed that Spain's legal system was incompatible with that of the United States.[32] In other words, devising new procedural rules was not enough—Spanish law itself was the problem. The Grand Jury of East Florida, for example, complained that Spanish laws were "inconsistent with the principles and genius of a republican Government."[33] Thus, in contrast to Louisiana, which incorporated the civil law practices of its former ruler, Florida rejected them. In September 1822, the break with Spanish law became complete when the legislative council adopted the common law of England.[34]

District Courts of East Florida and West Florida

Because Congress did not establish territorial courts in the act authorizing President Monroe to take possession of Florida, there was no need to delineate their jurisdiction. But when Monroe established two judicial districts—one for East Florida and the other for West Florida[35]—he created a conundrum: what was a judge appointed to one of these districts supposed to do? Attorney General Wirt argued that such a judge would have been an anomaly in the Spanish legal system in Florida at the time of the transfer and "could have found no functions apposite his commission."[36] Because Congress intended to leave the status quo in place, the only tasks for these judges was the enforcement of the revenue collection and slave importation laws. Overseeing these laws was among the duties assigned to the president by Congress and therefore delegable by him. Wirt had concluded as much when commenting on the power struggle that already had begun to develop between Jackson and Eligius Fromentin, the first judge of the District of West Florida.[37] Monroe later acknowledged that if these limitations were correct, then the "district judges have nothing to do . . . with the internal government of the province."[38]

Setting these issues aside, Monroe appointed William P. DuVal[39] as East Florida's first judge and Fromentin as his West Florida counterpart. Neither decision sat well with Jackson. In a letter to Monroe, Jackson wrote that DuVal "is a good private character, but of a very moderate capacity as a Lawyer."[40] As for Fromentin, Jackson had much more to say.[41] He wrote that a number of people, including himself and those who were familiar with Fromentin from their time in New Orleans, were "astonished at his being appointed . . . a Judge."[42]

As a former U.S. senator from Louisiana (1813–19), Fromentin undoubtedly was familiar with brass-knuckle politics, but in Pensacola, with Jackson as governor, he did not stand a chance. Within a month of his arrival, the members of the Pensacola Bar wrote to Monroe that:

> The Undersigned, the Members of the Bar of Pensacola, unanimously, and in the most respectful manner, represent, that they have seen, with extreme regret and mortification, the appointment, to a Judicial Office of high importance in this Province, by the Supreme Executive of the Federal Government, of a man, whose legal acquirements, and whose moral character, are equally unfitted to inspire those sentiments of respect, and that feeling of confidence, which are due to his elevated station, but which rank, however dignified, cannot alone confer. The dispensation of justice depends, not only on the wisdom and rectitude of the Bench, but on the integrity and consideration of the Bar. In a Court, in which it is deemed degrading to practice, honorable men will be reluctant to appear. . . . His incapacity, which might well have been argued from the defect of his education, has been rendered glaringly apparent from his first attempt to assume the exercise of power.[43]

The letter ended with a plea that even if West Florida was stuck with Fromentin for the time being, Congress should refrain from renewing his term at its next session. Henry Brackenridge, Pensacola's *alcalde*, was listed as one of the letter's endorsers.

Neither of Florida's new courts was up and running by the time of Spain's transfer. For his part, DuVal did not reach St. Augustine until four months later. When he finally did arrive in November 1821, however, he immediately made it clear that he viewed his jurisdiction as extending far beyond the revenue collection and slave importation laws. In his first address to the Grand Jury of the District of East Florida, DuVal advised: "You Gentlemen, as the Grand Inquest for the Nation, will examine into all cases where a breach of the laws of the United States has taken place."[44] Among the crimes he listed were murder on the high seas, piracy, and treason. But with only a handful of cases before the court, his expansive views were never tested. And after being in St. Augustine for only a month, DuVal departed the city for Washington, D.C.[45]

On the other side of the state, life for Fromentin was not nearly as placid. Fromentin had arrived in Pensacola in late July 1821, but the prosecuting attorney was still en route and the marshal had left without appointing a deputy. With time on his hands, Fromentin pondered his new appointment and voiced his disappointment with it. He had assumed he would have the same jurisdiction that was vested in territorial judges where no federal district court had been established.[46] But as Jackson soon would make clear in the Callava affair, he held the reins of judicial power in West Florida.

Of all the disputes that occurred during Jackson's brief tenure as governor, the most notable involved Colonel José Maria Callava, the outgoing Spanish governor of West Florida.[47] The basis for their disagreement was the estate of Nicolas Maria Vidal, the colony's one-time *auditor de guerra* (judge advocate), who had died in 1806.

Forbes and Company was responsible for settling Vidal's estate. Although ordered to do so by Callava, John Innerarity, an employee of Forbes, refused to deliver various papers relating to the estate. After Jackson took office, Vidal's daughter Mercedes presented her claims to Jackson. In the course of hearing her entreaties (Mercedes and her sister Carolina believed that Innerarity had fraudulently settled the estate and now was trying to cover up his misdeeds), Jackson learned that contrary to its treaty obligations, Spain had allowed various documents to be removed from the municipal archives. After numerous attempts to retrieve them failed, Jackson sent three of his closest associates, accompanied by armed guards, to Callava's home. There, they dragged him out of bed and hauled him before Jackson.

When he was unable to persuade Callava to return the documents, Jackson flew into a rage and had him jailed. As he had in the past, Jackson pursued his aims with no regard for "diplomatic obligations, evidence, law, propriety, and forms of procedure."[48] Not surprisingly, Callava complained bitterly about his ill-treatment.[49]

As soon as the documents were in his possession, Jackson ordered Callava released. While Callava was still in jail, however, Fromentin had signed a writ of *habeas corpus*. Upon hearing this, Jackson brought Fromentin in front of him "to show cause why he has attempted to interfere with my authority as Governor of the Floridas, exercising the powers of the Captain General and Intendant of the Island of Cuba over the said provinces, and of the Governors of said provinces respectively, in my judicial capacity as supreme judge over the same."[50]

According to Jackson, Fromentin had no power to issue a writ of *habeas corpus* because his jurisdiction began and ended with the revenue collection and slave importation laws. In this regard, Jackson had the support of Monroe and Wirt, who both believed Fromentin had overstepped his limited authority. Nevertheless, Wirt did not approve of Jackson's treatment of Fromentin, as he made clear in a letter to Monroe.[51]

Fromentin did not take well to being sidelined; neither did he relish the prospect of having to implement Spanish law. As a result, he refused to hear a case arising from the capture of the brig *Centinella*, a Colombian privateer seized by the U.S.S. *Hornet* for suspected piracy.[52] In a rather petulant letter to the captain of the *Hornet*, Fromentin explained that such activity did not fall within his jurisdiction, which now was limited to the revenue collection and slave importation laws.

To make his position crystal clear, Fromentin then added: "If no other consideration should induce me to hesitate, the summary mode of proceedings prescribed by the Spanish laws in cases of piracy does not agree with my idea of the obligations imposed upon a judge of the United States in a trial for a capital offense."[53]

County Courts

When Florida was transferred to the United States, Jackson assumed the judicial powers previously vested in the Spanish officials in both East and West Florida. He took this responsibility very seriously and considered "the Judiciary as by far the most important branch of the territorial government."[54] Yet despite having the authority to do so, he opted not to relegate all judicial power to himself and soon established county courts.[55]

The county courts were designed to administer justice in the vast areas beyond Pensacola and St. Augustine.[56] In those two cities, the governments inherited from Spain would continue. But in the rural areas, where the population was predominately American, there was a "necessity of assimilating the present institution to something which they can understand, and of administering the laws by means of tribunals not altogether foreign to their habits and feelings."[57]

Before Jackson could establish county courts, however, it was necessary for there to be counties. He therefore created two: Escambia and St. Johns. Escambia County extended from the Perdido River to the Suwanee River; the rest of the Florida peninsula constituted St. Johns County.[58] Each county court would be comprised of five justices of the peace.[59] Three justices would form a quorum.[60] The jurisdiction of the county court included all civil cases originating in the respective county if the sum in controversy exceeded $20.[61] For sums greater than $500, both parties had the right to appeal the county court's decision to the governor.[62]

The ordinance provided that "the judicial proceedings in all civil cases shall be conducted, except as to the examination of witnesses, according to the course of the existing laws, or the laws of Spain."[63] Jackson later asserted that the procedures provided in the ordinances he issued did not vary from Spanish practices except for the requirement that the testimony of all witnesses whose attendance could be procured would be *viva voce*.[64]

To begin a lawsuit, one simply had to file a complaint with the county clerk explaining the nature of the suit and the relief that was being sought.[65] Complaints could be filed in either English or Spanish.[66] But if at least one of the parties was a Spaniard, the pleadings had to be served in both English and Spanish.[67] Any documents supporting the claim were to be attached to the complaint.[68] After making a copy of the petition, the clerk placed the suit on the court docket and created a "citation" requiring the defendant to show up on a certain date to answer the complaint.[69] The *alguazil* (sheriff) would then serve both the complaint and the citation on the defendant.[70]

If the defendant appeared in court on the scheduled day, he or she had three days to answer the complaint, unless additional time was granted.[71] Each party was permitted to submit interrogatories to the other side.[72] Failing to answer the questions was deemed an admission (*pro confesso*).[73]

If the defendant did not appear on the designated day, the court could enter a default judgment, provided the requested remedy was "liquidated by proven [a]ccount."[74] In all other cases, the suit proceeded without the defendant.[75] Testimony was heard, damages were assessed, and a final judgment was rendered.[76] Final judgments were executed without further court order.[77] Any sale of property to satisfy the judgment was conducted according to Spanish law.[78]

The county court also had jurisdiction over criminal cases.[79] The common law, rather than Spanish law, governed criminal proceedings.[80] Only by a presentment, or an indictment by a grand jury, could a person be charged with a capital or infamous crime.[81] Those accused of a crime had the right to be informed of the nature of the charges against them and the right to a speedy and public trial in front of a jury composed of residents of the county in which the crime occurred.[82] The accused also had the right to confront his or her accusers and the right to compel the testimony of witnesses who could offer favorable testimony.[83] Perhaps most importantly, the accused had the right to have an attorney present.[84] In short, Jackson granted to criminal defendants the same rights U.S. citizens had under the Fifth and Sixth Amendments of the U.S. Constitution.

Applying Spanish law to disputes was not always easy. In a lawsuit in St. Augustine arising from the Army's occupation of public buildings, the issue was whether an officer could be held civilly liable for torts committed while acting in his official capacity. In 1821 Captain John R. Bell arrested "a Mr. Fairbanks [after he] attempt[ed] to carry off by force a negro woman and her two children then in the possession of the law [i.e., in custody]."[85] Bell confined Fairbanks in Fort Marion (formerly the Castillo de San Marcos) for four days. Subsequently, Fairbanks sued Bell in the St. Johns County Court for false imprisonment and sought $450 in damages.[86] In a letter to Jackson, Bell claimed he was immune from suit.[87] Eventually, the lawsuit came to the attention of Attorney General Wirt.[88]

Wirt maintained that according to federal law, government officers were liable for torts committed by them while "under color of their office."[89] However, if the act was lawful, the officer could offer this fact as a defense.[90] Wirt urged Monroe not to intervene in Fairbanks's lawsuit, because doing so would contravene both U.S. constitutional and statutory law.[91] In this case, however, Spanish law still applied. Thus, determining whether Jackson, who had assumed the powers of the governor and captain-general of Cuba, could shield Bell from civil liability required "access to the records and archives of the provinces while under the Government of Spain."[92] It is unclear whether Bell or Fairbanks ever undertook such an effort (one presumes they did not).

Some information regarding the activities of the courts during this time can be gleaned from local newspapers. One announced on September 1, 1821, that the judges of the St. Johns County Court had been sworn in.[93] The actual number of cases before the court is uncertain, but by December 1821 the foreman of the grand jury reported that there were only "[a] few cases of misdemeanor and larceny on the docket of the term."[94]

Florida's Judicial System: 1822–1845

On March 30, 1822, a little more than eight months after the transfer of Florida to the United States, Congress enacted legislation establishing the territorial government of Florida.[95] The new statute vested executive power in a governor, who was to be appointed by the president for a three-year term.[96] In addition to serving as the commander-in-chief of the territorial militia, the governor

Figure 3. William P. DuVal, Judge, U.S. District Court for the District of East Florida and Territorial Governor of Florida. Courtesy of the State Library and Archives of Florida.

would be the *ex officio* superintendent of Indian affairs.[97] The governor had the power to pardon offenses against the territory, but pardons for offenses against the United States required the consent of the president.[98]

Initially, the governor was to appoint all of the officials of the civil government and the militia except for those appointed by the president.[99] In 1829 Congress (with some exceptions) granted voters the power to elect these officials.[100] Due to the lengthy absences of William DuVal, Florida's first territorial governor, Congress also passed legislation requiring the governor to obtain permission from the president prior to leaving the territory.[101]

Congress further directed that there should be a Secretary of the Territory,[102] whose duty was to "record and preserve all the papers and proceedings of the executive, and all the acts of the governor and legislative council, and transmit authentic copies of the proceedings of the governor, in his executive department, every six months, to the President of the United States."[103] The secretary also would assume the governor's duties in the event of the latter's death, resignation, removal, or absence.[104]

Congress vested the legislative power in the governor and a unicameral council.[105] This body consisted of thirteen members appointed by the president.[106] In 1829 the power to elect the council was extended to the territory's eligible voters.[107] In 1838 Congress split the council into two bodies: the Senate and the House of Representatives.[108] The territory was permitted to send one non-voting delegate to Congress.[109]

The governor, with the consent of a majority of the council, had the power to alter, modify, or repeal any law that was in force prior to the effective date of the act establishing the territorial government.[110] Unless repealed or amended by the council, such laws would remain in force as long as they did not conflict with the provisions of the territorial act.[111] The council could pass laws on "all the rightful subjects of legislation," provided that these laws did not conflict with the constitution and laws of the United States.[112]

Although the territorial act did not explicitly mention a veto power, one can be inferred from the fact that the governor was required to forward all legislative proposals to Congress.[113] It is unlikely that the governor would have forwarded proposals he did not support. In 1823 Congress granted the governor the power to veto legislation proposed by the council.[114] The council could override the veto with the agreement of two-thirds of its members.[115]

Legislation passed by the council and forwarded to Congress did not require the approval of Congress to become effective. However, Congress retained the power to repeal such legislation.[116] Between 1822 and 1845 Congress rarely took this step. In 1822, however, it did annul an ordinance[117] issued by Jackson in July 1821 regarding the naturalization of Florida's foreign residents,[118] as well as an ordinance passed in October 1821 by the St. Augustine city council concerning the imposition of certain taxes.[119] Likewise, in 1834 Congress annulled all territorial acts that imposed higher property taxes on non-residents than on residents.[120] Also in 1834 Congress repealed an act regulating civil procedure, declaring that it "affects existing remedies, prevents the execution of judgments rendered in obedience to existing laws, and impairs the obligation of contracts."[121]

In 1836 Congress annulled several acts regarding the incorporation of banks and the extension of banking powers to other institutions.[122] In fact, Congress stipulated that no law passed by the legislative council pertaining to the incorporation of banks could go into effect unless Congress confirmed it.[123]

The governor and the council were not granted power "over the primary disposal of the soil, nor to tax the lands of the United States, nor to interfere with the claims to lands within said territory."[124] Though unsettled land claims dating back to the Spanish and British eras heavily impacted the development of Florida for decades after the cessation, settling these claims was not initially within the power of the territorial government.

To settle claims to titles granted prior to January 24, 1818,[125] Congress established a board of three commissioners with the "power to inquire into the justice and validity of the claims filed with them."[126] For claims under 1,000 acres, the board could confirm the claim and release any interest the United States might have in the land.[127] For claims exceeding 1,000 acres, or if the amount of land granted was uncertain, the board had to file a report with the U.S. Secretary of the Treasury indicating whether it thought the claim was valid.[128]

Superior Courts and Court of Appeals

In the act creating the territorial government, Congress established two superior courts: one for East Florida and one for West Florida.[129] Each court was assigned one judge, who was required to hold court on the first Monday in January, April, July, and October.[130] The court was to remain in session until all the cases on the docket had been reviewed or continued to the next term. Sessions were to take place in St. Augustine for East Florida and in Pensacola for West Florida.[131] The legislative council was given the authority to designate additional times and locations.[132]

Congress subsequently created additional superior courts. In 1824 it added a third court between the Apalachicola and Suwanee Rivers,[133] and in 1828 a fourth court known as the Southern District.[134] In 1838 it created the fifth and final territorial judicial district, composed of the counties of Franklin, Washington, and Jackson, and named it the Apalachicola District.[135]

Initially, Congress granted the superior courts jurisdiction in all criminal cases and exclusive jurisdiction in all capital cases.[136] For criminal offenses arising under the laws of the United States, the superior courts had the same jurisdiction as the federal court in the Kentucky District.[137] In later legislation, this criminal jurisdiction became more nuanced. In 1826 the superior courts were granted original and appellate jurisdiction for criminal offenses under territorial law and exclusive jurisdiction for all crimes arising under the laws of the United States.[138]

Congress granted the superior courts jurisdiction over civil suits based on the laws of the Florida territory if the amount was $100 or more.[139] In 1826 this was extended to exclusive jurisdiction of civil causes of action based on admiralty and maritime law.[140] Although Congress initially did not give the superior courts a role in the unsettled land claims from the Spanish era, it eventually granted them the power to adjudicate claims exceeding 3,500 acres.[141] Due to its unique location, the superior court in the Southern District was given special instructions for handling cases involving the salvage of shipwrecks.[142] In 1834 the judge of the Eastern District was granted, for one year, the authority to adjudicate claims put forward by subjects of the Spanish government who suffered damages as a result of the U.S. Army's presence in East Florida in 1812–13 (during the so-called Patriot War).[143]

The act establishing the territorial government did not provide a right to appeal decisions of the superior courts based on territorial law. However, decisions based on U.S. law could be appealed to the U.S. Supreme Court.[144] In a letter to President Monroe in September 1822, the legislative council expressed its concern that the failure to provide a right to appeal decisions based on territorial law concentrated a "novel and dangerous power" in the hands of each superior court judge.[145] In 1824 Congress responded by enacting legislation that created a territorial court of appeals consisting of all the superior court judges.[146] Congress also granted the right to appeal decisions from the court of appeals if the amount in dispute exceeded $1,000.[147]

Superior court judges were appointed by the president for a term of four years.[148] Though the act made no provision for the renewal of terms and mandated no term limits, re-appointments were common. However, the prospect of long hours, low pay, and arduous travel deterred some nominees. In 1841, for example, William H. Brockenbrough, a Tallahassee lawyer, declined an appointment to the Middle District due to the meager salary.[149]

Failure to publish the territory's acts was a recurring problem and, on at least one occasion, the Superior Court of West Florida suspended all civil cases until the laws were published.[150] Lack of money was the main culprit, and the reluctance, or inability, of the federal government to fund the territorial government was a perpetual source of frustration for local officials (who often had to pay for necessaries out of their own pockets). Though many territorial laws and municipal ordinances did appear in local newspapers, this piecemeal approach was not an adequate substitute for a printed compilation of the territorial acts indexed by topic.

Circuit Courts

In August 1822 the legislative council created two circuit courts, composed of one judge each.[151] The courts had exclusive jurisdiction over civil suits for sums of $20 to $100 and appellate jurisdiction for sums under $20.[152] These courts also shared concurrent civil jurisdiction with the superior courts in suits for sums exceeding $100 arising under territorial law.[153] For reasons not specified, the legislative council granted the circuit courts criminal jurisdiction only over crimes that occurred in Jackson and Duval counties.[154]

A party had the right to appeal a circuit court's decision to the superior court.[155] If it failed to do so, it still had the right to submit a copy of the record to the superior court prior to the final execution of the judgment.[156] If the superior court found that an injustice had been committed, or there was a defect in the lower court's proceedings, it could issue a writ of *supersedeas* (suspension), which stopped execution of the judgment.[157] No provision was made for remanding the case to the lower court to correct its error.

The circuit court judges were appointed by the governor and remained in office unless removed by the governor and the legislative council.[158] For contempt of court, the judges were authorized to impose fines in amounts up to $20 and order imprisonment for no more than six days.[159]

Within a few months of the creation of the circuit courts, the inhabitants of East Florida questioned whether the burdensome taxes that were imposed to fund them were worth the expense.[160] The territory's current population did not justify a two-tiered trial court system; it made more sense to simply expand the jurisdiction of the superior courts. Within a year of their creation, the circuit courts were replaced by the county courts.

County Courts

The county courts that had been established by Jackson were abolished when Congress created the territorial government in March 1822.[161] In September 1822, however, the legislative council reestablished them.[162] This legislation was repealed by Congress in March 1823.[163] Another attempt, in June 1823, fared better and survived scrutiny.[164] A few weeks later, in July 1823, the council passed legislation advising that "whenever the word 'circuit courts' shall occur in the act of the last session of the legislative council, the county court shall be understood, and have jurisdiction."[165] This act effectively ended the territory's short experiment with circuit courts. All cases that had been pending in the circuit courts were transferred to the county courts and superior courts.[166]

By the end of the 1823 legislative session, Florida had five counties: Duval, Escambia, Gadsden, Jackson, and St. Johns. In each of them, the legislative council established a county court, which consisted of one judge.[167] The number of judges in each county court was increased to three in 1824.[168] The governor and the legislative council jointly appointed county court judges.[169]

The county courts initially had jurisdiction over suits for sums of $20-$100 and appellate jurisdiction for sums below $100.[170] For sums above $100, the county court shared jurisdiction with the superior court.[171] In such cases, litigants had the right to appeal the county court's decision to the superior court.[172] Additionally, the county courts were the probate courts for their respective counties.[173]

The county courts had concurrent jurisdiction with the superior courts over non-capital criminal offenses.[174] The criminal jurisdiction of the county courts was later refined to include concurrent jurisdiction in affray, assault and battery, breach of the peace, case, covenant, and trespass actions.[175] Whenever a difficult question of criminal law arose in the county courts, the proceedings had to be suspended and the question sent to the superior court for review.[176] In November 1828 the legislative council stripped the county courts of their criminal jurisdiction except when the accused was the judge of the superior court.[177]

A county court's decision affirming a justice of the peace was final except for matters involving only questions of law.[178] In such cases, the parties could appeal the county court's decision to the superior court.[179] If an appeal was taken, the county court judge was required to certify that the record filed by the appellant accurately reflected the evidence presented and the resulting decision.[180]

County courts also performed many non-judicial functions, including some that later would be handled by specialized administrative agencies. For example, the county courts were charged with keeping the roads in good repair, assisting the poor, and levying taxes to provide for the upkeep of public buildings.[181] They also were tasked with appointing cattle inspectors.[182]

Municipal Courts

In addition to the aforementioned courts, the legislative council occasionally created courts to serve specific cities. These included an Apalachicola court of common pleas (1831) to handle minor civil and criminal cases,[183] a St. Joseph mayor's court (1837) to hear disputes not exceeding $500,[184] and an Apalachicola mayor's court (1844) to enforce municipal ordinances.[185]

Justices of the Peace

Justices of the peace were important officials in territorial Florida. They had both judicial and administrative functions, and depending on the circumstances, performed the roles of magistrate, city manager, county commissioner, and chief of police. Although originally selected by the governor,[186] in 1829 they became appointees of the legislative council.[187]

Justices of the peace had jurisdiction over all causes of action in which the amount in dispute was $20 or less if "founded on any bond, bill, note, or account in writing, or assumpsit."[188] They could render judgments and order that these judgments be executed.[189] For judgments under $10, the parties had no right of appeal.[190] For judgments exceeding $10, the parties could appeal to the circuit court.[191] A justice of the peace could hold court to hear civil cases as often as needed [192] and could take depositions that could be introduced as evidence anywhere in the territory.[193]

While justices of the peace had no authority to try defendants for criminal offenses, upon receiving information that an individual had breached the peace he could have the person arrested and brought forward to answer for the offense.[194] He could then order the person to appear before the circuit court.[195] He also could set bail and if its conditions were not met, he could have the person put in jail until the circuit court's next term.[196]

Court Officers

To assist the territory's judges, both Congress and the legislative council authorized the creation of various offices, including clerks, constables, marshals, prosecuting attorneys, and sheriffs. When the territorial government established the county courts and appointed officials to serve them, the expense of maintaining two judicial systems quickly became apparent. Efforts by local officials to adapt to the conditions confronting them often were rebuffed by Congress, although federal interest in maintaining tight control over the territory waned as Florida approached statehood. In 1828 the legislative council made assessors, coroners, county court clerks, sheriffs, surveyors, and tax collectors elective positions.[197]

In 1789 Congress had created the office of U.S. Marshal to execute throughout the federal judicial districts "all lawful precepts directed to him, and issued under the authority of the United States."[198] In the act to establish the territorial government in Florida, Congress provided that each superior court would have one marshal.[199] These marshals were to perform the same duties as the marshals in other federal districts and, like them, would be appointed by the president with the advice and consent of the U.S. Senate.[200] At the county level, the legislative council assigned to each county a sheriff to "perform all duties required by law."[201]

Because the superior courts acted as both a territorial court and a federal court, the issue of the respective duties of the marshals and sheriffs, as well as the power to define them, resulted in a power struggle between Joseph L. Smith, the Judge of East Florida, and Waters Smith, the newly appointed Marshal of East Florida. James R. Hanham, the Sheriff of St. Johns County, had been recommended by Judge Smith and by the justices of the St. Johns County Court for the position of East Florida marshal.[202] When President Monroe passed over Hanham, Judge Smith decided to see to it that Marshal Smith had as little to do as possible.

In April 1823 Marshal Smith wrote to Secretary of State John Quincy Adams to complain that Judge Smith had "directed that all process issuing from that Court in the name and by authority of the Territory, shall be directed to, and served by the Sheriffs of the Counties of St. Johns and Duval."[203] This raised the question of whether Judge Smith had exceeded his authority.

In June 1823 the legislative council passed a law making marshals the executive officers of the superior courts and transferred to them "all business confided to the sheriffs of the several counties of this territory, emanating from the [Superior Courts] of their respective district."[204] Because the act creating the territorial government granted the legislative council the authority to pass laws that were not inconsistent with the laws of the United States, expanding the role of the marshals was not, *ipso facto*, inconsistent with anything Congress had done. In 1824 Congress seemed to agree and provided that marshals "shall, also, be subject to such regulations and penalties as the legislative council shall impose, while acting under, and in virtue of, the territorial laws."[205] This meant, in effect, that marshals had one set of rules when acting under U.S. law and another when acting under territorial law.

A year later, the council changed its mind and enacted legislation in which "all business confided to the marshals of this Territory shall be transferred to the sheriffs of the respective counties."[206] Some East Florida inhabitants were not in favor of this transfer. In a petition to Congress, they argued that creating a "multiplicity of officers to the Superior Court (if the Legislative Council have authority to do so) will be productive of great inconvenience to the inhabitants of this district and occasion much embarrassment in the administration of Justice."[207] Eventually, the U.S. House of Representatives' Committee on the Territories stepped in and settled the matter by reversing the council.[208]

Crimes and Misdemeanors

Although common law offenses were recognized in the Florida territory, criminal law was largely rooted in statutes. In September 1822 the legislative council passed detailed laws on crimes and criminal procedure.[209] Crimes included arson, assault and battery, bigamy, burglary, cattle stealing, counterfeiting, falsifying records, forgery, fraud, horse stealing, larceny, manslaughter, murder, perjury, rape, receiving stolen goods, and subornation of perjury.

The criminal justice process began when a warrant for the arrest of a person accused of a crime was issued by a justice of the peace.[210] To bring the accused into custody, the sheriff had the authority to form a *posse comitatus* and requisition horses for the search.[211] Within ten days of the arrest, two justices were required to meet at the county courthouse to review the allegations.[212] If they concluded there was sufficient evidence, the case was referred to the appropriate court for prosecution, accompanied by the testimony, reduced to writing, of any witnesses the justices had relied on in arriving at their decision.[213] If the justices decided there was insufficient evidence to move forward, the suspect was released.[214] The decision to release a suspect did not bar future prosecution based on the same allegations.[215]

If the suspect was referred for prosecution, the justices had to state for the record whether the accused was eligible for bail and, if so, recommend an amount.[216] The court having jurisdiction over the offense was not bound by the decision of the justices and could release the suspect on bail even if the justices had determined that the suspect was ineligible for bail.[217] Once bail was granted and the suspect was released, he or she was required to appear on the first day of the court's next term.[218] Failure to do so forfeited the securities guaranteeing bail.

To proceed to trial, the accused had to be indicted by a grand jury.[219] Prior to the start of the court term, the sheriff (or the court's executive officer) was required to summon "twenty[-]four of the most discreet house[-]keepers" residing within the court's jurisdiction.[220] The grand jury had to consist of at least sixteen individuals.[221] If an insufficient number of prospective jurors showed up, the sheriff could press any otherwise-qualified bystanders into service.[222]

According to the statutes, the grand jury was to "enquire of and present all murders, felonies, crimes, and misdemeanors."[223] If indicted, a bill of indictment was sent to the judge, who would issue a writ of *capias* (capture) if the accused was not already in custody.[224] If the accused was in custody and was charged with a felony, he or she had to be arraigned and tried in the same court term, unless a continuance was granted because "the witnesses could not be procured."[225]

The accused could file a motion on the first day of the court's term to have the trial during that term.[226] If the grand jury did not indict the accused during the term, the judge could release the accused on bail.[227] If the accused was still in custody during the following term, the judge had to release him or her without bail in the absence of an indictment.[228] If the accused was not indicted by the third term, the charges had to be permanently dismissed.[229] All crimes had to be prosecuted within two years of their occurrence.[230]

For criminal offenses, there were two types of juries: grand and trial ("petit"). In the act establishing the territorial government, Congress limited service on these juries to free white male landowners who had resided in the territory for at least one year.[231] The legislative council was granted the power to prescribe the method of choosing jurors.[232] Otherwise, the judge of each court had the authority to do so.

Later legislation modified the requirements for jury service. In 1829 the council stipulated that jurors had to be between the ages of twenty-one and sixty.[233] Clergymen and physicians were exempted.[234] Beginning in 1832, the sheriff was required to file with the county clerk the names of all of the men in the county who were eligible to serve as jurors.[235] The justices of the peace would then examine the sheriff's list and could add or delete names as they saw fit.[236] They also had the final say in determining whether a particular individual was qualified to be a juror.[237]

Obtaining the required number of jurors was a perennial problem due to the small pool of eligible citizens and the refusal of many jurors to show up when called. Anyone accused of a high crime or misdemeanor was allowed to peremptorily challenge fifteen jurors (and even more if good cause was shown).[238] As a result, seating a jury sometimes proved impossible. In 1836 the legislative council divided Monroe County, with the eastern portion becoming Dade County.[239] This decision caused an uproar in Monroe County, which already was having trouble finding jurors.[240]

Criminal penalties included corporal punishment, fines, imprisonment, restitution, and time in a pillory. Murder and rape were capital crimes.[241] Executions were by hanging[242] and had to be carried out within fifty days of conviction.[243] For manslaughter, the defendant could be fined $1,000 and imprisoned for up to one year.[244] For a second larceny conviction, a person could be fined up to four times the value of the item stolen and had to be whipped, with the lashing not to "exceed[] 75 stripes, to be well laid on his, her or their bare back."[245] A fine of $5 could be levied on a person for profane swearing.[246]

The lack of adequate jails limited the options available to sentencing judges. A grand jury in Monroe County complained that its dilapidated jail was full of those convicted of crimes against the United States, but Congress "has hitherto never appropriated one cent to the building or repairing [of] a jail in this entire Judicial District."[247] Similarly, a grand jury of Calhoun County strongly urged that jails be built so that corporal punishment could be abolished.[248]

Documents and letters sent to federal officials, newspaper articles, and correspondence between territorial leaders are important sources of information about criminal activity in territorial Florida.[249] Examples of criminal cases include the indictment and conviction of Martin Hutto, a resident of Walton County, for armed robbery;[250] the conviction of three men in Leon County for assault and battery;[251] "six Bills of Indictment: viz. one against a colored boy, for passing counterfeit coin: two against Negroes for Petit Larcenies: and three for trifling cases of Assault and Battery";[252] charges against three men for disturbing the peace in St. Augustine and rioting;[253] and the case of Isaac Nathans, who was convicted of assault and battery for pummeling Robert W. Bell after the latter insulted a female member of Nathans's family.[254]

Civil Cases

Legislation governing civil matters in the courts were among the first acts passed by the council. Rules regarding actions in equity,[255] actions in law,[256] attachments,[257] execution of judgments,[258] and statutes of limitations[259] were all approved within six months of Florida becoming a territory. These rules frequently were amended, especially during the first decade after the cessation of Florida. Procedural rules for filing claims in the superior courts also were adopted by the court of appeals after the legislative council ordered it to "make all necessary rules for the regulation of the Superior Courts[.]"[260]

The procedure for commencing a lawsuit was fairly straightforward. The plaintiff was required to file a complaint in the clerk's office describing the cause of action, along with any documentation supporting the claim.[261] Suits normally were brought in the county in which the defendant resided. If process was served at least thirty days before the first day of the court's next term, the plaintiff had the right to demand that a trial be held once the term began.[262] If service occurred less than thirty days prior to the first day of the term, the defendant had the right to continue the trial until the subsequent term.[263] A default judgment could be issued if the defendant did not show up on the first day of the term in which the suit was docketed.[264] The court clerk was authorized to add five percent to the total amount of the resulting judgment to help defray the attorneys' fees of the winning party.[265]

As with criminal cases, civil cases frequently were mentioned in local newspapers. Examples include a notice that a lawsuit had been commenced in Gadsden County;[266] an announcement of a public auction of land to satisfy a judgment;[267] a notice to file claims against an estate that was in probate;[268] an order that non-resident defendants return to Florida to answer a lawsuit filed against them;[269] an announcement that a tract of land was being partitioned;[270] and a declaration by an attorney in Pensacola that he intended to file a lawsuit in the Western District of Florida to collect on a debt of $684 that was secured by land on the Escambia River.[271]

Although Spanish civil law had been rejected in favor of English common law, at times interesting choice of law problems arose. A Pensacola newspaper published a notice about a foreclosure action filed on December 15, 1823, in the Superior Court of the Western District of Florida.[272] On June 16, 1821, a mortgage had been executed on land located along the Perdido River. Later, when the borrower failed to pay the amount owed, the lender sued. In his complaint, the plaintiff sought recovery for the outstanding debt (as well as the costs incurred in filing the suit) and asked the court not to grant the defendant the equity of redemption.[273] Because the transfer of West Florida to the United States was not completed until July 1821, the mortgage's execution was governed by Spanish law; however, the plaintiff's foreclosure action was subject to U.S. law.

In another case, Alexander Hamilton Jr., the U.S. Attorney for East Florida (and the second son of the famed Federalist), got into a dispute with John

England, the Roman Catholic bishop of Charleston, South Carolina. When St. Augustine's last Spanish priest (Father Michael Crosby, who was from Ireland) died, Hamilton claimed that all of the Church's properties in the city passed to the United States.

In legal terms, the issue was whether, at the time of the cessation of Florida, the properties were held by the Spanish Crown or were privately owned by the Church. If the former, they now belonged to the United States. Attorney General William Wirt ultimately sided with England's position,[274] and Congress removed all doubt several years later when it formally conveyed the property to the Church.[275]

Admission to the Bar

To practice law in the Florida territory, an aspiring attorney needed a license from the governor or a superior court judge.[276] No person convicted of "perjury, bribery, corruption, or other infamous crime" was eligible for a license.[277] By statute, sheriffs, court clerks, and their deputies were not permitted to practice law.[278]

In 1832 the legislative council directed the court of appeals to draft rules for the superior courts.[279] Under the new rules, an applicant had to be at least twenty-one years old and of good moral character.[280] In addition, a superior court judge had to find the petitioner fit to practice.[281]

The rules did not include a code of ethics, nor did they provide for disciplinary actions. However, grounds for disbarment did appear in several territorial laws. Thus, for example, attorneys who failed to turn over money to clients were to be "stricken from the list of attorneys."[282] Likewise, an attorney convicted of barratry (i.e., inciting litigation) was "disqualified from practicing [in] the future."[283]

Conclusion

In 1838, in preparation for statehood, Florida held a constitutional convention in the town of St. Joseph.[284] The document that emerged vested judicial power in a Supreme Court and various circuit courts, chancery courts, and justices of the peace.[285] The Supreme Court was to be primarily an appellate court,[286] whereas the circuit courts were to be primarily trial courts.[287] The Florida legislature was granted the authority to create equity courts, but circuit courts would perform as both courts of law and courts of equity if the chancery courts were not formed.[288] The legislature was to determine the jurisdiction of the county-based justices of the peace.[289]

Although Florida was granted statehood in March 1845,[290] the territorial courts were not abolished until July 1845, when the legislature directed that the actions being heard by them were to be transferred to the new state courts.[291] In the meantime, Congress established the state as a single federal judicial district called the District of Florida and allotted to it one judge.[292]

With the establishment of the District of Florida and the creation of the state court system, the federal courts and the state courts went their separate ways, ending the unique blend of federal and territorial law that characterized Florida's legal system from 1821 to 1845. Soon after the creation of the Florida Supreme Court, its decisions began to be compiled, indexed, and printed.[293] The availability of this information, along with improved modes of transportation and freedom from outside interference, marked the beginning of a new period in Florida's judicial development.

Notes

1. For detailed accounts of these negotiations, see Hubert Bruce Fuller, The Purchase of Florida: Its History and Diplomacy (1964); Philip Coolidge Brooks, Diplomacy and the Borderlands: The Adams-Onís Treaty of 1819 (1939).

2. The boundaries of the land that had been purchased from France were unclear. When the British acquired Florida in 1763, they extended the area's western boundary to the Mississippi River. Twenty years later, Spain re-acquired Florida and set the boundary between West Florida and colonial Louisiana at the Mississippi River. In 1800, France acquired Louisiana from Spain. The United States claimed that the land between the Mississippi River and the Perdido River was part of the territory it had acquired from France in 1803 and, as a result, Spanish Florida ended at the Perdido. Spain disputed this claim but was in no position to push back the American settlers through military action. *See further* Samuel C. Hyde Jr., *Setting a Precedent for Regional Revolution: The West Florida Revolt Considered*, 90 Fla. Hist. Q. 121 (2011); Henry S. Marks, *Boundary Disputes in the Republic of West Florida in 1810*, 12 La. Hist. 355 (1971); Isaac Joslin Cox, *The American Intervention in West Florida*, 17 Am. Hist. Rev. 290 (1912).

3. *See* Treaty of Amity, Settlement, and Limits between the United States of America and his Catholic Majesty, U.S.-Spain, Feb. 22, 1819, 8 Stat. 252, more commonly referred to as the Adams-Onís Treaty (in recognition of the diplomats who negotiated it: U.S. Secretary of State John Quincy Adams and Spanish ambassador Luis de Onís y Gonzalez-Vara).

4. 8 Stat. at 264 (art. 16).

5. An English translation of Spain's ratification can be found at 3 U.S.T.I.A. (Miller) 3, 18–20 (1933).

6. *See* An Act to Authorize the President of the United States to take Possession of East and West Florida and Establish a Temporary Government Therein, 3 Stat. 523 (1821). This act originally was passed on March 3, 1819, but was reenacted due to the long delay in the ratification of the Adam-Onís treaty.

7. *Id.* at 524. Congress had gained experience in establishing territorial governments from

its oversight of the Northwest Territory. *See* Denis P. Duffey, Note, *The Northwest Ordinance as a Constitutional Document*, 95 Colum. L. Rev. 929 (1995). It therefore is unclear why Florida's territorial government was not immediately established, especially in light of the fact that there was a two-year gap between the signing of the treaty and the actual transfer.

8. 3 Stat. at 524.

9. Monroe outlined his appointments in a letter to Andrew Jackson. *See The President to Commissioner and Governor Jackson, in* 22 Territorial Papers of the United States: The Territory of Florida, 1821–1824, at 53–57 (Clarence Edwin Carter ed. 1956) [hereinafter Carter v. 22].

10. This division also was adopted by Spain during its second period of rule (1783–1821). The lack of a central government during the colonial era helps to explain the cultural, economic, and political differences between East and West Florida. *See further* Chapters 1 and 2 of this book.

11. 3 Stat. at 524 (§ 2). The limited application of U.S. laws to the territory would cause problems when judicial districts were created. *See infra* notes 35–38 and accompanying text.

12. 3 Stat. at 524 (§ 2).

13. *Id.*

14. *See Commission of Andrew Jackson as Governor, in* Carter v. 22, *supra* note 9, at 9–11. For an overview of Jackson's tenure as governor, see, e.g., Herbert J. Domherty Jr., *The Governorship of Andrew Jackson*, 33 Fla. Hist. Q. 3 (1954).

15. *See* Carter v. 22, *supra* note 9, at 10.

16. *See Special Commission of Andrew Jackson as Governor, in* Carter v. 22, *supra* note 9, at 18–19.

17. *Id.* at 18.

18. *See The Secretary of State to Commissioner and Governor Jackson, in* Carter v. 22, *supra* note 9, at 15.

19. Thomas Edward Watson, The Life and Times of Andrew Jackson 262 (1912).

20. William Graham Sumner, Andrew Jackson as a Public Man: What He Was, What Chances He Had, And What He Did with Them 69 (1890).

21. *The Attorney General to the President, in* Carter v. 22, *supra* note 9, at 251 (italics in original).

22. For a variety of reasons, a full-fledged legal system never developed in Spanish Florida. *See further* Chapter 1 of this book.

23. For an account of the transfer, see Rogers W. Young, *The Transfer of Fort San Marcos and East Florida to the United States*, 14 Fla. Hist. Q. 231 (1946).

24. *Proclamation by Commissioner and Governor Jackson*, in Carter v. 22, *supra* note 9, at 110–11.

25. *Governor Jackson to the Secretary of State, in* Carter v. 22, *supra* note 9, at 150.

26. *Id.*

27. The 1812 Constitution of Cádiz contained provisions on the structures of municipal government. *See* M.C. Mirow, Florida's First Constitution: The Constitution of Cádiz (2012). Whether these provisions applied to East and West Florida was unresolved at the time of Florida's transfer to the United States. *See further* Chapter 1 of this book.

28. *Governor Jackson to the Secretary of State, in* Carter v. 22, *supra* note 9, at 151. For a description of the Spanish legal system in St. Augustine, see John Harry Matthews, *Law Enforce-*

ment in Spanish East Florida: 1783–1821 (unpublished Ph.D. dissertation, Catholic University of America, 1987). *See also* Chapter 1 of this book.

29. *See Report of Mr. Brackenridge to Governor Jackson* (July 26, 1821), *in* 2 American State Papers: Documents, Legislative and Executive of the Congress of the United States—Miscellaneous 902 (Walter Lowrie & Walter S. Franklin eds. 1834).

30. *Id.* at 903. Brackenridge argued that the introduction of easy-to-understand rules of procedure and the creation of a tribunal before which a trial could be conducted would suffice until the territorial government was established.

31. *Governor Jackson to the Secretary of State, in* Carter v. 22, *supra* note 9, at 150.

32. *See, e.g., From Pensacola,* Raleigh Reg., Sept. 7, 1821, at 1 (reprinting an extract from a letter written by a resident of Pensacola dated July 23, 1821).

33. *Presentment of the Grand Jury of East Florida, in* Carter v. 22, *supra* note 9, at 295.

34. *See* An Act Providing for the Adoption of the Common Law and Certain Statutes of Great-Britain and for Repealing the Laws and Ordinances Now in Force, 1822 Fla. Terr. Acts 53 (§ 1). This act embraced the common law as it existed prior to the fourth year (1606) of the reign of James I. (In 1606, following the failed Guy Fawkes Gunpowder Plot, James introduced a series of repressive measures aimed chiefly at Catholics.)

35. *See The President to Commissioner and Governor Jackson, in* Carter v. 22, *supra* note 9, at 55.

36. *The Attorney General to the President, in* Carter v. 22, supra note 9, at 251.

37. *Id.* at 250–53.

38. *The President to the Attorney General, in* Carter v. 22, *supra* note 9, at 242.

39. For background information on DuVal, see James M. Denham, Florida Founder William P. DuVal: Frontier Bon Vivant (2015).

40. *Governor Jackson to the President, in* Carter v. 22, *supra* note 9, at 160.

41. *Id.* at 160–61.

42. *Id.* at 161.

43. *Memorial to the President by Members of the Pensacola Bar, in* Carter v. 22, *supra* note 9, at 183.

44. *Charge,* Fla. Gazette, Dec. 10, 1821, at 3.

45. DuVal apparently made a favorable impression in the nation's capital, because in April 1822 Monroe appointed him to succeed Jackson as Florida's governor.

46. *See Judge Fromentin to the Secretary of State, in* Carter v. 22, *supra* note 9, at 173–75. In 1805, Congress had passed legislation that granted the same jurisdiction to superior courts in territories that did not have a federal district court as was exercised by the district court of Kentucky. *See* An Act to Extend Jurisdiction in Certain Cases to the Territorial Courts, 2 Stat. 338 (1805).

47. The incident is discussed further in Herbert J. Doherty Jr., *Andrew Jackson vs. The Spanish Governor: Pensacola 1821,* 34 Fla. Hist. Q. 141 (1955). *See also* Virginia Meacham Gould, *"A Chaos of Iniquity and Discord": Slave and Free Women of Color in the Spanish Ports of New Orleans, Mobile, and Pensacola, in* The Devil's Lane: Sex and Race in the Early South 232–33, 238–39 (Catherine Clinton & Michele Gillespie eds. 1997).

48. William Graham Sumner, Andrew Jackson 89 (1910).

49. *See Col. Callava's Statement,* Daily Nat'l Intelligencer, Oct. 3, 1821, at 2.

50. *Order of Governor Jackson* (Aug. 23, 1821), *in* Lowrie & Franklin, *supra* note 29, at 810.

51. *See The Attorney General to the President*, *in* Carter v. 22, *supra* note 9, at 256.

52. *See Acting Governor Walton (West Florida) to the Secretary of State*, *in* Carter v. 22, *supra* note 9, at 292–93.

53. *Mr. Fromentin to Captain Henley* (Dec. 1, 1821), *in* Lowrie & Franklin, *supra* note 29, at 869.

54. *Governor Jackson to the Secretary of State*, *in* Carter v. 22, *supra* note 9, at 237.

55. *See* Ordinance No. 4, at § II, *in* Ordinances by Major-General Andrew Jackson, Governor of the Provinces of the Floridas, Exercising the Powers of the Captain-General, and of the Intendant of the Island of Cuba, over the said Provinces, and of the Governors of said Provinces Respectively (R.W. Edes ed. 1821).

56. *See Governor Jackson to the Secretary of State*, *in* Carter v. 22, *supra* note 9, at 151.

57. *Id.*

58. *See* Ordinance No. 4, at § I, in Edes, *supra* note 55.

59. *Id.* § II.

60. *Id.*

61. *Id.*

62. *Id.*

63. *Id.* § III.

64. *See Governor Jackson to the Secretary of State*, *in* Carter v. 22, *supra* note 9, at 151.

65. Ordinance No. 5, at § I, *in* Edes, *supra* note 55.

66. *Id.* § VII.

67. *Id.*

68. *Id.* § X.

69. *Id.* § II.

70. *Id.*

71. *Id.* § V.

72. *Id.* § X.

73. *Id.*

74. *Id.* § III.

75. *Id.*

76. *Id.*

77. *Id.* § VI.

78. *Id.*

79. Ordinance No. 4, at § II, *in* Edes, *supra* note 55.

80. *Id.* § III.

81. *Id.*

82. *Id.*

83. *Id.*

84. *Id.*

85. *John R. Bell to Governor Jackson*, *in* Carter v. 22, *supra* note 9, at 246.

86. *Id.*

87. *Id.*

88. *See The Attorney General to the President*, in Carter v. 22, *supra* note 9, at 267–69.

89. *Id.* at 268.

90. *Id.*

91. *Id.*

92. *Id.* at 269.

93. *New Appointments*, Daily Nat'l Intelligencer, Sept. 24, 1821, at 3. According to the paper:

> On Saturday last, Mr. Secretary *Worthington*, exercising the powers of Governor of this province, under the Captain General Jackson, proceeded to the farther organization of the Civil Authority of the County of St. John's and of this city, in conformity to certain Ordinances which have been promulgated.
>
> The Governor, accompanied by Capt. *Bell*, of the Artillery, commanding the United States' troops, Capt. *Hammersley*, of the navy, and many Floridians, met the Civil Officers in the Council Chamber at 10 o'clock, when, after a short and appropriate address, the [new judges] were sworn into office. . . .
>
> The oaths were administered with much ceremony, under the auspicious waving of the *Star Spangled Banner*; and the novelty of the scene was much increased by the presence of about 50 Indians of the Chehaw tribe, who had just came into town to visit the new authorities.

Id. (italics in original).

94. *County Court of St. John's [sic]—Charge*, Fla. Gazette, Dec. 22, 1821, at 3.

95. *See* An Act for the Establishment of a Territorial Government in Florida, 3 Stat. 654 (1822).

96. *Id.* at 655 (§ 2). The governorship would not become an elective position until 1845.

97. *Id.*

98. *Id.*

99. *Id.*

100. *See* An Act to Authorize the Citizens of the Territories of Arkansas and Florida to Elect their Officers and for Other Purposes, 4 Stat. 332 (1829). Excluded from this legislation were the offices of auditor, justice of the peace, and treasurer (these positions were filled by the legislative council).

101. *See* An Act to Amend "An Act for the Establishment of a Territorial Government in Florida" and for Other Purposes, 3 Stat. 750, 751, at § 4 (1823). This provision was repealed on March 26, 1824. *See* An Act to Amend an Act Entitled "An Act to Amend an Act for the Establishment of a Territorial Government in Florida and for Other Purposes," 4 Stat. 45, 47, at § 6 (1824).

On one occasion, DuVal's absence created a problem for Joseph Smith, the incoming judge of the Eastern District of Florida. As a new appointee, Smith feared that DuVal's absence would cause Smith to miss at least two court terms because judges were required to take their oaths in front of the governor. *See* 3 Stat. at 657 (§ 8). In a letter to Secretary of State John Quincy Adams, Smith urged Congress to pass legislation to allow other officials to administer the oath. *See Judge Smith to the Secretary of State*, *in* Carter v. 22, *supra* note 9, at 554, 555.

102. 3 Stat. at 655 (§ 3).

103. *Id.*

104. *Id.*

105. *Id.* § 5. For a description of the early Florida legislature, see Allen Morris & Amelia Rea Maguire, *The Unicameral Legislature in Florida*, 58 Fla. Hist. Q. 303 (1980).

106. 3 Stat. at 655 (§ 5). The number of members of the legislative council varied over

time. *See, e.g.*, An Act to Equalize Representation in the Territory of Florida and for Other Purposes, 4 Stat. 677 (1834).

107. *See* 4 Stat. at 333 (§ 5). This act provided that Escambia, Gadsden, Jackson, Leon, Mosquito, and St. Johns counties would each have two members while Alachua, Duval, Hamilton, Jefferson, Madison, Monroe, Nassau, Walton, and Washington counties would each have one member.

108. *See* An Act to Reorganize the Legislative Council of Florida and for Other Purposes, 5 Stat. 263 (1838).

109. *See* 3 Stat. at 659 (§ 14).

110. *Id.* at 655 (§ 5).

111. *Id.* at 659 (§ 13).

112. *Id.* at 655 (§ 5). The existence of such a conflict was alleged but found not to exist in American Ins. Co. v. 356 Bales of Cotton (Canter), 26 U.S. (1 Pet.) 511, 546 (1828).

The *356 Bales* case involved a territorial statute that created a so-called "Wreckers' Court" in Key West. *See* An Act Concerning Wreckers and Wrecked Property, 1823 Fla. Terr. Acts 128. In actuality, the Wreckers' Court was an *ad hoc* form of arbitration consisting of five persons convened by the "justice of the peace or notary public as may reside next adjacent to the place of arrival" of the salved goods. *Id.* § 1. The panel's members had to include "two . . . persons . . . nominated by the owners of the property . . . and two . . . persons . . . nominated by the salvors . . . and [a] fifth person . . . nominated by the justice or notary. . . ." *Id.* § 3. In 1826, Congress repealed the Wreckers' Act. *See* An Act to Annul "An Act Concerning Wreckers and Wrecked Property," Passed by the Governor and Legislative Council of the Territory of Florida, 4 Stat. 138 (1826). As a result, how salvage cases were to be resolved, and by whom, suddenly became uncertain. To address this problem, Congress authorized creation of a new superior court at Key West and, based on the *356 Bales* decision (which had been handed down two months earlier) granted it jurisdiction over the local wrecking industry. *See* An Act to Establish a Southern Judicial District in the Territory of Florida, 4 Stat. 291, 292, at §§ 3–6 (1828). For a further discussion, see, e.g., W. Randy Miller, *The Case of the Brig Halcyon: A Study in Old Key West Admiralty Law*, 27 J. Mar. L. & Com. 311 (1996); Dorothy Dodd, *The Wrecking Business on the Florida Reef 1822–1860*, 22 Fla. Hist. Q. 171 (1944).

113. 3 Stat. at 655 (§ 5).

114. *See* 3 Stat. at 751–52 (§ 6).

115. *Id.* at 752 (§ 6). In 1823, for example, the legislative council overrode DuVal's veto of An Act Providing for the Adoption of the Common and Statute Laws of England and for Repealing Certain Laws and Ordinances, 1824 Fla. Terr. Acts 136, 137.

116. 3 Stat. at 655 (§ 5).

117. *See* An Act to Relieve the People of Florida from the Operation of Certain Ordinances, 3 Stat. 685 (1822).

118. *See* Ordinance No. 3, *in* Edes, *supra* note 55. Presumably this ordinance was repealed because only Congress can make rules regarding naturalization. *See* U.S. Const., art. I, § 8, cl. 4.

119. *See An Ordinance Passed in [the] City Council on the 17th October, 1821*, Fla. Gazette, Oct. 20, 1821, at 1, *repealed*, 3 Stat. at 685.

120. *See* An Act Repealing Certain Acts of the Legislative Council of the Territory of Florida, 4 Stat. 740 (1834).

121. *See Report of the House Committee on the Territories*, *in* 25 Territorial Papers of the United States: The Territory of Florida, 1834–1839, at 5 (Clarence Edwin Carter ed. 1960) [hereinafter Carter v. 25].

122. *See* An Act to Disapprove and Annul Certain Acts of the Territorial Legislature of Florida and for Other Purposes, 5 Stat. 61, at § 2 (1836).

123. *Id.* § 1.

124. 3 Stat. at 655–56 (§ 5).

125. Treaty of Amity, *supra* note 3, at art. 8 (8 Stat. at 258).

126. *See* An Act for Ascertaining Claims and Titles to Land within the Territory of Florida, 3 Stat. 709, 717, at § 5 (1822). The board is discussed further in Chapter 1 of this book.

127. 3 Stat. at 718 (§ 5).

128. *Id.*

129. 3 Stat. at 656 (§ 6).

130. *Id.*

131. *Id.*

132. *Id.* Although designating a particular location for a particular session did not create a new superior court, when sitting in Gadsden County the Middle District sometimes was referred to as the Superior Court of Gadsden County. The legislative council added sessions, and changed the dates of existing sessions, on a frequent basis. *See* An Act to Provide for Holding Terms of the Superior Courts in Different Counties within this Territory and for Other Purposes, 1826–1827 Fla. Terr. Acts 153.

133. *See* 4 Stat. at 45. The sessions of this court were to be held "at the seat of government in said territory." In time, this district became known as the Middle District (due to its physical location between the East and West districts).

134. *See* 4 Stat. 291. The sessions of this court were held at Key West.

135. *See* An Act to Establish a New Judicial District in the Territory of Florida, 5 Stat. 294 (1838).

In 1835, the legislative council had petitioned Congress to create a superior court in a district to be called the Judicial District of Suwannee composed of Alachua, Columbia, Hamilton, Hillsborough, and Madison counties. *See Resolution of the Legislative Council*, *in* Carter v. 25, *supra* note 121, at 107. A group of local citizens protested to Congress that a new judicial district was not needed and that the creation of additional districts should await statehood. *See Remonstrance to Congress by Citizens of the Territory*, *in* Carter v. 25, *supra* note 121, at 477–78.

136. 3 Stat. at 656 (§ 6).

137. *Id.* (§ 7).

138. *See* An Act to Amend the Several Acts for the Establishment of a Territorial Government in Florida, 4 Stat. 164 (1826).

139. 3 Stat. at 654 (§ 6).

140. 4 Stat. at 164.

141. *See* An Act Supplementary to the Several Acts Providing for the Settlement and Confirmation of Private Land Claims in Florida, 4 Stat. 284, 285, at § 6 (1828).

142. *Id.* at 292 (§§ 3–6).

143. *See* An Act for the Relief of Certain Inhabitants of East Florida, 1 Acts Passed at the First Session of the Twenty-Third Congress of the United States 48 (1834).

144. 3 Stat. at 656 (§ 7).

145. *See Memorial to the President by the Legislative Council, in* Carter v. 22, *supra* note 9, at 523–24.

146. 4 Stat. at 46 (§ 4).

147. 3 Stat. at 752 (§ 7).

148. 3 Stat. at 657 (§ 8). Volumes 22–26 of The Territorial Papers of the United States: The Territory of Florida (Clarence Edwin Carter ed. 1956–62) contain copies of the presidential commissions for judges of the superior courts. For short biographies of select judges from territorial Florida, see Walter W. Manley, II et al., The Supreme Court of Florida and Its Predecessor Courts, 1821–1917 (1997).

149. *See Judge Brockenbrough to the President, in* 26 Territorial Papers of the United States: The Territory of Florida, 1839–1845, at 377 (Clarence Edwin Carter ed. 1962) [hereinafter Carter v. 26].

150. *See Non-Publication of the Laws*, Pensacola Gazette & W. Fla. Advertiser, July 6, 1827, at 2.

151. *See* An Act to Regulate the Counties and Establish Inferior Courts in the Territory of Florida, 1822 Fla. Terr. Acts 3 (§ 2).

152. *Id.* at 3 (§ 3).

153. *Id.*

154. *Id.* at 5 (§ 13).

155. *Id.* at 4 (§ 4).

156. *Id.* (§ 5).

157. *Id.*

158. *Id.* at 3 (§ 2).

159. *Id.* at 4 (§ 9).

160. *See Memorial to Congress by Inhabitants of East Florida, in* Carter v. 22, *supra* note 9, at 572–73.

161. The county courts were terminated by default. Once Congress established the territorial government, the temporary governing arrangements ended.

162. *See* An Act Authorising the Appointment of Justices of the Peace and Defining their Powers and Establishing County Courts, 1822 Fla. Terr. Acts 91, 93–94, at §§ 12–20.

163. *See* 3 Stat. at 754 (§ 16). The reasons why Congress repealed this territorial act are uncertain.

164. *See* An Act to Regulate the Counties and Establish County Courts in the Territory of Florida, 1823 Fla. Terr. Acts. 8.

165. *See* An Act to Extend the Authority of the Judges and Clerks of the County Courts in Certain Cases, 1823 Fla. Terr. Acts 138.

166. *See* An Act for the Removal and Prosecution of Proceedings at Law and in Equity, Begun and Remaining Unfinished in any of the Former Courts of this Territory, 1823 Fla. Terr. Acts 15.

167. *See* 1823 Fla. Terr. Acts at 8 (§ 2). For a brief time, the legislative council authorized the position of associate judge, but it abolished this office in 1825. *See* An Act to Alter and Amend "An Act to Regulate the Counties and Establish County Courts in the Territory of Florida," 1825 Fla. Terr. Acts 84.

168. *See* An Act to Regulate the Counties and Establish County Courts in the Territory of Florida, 1824 Fla. Terr. Acts 247.

169. 1823 Fla. Terr. Acts at 8 (§ 2).

170. *Id.* (§ 3). In 1828, the minimum amount in dispute was raised to $50. *See* An Act to Establish County Courts and Prescribing their Jurisdiction, 1828 Fla. Terr. Acts 213, at § 4.

171. 1823 Fla. Terr. Acts at 8–9 (§ 3).

172. *Id.*

173. *Id.* at 9 (§ 7).

174. *Id.* at 8 (§ 3). For capital offenses, the superior courts had exclusive jurisdiction.

175. *See* An Act to Amend the Act Establishing County Courts in this Territory, 1826–27 Fla. Terr. Acts 106, 107 (§ 3).

176. *See* 1823 Fla. Terr. Acts at 11 (§ 17).

177. *See* An Act to Establish County Courts and Prescribe their Jurisdiction, 1829 Fla. Terr. Acts 41, 42, at § 4.

178. 1823 Fla. Terr. Acts at 12 (§ 20).

179. *Id.*

180. *Id.* at 9 (§ 4).

181. *Id.* at 9–10 (§ 9).

182. *See* An Act to Authorise the County Courts in this Territory to Appoint Inspectors of Cattle in their Respective Counties, 1834 Fla. Terr. Acts 53 (§ 1).

183. *See* An Act to Establish and Organize a Court of Common Pleas, and of Oyer and Terminer, in the Town of Apalachicola, 1831 Fla. Terr. Acts 9.

184. *See* An Act to Amend the Incorporation of the City of St. Joseph, 1837 Fla. Terr. Acts 48, 49, at § 2.

185. *See* An Act to Establish and Organize a Mayor's Court for the City of Apalachicola, 1844 Fla. Terr. Acts 49.

186. *See* 1822 Fla. Terr. Acts at 91 (§ 1).

187. In 1828, the legislative council made justices of the peace elective. *See* An Act to Provide for the Election of County Officers, 1828 Fla. Terr. Acts 172. In 1829, Congress overrode this decision and transferred responsibility for appointing them from the governor to the council. *See* 4 Stat. at 332 (§ 1). In 1845, four days after the advent of statehood, the positions again were made elective. *See* An Act to Provide for the Election of the Justices of the Peace, 1845 Fla Terr. Acts 17.

188. 1822 Fla. Terr. Acts at 91 (§ 3).

189. *Id.*

190. *Id.* (§ 4).

191. *Id.* After the circuit courts were abolished in 1823, appeals went to the county courts.

192. *See* An Act Authorising the Appointment of Justices of the Peace and Defining their Powers, 1824 Fla. Terr. Acts 239 (§ 3).

193. *See* An Act Respecting Depositions, 1826–1827 Fla. Terr. Acts 137.

194. *See* 1822 Fla. Terr. Acts at 93 (§ 10).

195. *Id.*

196. *Id.*

197. *See* An Act to Provide for the Election of County Officers, 1827–1828 Fla. Terr. Acts 172. This act was vetoed by Governor DuVal but his veto was overridden by the legislative council.

198. An Act to Establish the Judiciary Courts of the United States, 1 Stat. 73, 87 (1789).

199. *See* 3 Stat. at 656 (§ 7).

200. *Id.* at 656–57 (§§ 7–8).

201. *See* 1822 Fla. Terr. Acts at 4 (§ 10).

202. *See Commission of Waters Smith as United States Marshal (East Florida), in* Carter v. 22, *supra* note 9, at 639 n.13.

203. *See Waters Smith to the Secretary of State*, in Carter v. 22, *supra* note 9, at 666.

204. *See* An Act Assigning Duties to the Marshals of the United States for the Territory of Florida, 1823 Fla. Terr. Acts 59, 60 (§ 5).

205. 4 Stat. at 46 (§ 3).

206. *See* An Act Repealing the Act "Assigning the Duties of the Sheriffs to the Marshals of the Territory of Florida," 1824 Fla. Terr. Acts 173 (§ 2).

207. *See Petition to Congress by Inhabitants of East Florida, in* 23 Territorial Papers of the United States: The Territory of Florida, 1824–1828, at 186, 187 (Clarence Edwin Carter ed. 1958) [hereinafter Carter v. 23].

208. *See Report of House Committee on the Territories, in* Carter v. 23, *supra* note 207, at 426, 427 ("It is not perceived what authority the legislative council had to transfer from the Marshals to other officers, any portion of their ministerial duties—and more especially as the marshals and the court are appointed . . . by the United States, and derive their authority from them. To prevent all further doubt and difficulty, your committee have thought it advisable to make these marshals the only ministerial officers of the Superior Courts and of the Court of appeals within the counties in which they reside.").

209. *See* An Act for the Apprehension of Criminals and the Punishment of Crimes and Misdemeanors, 1822 Fla. Terr. Acts 151.

210. *Id.* (§ 1).

211. *Id.* at 152 (§ 6).

212. *Id.* at 151 (§ 2).

213. *Id.* at 152 (§§ 3 and 5).

214. *Id.* at 151 (§ 2)

215. *Id.* at 151–52 (§ 2).

216. *Id.* at 152 (§ 3)

217. *Id.* at 153 (§ 8).

218. *Id.* at 152 (§ 3).

219. *Id.* at 153 (§§ 11–12).

220. *Id.* (§ 11).

221. *Id.* The territorial law read "twenty four house[-]keepers or sixteen of them shall be a grand jury."

222. *Id.*

223. *Id.*

224. *Id.* (§ 12).

225. *Id.* at 153–54 (§ 13).

226. *Id.*

227. *Id.*

228. *Id.*

229. *Id.*

230. *Id.* (§ 19).

231. 3 Stat. at 658–59.

232. *Id.* at 659.

233. *See* An Act to Amend an Act for the Summoning of Grand and Petit Jurors and for Other Purposes, 1829 Fla. Terr. Acts 97. In 1823, the maximum age for petit jurors had been increased to 50. *See* An Act for the Summoning of Grand and Petit Jurors and for Other Purposes, 1823 Fla. Terr. Acts 107, 109–10, at § 8.

234. *Id.* at 110 (§ 9).

235. *See* An Act to Prescribe the Mode of Summoning Grand and Petit Jurors, 1832 Fla. Terr. Acts 133.

236. *Id.* (§ 2).

237. *Id.*

238. *See* An Act to Amend an Act to Define Crimes and Misdemeanors and to Prescribe Punishments for the Same, 1825 Fla. Terr. Acts 79.

239. *See* An Act to Organize a County to be called Dade County, 1836 Fla. Terr. Acts at 19.

240. *See Petition and Remonstrance to Congress by Inhabitants of Monroe and Dade Counties, in* Carter v. 25, *supra* note 121, at 240–43.

241. 1822 Fla. Terr. Acts at 154–55 (§ 21).

242. *Id.*

243. *Id.* at 165 (§ 45).

244. *Id.* at 155 (§ 21). If a slave was convicted of manslaughter, the punishment was death. *See* An Act Regulating Slaves and Prescribing their Punishment in Certain Cases, 1826–1827 Fla. Terr. Acts 141 (§ 3).

245. 1822 Fla. Terr. Acts at 156–57 (§ 25).

246. *Id.* at 166 (§ 55).

247. *Presentment of the Grand Jury for Monroe County, in* Carter v. 26, *supra* note 149, at 404–5.

248. *General Presentments of the Calhoun County Grand Jury, in* Carter v. 26, *supra* note 149, at 143, 145 (underlining in original).

249. *See generally* James M. Denham, "A Rogue's Paradise": Crime and Punishment in Antebellum Florida, 1821–1861 (1997).

250. *See Indictment and Judgment against Martin Hutto, in* 24 Territorial Papers of the United States: The Territory of Florida, 1828–1834, at 17–19 (Clarence Edwin Carter ed. 1959) [hereinafter Carter v. 24]. On July 14, 1827, Hutto was accused of assaulting Thomas G. Jones in order to steal the mail that Jones was carrying. Hutto was convicted and sentenced to two years in prison and ordered to pay court costs of $101.36.

251. *See Secretary Walker to the President, in* Carter v. 25, *supra* note 121, at 154, 155–56 (excerpt from the executive proceedings of the Florida Territory).

252. *Superior Court*, Pensacola Gazette & Fla. Advertiser, May 12, 1829, at 2.

253. *See Minutes of [the] Territorial Supreme Court: East Florida District, in* Carter v. 24, *supra* note 250, at 291–93. Judge Joseph Smith had to halt the court proceedings after the defendants began engaging in "high handed contempts [and] violent and tumultuous conduct and [made] threats towards me while acting in my Judicial Capacity." In particular, Smith took exception to an utterance by one of the defendants that he "should be put down." The defendants were fined $5 for contempt of court and jailed for four hours. Bail for the other charges was set at $400 apiece.

254. *See Secretary Walker to the President, in* Carter v. 25, *supra* note 121, at 154, 160. Governor John Eaton pardoned Nathans because he felt the fine was disproportionate to the offense

and Bell's abusive words had "rendered [Nathans's] conduct and course in a great degree excusable if not entirely justifiable."

255. *See* An Act Regulating Proceedings in Chancery, 1822 Fla. Stat. Terr. 23.

256. *See* An Act Regulating Civil Proceedings, 1822 Fla. Stat. Terr. 33.

257. *See* An Act Regulating the Mode of Proceeding on Attachments, 1822 Fla. Terr. Acts 14.

258. *See* An Act Regulating Executions, 1822 Fla. Terr. Acts 19.

259. *See* An Act Concerning Limitation of Actions, 1822 Fla. Stat. Terr. 80.

260. *See* An Act Regulating the Mode of Suing Out Writs of Error and Prosecuting Appeals in the Court of Appeals of the Territory of Florida, 1832 Fla. Terr. Acts 93, 95, at § 12.

261. *See* An Act to Amend an "An Act Regulating Judicial Proceedings Approved December 30th 1824," 1825 Fla. Terr. Acts 17.

262. *Id.* at 18 (§ 3).

263. *Id.*

264. *Id.* at 20 (§ 11).

265. *Id.* at 23–24 (§ 26).

266. *See Gadesden [sic] County Court*, Floridian, Jan. 10, 1835, at 3 ("John R. Chapman v. John R. Hardgrove").

267. *See Sheriff's Sale*, Pensacola Gazette & W. Fla. Advertiser, Sept. 24, 1825, at 4 ("Sarah Boon v. Nathan Shackleford").

268. *See Notice*, Pensacola Gazette & Fla. Advertiser, May 16, 1828, at 3 (estate of Manuel Bonifay).

269. *See In the Superior Court of the Middle District of Florida*, Floridian, Jan. 23, 1841, at 4 ("Oliver Besley v. Urelius Birge").

270. *See In Partition*, Pensacola Gazette & W. Fla. Advertiser, June 10, 1826, at 4 ("John de la Rua v. Heirs of Turner Stark").

271. *See Notice*, Pensacola Gazette, Jan. 14, 1826, at 4 (mortgage from Charles Beeler to Charles Ivy).

272. *See Foreclosure of Mortgage*, Pensacola Gazette & W. Fla. Advertiser, Mar. 13, 1824, at 4 (mortgage from Alexander Love to Thomas English).

273. The equity of redemption allows a borrower to retain his or her property by paying the amount owed. *See, e.g.*, Hodgson v. Butts, 7 U.S. (3 Cranch) 140, 144 (1805).

274. *See The Attorney General to the Secretary of State, in* Carter v. 22, *supra* note 9, at 492–93.

275. *See* An Act to Provide for the Confirmation and Settlement of Private Land Claims in East Florida and for Other Purposes, 4 Stat. 202, at § 3 (1827). For a further discussion, see Michael J. Curley, *Book Review*, 44 Catholic Hist. Rev. 250, 251 (1958) (reviewing Carter v. 22, *supra* note 9).

276. *See* An Act for the Admission of Attorneys at Law into this Territory, 1822 Fla. Terr. Acts 12, at § 1.

277. *Id.* at 13 (§ 5).

278. *See* An Act to Prescribe the Mode by which Attorneys and Counselors at Law may be Admitted to Practice in the Courts of this Territory, 1827–28 Fla. Terr. Acts 59, 60 (§ 5).

279. *See* 1832 Fla. Terr. Acts 92, 94 (§ 12).

280. *See* Rules Adopted by the Court of Appeals for the Government of the Practice in the Superior Courts of Florida § VI (1833).

281. *Id.*

282. 1827–28 Fla. Terr. Acts at 61 (§ 7).

283. *See* An Act Relating to Crimes and Misdemeanors, 1828 Fla. Terr. Acts 48, 66 (§ 63).

284. *See* James B. Whitfield, *Florida's First Constitution*, 17 Fla. Hist. Q. 73 (1938).

285. *See Constitution or Form of Government for the People of Florida, Dec. 3, 1838*, at art. V, *in* The Acts and Resolutions of the First General Assembly of the State of Florida 5, 12, at § 1 (1845).

286. *Id.* § 2.

287. *Id.* at 13 (§ 6).

288. *Id.* § 8.

289. *Id.* § 10.

290. *See* An Act for the Admission of the States of Iowa and Florida into the Union, 5 Stat. 742 (1845).

291. *See* An Act to Organize the Circuit Courts of the State of Florida, 1845 Laws of Fla. 8, 9 (§ 5); An Act to Organize the Supreme Court of the State of Florida, 1845 Laws of Fla. 12, 13–14 (§ 14).

292. *See* An Act Supplemental to the Act for the Admission of Florida and Iowa into the Union and for Other Purposes, 5 Stat. 788, at § 3 (1845). Isaac H. Bronson was named the district's first judge. Because Florida was not assigned to a particular judicial circuit, its district court exercised the same jurisdiction as the U.S. circuit courts except as to appeals and writs of error (which were heard by the U.S. Supreme Court). For a further discussion, see James M. Denham, *From a Territorial to a State Judiciary: Florida's Antebellum Courts and Judges*, 73 Fla. Hist. Q. 443 (1995).

293. As it happens, the very first case to be officially reported involved a question about the jurisdiction of the new state courts. *See* Stewart v. Preston, 1 Fla. 1, 1 (1846) ("The Act of the General Assembly, 'that all cases now pending in said Court of Appeals, shall be transferred to said Supreme Court, and tried and decided therein and thereby, except cases cognizable by the Federal Courts' is imperative, and there is no cause for questioning the power of the General Assembly to pass such a law.").

4

Confederate Courts

ROBERT W. LEE

On Tuesday, November 6, 1860, Abraham Lincoln was elected president of the United States. Three weeks later, the Florida General Assembly[1] passed a bill calling for a state convention to be held in Tallahassee to consider the possibility of seceding from the United States.[2] Signed into law by Governor Madison S. Perry on November 30, the legislation designated December 22 for the election of delegates and set Thursday, January 3, 1861, as the convention's opening day.

Perry, an ardent secessionist, was concerned that the delegates from Key West, whose support was considered critical, would not arrive in time to participate.[3] As a result, the General Assembly called on the Monroe County probate judge[4] to promptly canvass and certify the results so that the winners could immediately board a steamer for the capital.[5]

Secession Convention

The "Florida Convention of the People" (the gathering's official name) commenced on January 5, 1861, with sixty-nine delegates in attendance. Of these men, nearly a dozen were lawyers or judges.[6] The latter group included Circuit Judge John C. McGehee of Madison County,[7] who was elected the convention's president, and County Judges James H. Chandler of Volusia County[8] and James B. Dawkins of Alachua County.[9] No one, however, played a more important role at the convention than McQueen McIntosh, until recently the judge of the U.S. District Court for the Northern District of Florida. A prosperous slave owner, McIntosh lobbied for immediate secession. A competing proposal, championed by Dr. George W. Parkhill, a physician from Leon County, took a much more cautious approach. It required any decision regarding secession to be approved by the people before being put into effect.[10]

On January 10, 1861, the delegates overwhelmingly sided with McIntosh,[11] voting 62–7 to secede from the Union and form the independent "nation of

Florida."[12] The next day, they affixed their signatures to the Ordinance of Secession.[13] This relatively brief instrument, drafted with the assistance of the Florida Supreme Court,[14] announced:

> We, the people of Florida, in Convention assembled, do solemnly ordain, publish, and, declare that the State of Florida hereby withdraws herself from the Confederacy of States existing under the name of the United States of America, and from the existing Government of the said States; and that all political connection between her and the Government of said States ought to be, and the same is hereby totally annulled, and said Union of States dissolved; and the State of Florida is hereby declared a sovereign and independent nation; and that all ordinances heretofore adopted, in so far as they create or recognize the said Union, are rescinded; and all laws, or parts of laws, in force in this State, in so far as they recognize or assent to the said Union, be and are hereby repealed.[15]

Along with the Ordinance of Secession, the delegates promulgated a new state constitution. Other than striking references to the "United States," however, this new version merely repeated its predecessor.[16] On February 8, 1861, after less than a month as its own country, Florida joined the other Southern states to form the Confederate States of America ("CSA").[17]

Federal Courts

The decision to secede from the Union raised an immediate question: what to do with the federal courts located in Florida? In 1847, Florida had been divided into two U.S. judicial districts, each with its own seat, with one (the Northern District at Tallahassee) occupied by McQueen McIntosh (appointed 1856) and the other (the Southern District at Key West) by William Marvin (appointed 1847).[18] McIntosh's resignation in January 1861 (to protest Lincoln's election) left the Northern District temporarily without a judge, but Marvin, who opposed secession (despite owning slaves), continued to run the Southern District as before.[19]

In June 1862, President Lincoln appointed Philip Fraser, a former mayor of Jacksonville, as McIntosh's successor. During the war, Fraser was unable to hold any sessions, but following the end of hostilities he heard cases until his death in 1876.[20]

The federal court problem, of course, also existed in the other Southern states.[21] To address it, in March 1861 the CSA promulgated its own constitution.[22] In Florida, this resulted in two new courts: a Confederate District Court for the District of Florida[23] at Marianna (covering the entire state and staffed by

Figure 4. Jesse J. Finley, Judge, C.S.A. District Court for the District of Florida and C.S.A. General. Courtesy of the State Library and Archives of Florida.

former Circuit Judge Jesse J. Finley), and a Court of Admiralty and Maritime Jurisdiction at Key West (headed by McIntosh).[24]

With paper in short supply, the confederate courts were forced to use the forms that had been printed for their predecessors, striking, whenever necessary, the word "United" and substituting in its place the word "Confederate."[25] As matters turned out, this was only the beginning of their problems:

> Nobody paid a great deal of attention to the Confederate district courts which, by the [CSA's] failure to create a Supreme Court, were kept hanging in the air. They had no final jurisdiction under the Constitution and laws, and at best had only concurrent jurisdiction with the state courts over which they had no authority, appellate or otherwise. In most of the districts they scarcely functioned at all, and since their decisions were only scatteringly published in the newspapers, little was known of them at the time and far less today.[26]

After less than a year, Finley resigned his judgeship in March 1862 to enter military service (eventually rising to the rank of general) and was not replaced.[27] Prior to his departure, however, he did appoint several court clerks. At least one of these orders has survived and reads as follows:

> By virtue of the authority vested in me, by the 4th section of an Act of the Provisional Congress of the Confederate States of America entitled, An Act to establish the Judicial Courts of the Confederate States of America, approved the 16th day of March, A.D. 1861, I, J.J. Finley, Judge of the District Court of the District of Florida, Do hereby appoint Samuel W. Spencer, Esq., Clerk and Commissioner of the District at Apalachicola, in the said District of Florida, to continue in said office, during the existence of the said Provisional Government of the Confederate States of America or until removed by me.
> Witness my hand and seal this 23rd day of May, A.D. 1861.[28]

Due to the North's continuous control of Key West, McIntosh accomplished even less than Finley. Indeed, when he journeyed to the island in May 1861 to organize his new court, he was nearly arrested and would have been had it not been for the timely intercession of Marvin, who allowed McIntosh to leave peacefully.[29] Thwarted in their effort to incarcerate McIntosh, the Union officers ejected the city's confederate sympathizers.[30]

State Courts

Because of the impotence of the confederate courts, the jurisdiction of Florida's circuit courts expanded to fill the void.[31] The Florida Supreme Court's operations also changed. In addition to its annual terms in the four prewar judicial circuits (eastern, middle, southern, and western), the General Assembly now required the court to meet yearly in the Suwannee Judicial Circuit at Lake City, a town midway between Jacksonville and Tallahassee.[32] Some things, however, remained the same. For example, the General Assembly continued to authorize the court to exchange copies of its bound law reports "for the reports of the other States," with twenty-five copies reserved for this purpose.[33]

With the apparent exception of justices of the peace, the judiciary remained exempt from military duty.[34] Nevertheless, judges were active in the war effort and helped raise funds to equip Florida's troops.[35]

In addition to being exposed to the draft, justices of the peace were delegated various war administration duties. For example, the General Assembly appropriated funds for the relief of soldiers' families and gave justices of the peace the responsibility of compiling lists of eligible families. These lists were then transmitted to the local probate judge for forwarding to Tallahassee.[36]

As the fighting continued, the courts began to experience difficulties in conducting their day-to-day affairs.[37] In time, these became major headaches:

> [Florida's] courts were almost paralyzed by the suspension of action[s] concerning debts. All process at law for debts was arrested until the first Monday of 1862. All process at law was also forbidden to any resident of the United States of America until that government recognized the independence of the Confederate States. Active warfare brought such disorganization that the courts voluntarily suspended much of their business. The holding of court became uncertain.[38]

In 1862, Pensacola was occupied by federal troops, and "[t]he duly elected city officials . . . fled the town along with over ninety per cent of the population."[39] Just a few months later, Fernandina also came under military rule.[40] Drawing juries from the population, limited to white men, grew increasingly difficult.[41]

Due to the disruptions caused by the war, the General Assembly authorized circuit court judges to "grant licenses for the building of toll bridges and turnpikes, and to establish ferries, to regulate the tolls of the same, to construct dams across streams not navigable, and to ascertain and declare what streams are navigable or not."[42]

The General Assembly also gave judges considerable discretion in moving court proceedings to places not occupied by Union troops.[43] In some instances, circuit courts had to meet in places other than their county seats. For example, in 1862 Jacksonville was occupied by Union forces, and the General Assembly was forced to move its circuit court to Baldwin, a small town about thirty miles to the west, "until such time as it may be safe . . . to return to Jacksonville."[44]

Despite the numerous hardships imposed by the war, the General Assembly remained committed to "the independence of the Judiciary" and strove to foster a strong state legal system.[45] Nevertheless, the only local tribunals that managed to keep functioning were the state's probate courts, whose judges continued to operate the "common schools" and played an active role in the appointment of teachers.[46] New election laws also made them the chairs of the county canvassing boards, which were given ten days to review and certify election results.[47] In some cases, however, the state had to authorize the clerks of the circuit courts to act in the absence of probate judges.[48] And criminal cases routinely languished, with enforcement and punishment being left to other officials, primarily city mayors.[49]

Because of a lack of access to the courts, the General Assembly continued to rely on the "patrol system" it had established in the 1830s to guard against slave violence. Taking the place of the courts in many instances, the patrols were authorized to mete out their own brand of justice, not to exceed thirty-nine lashes for an offense. The lack of men available to serve on patrols, however, made the system fairly ineffective.[50] Moreover, the patrols had no authority if the offense was a capital crime.

If a slave was charged with a capital offense, a special "slave court" was convened to address the matter, thereby avoiding the difficult problem of locating a circuit or county court judge. The slave courts initially consisted of two justices of the peace and twelve citizens, who collectively considered the evidence and made a decision. Toward the end of the war, this procedure was modified to provide that only the twelve jurors decided the matter, with the two justices of the peace presiding over the trial.[51] In one reported case, murder charges were brought in Alachua County against three slaves: "Alic, belonging to Mr. McLeod, and London and Paul, belonging to Mr. Hicks." After hearing the case, the jury found each of the slaves not guilty.[52]

Notwithstanding these challenges, the General Assembly created two new counties during this time: Baker near Jacksonville and Polk near Tampa.[53] In addition, the name of New River County was changed in 1861 to Bradford to honor a soldier who had died during a battle near Pensacola.[54]

Jurisprudence

The wartime decisions of the Florida Supreme Court demonstrate that despite the state's membership in the CSA, its legal philosophy remained closely tied to that of the United States. In a case involving statutory construction, for example, the high court wrote, "In *our own country*, the following language is used," and cited to the U.S. Supreme Court.[55] A number of other decisions also relied for authority on the U.S. Supreme Court[56] or the courts of Northern states.[57] In still another case, the Florida Supreme Court explained that it had adopted the "rules of equity in the Circuit Courts of the United States."[58]

Preemption

On many occasions, commanders on both sides of the war preempted the judicial system. The General Assembly expressed its strong disapproval of the military usurping the role of the civilian government and the state courts:

> This General Assembly, in the name of the people of the State of Florida and of their sovereignty, expresses its profound disapproval and censure of all officers in the military service who are forgetful that the tenure of

> their authority is derived from the will of the people, expressed through the forms of civil law, and will tolerate no assumption of arbitrary authority within their limits.[59]

One such incident occurred in the spring of 1864, as the army was attempting to build a railroad link from central Florida to Georgia. To complete the project, the military needed to "impress" iron, a process by which the government would confiscate goods for military purposes and reimburse the owners with almost worthless Confederate currency at government-set prices.[60]

The owner of the iron, Senator David L. Yulee, strenuously objected and sought protection from the Suwannee Circuit Court. Agreeing with Yulee, the court entered an injunction prohibiting the military authorities from appropriating the iron. Although this delayed the implementation of the military's order, it ultimately proved ineffectual as the army simply ignored the injunction and took the iron by force.[61]

Notwithstanding the pleas of the General Assembly, Governor John Milton supported the confiscation.[62] As noted by one historian, Florida acted as a "supermarket [for] the Confederate armies," and was the primary supplier of beef and salt throughout the Southern states.[63] The railroad therefore was vital if foodstuffs were to continue flowing. As for the quarrel between Yulee and the CSA, it continued until the end of the war, at which time it became moot.[64]

Conclusion

On May 10, 1865, federal troops began entering Tallahassee. Because only minor military skirmishes had taken place in Florida, the state had suffered relatively little destruction.[65] Nevertheless, the government of Florida "stood in humiliating confusion."[66]

On April 1, 1865, Governor Milton committed suicide.[67] Abraham K. Allison, the president of the Florida Senate, had taken Milton's place and had appointed a small group of "commissioners" to travel to Washington, D.C., to discuss the restructuring of Florida's government. The federal government, however, refused to recognize the delegation. Moreover, General Quincy A. Gillmore informed Allison that any state official who attempted to interfere with the authority of the federal government would be arrested.

On May 19, 1865, Allison resigned and went into hiding (he later was captured and briefly imprisoned for disloyalty to the Union).[68] Five days later, Gillmore imposed martial law on Florida. His order suspended the justices of the Florida Supreme Court but allowed the trial courts to continue operating.[69] On July 13,

1865, Judge William Marvin, who had defied the secessionists by continuing to operate the federal court at Key West until 1863, was named the state's provisional governor.[70]

While local judges were commanded to return to their offices, the military took over the handling of major offenses.[71] On October 28, 1865, a state constitutional convention, meeting in Tallahassee, annulled the Ordinance of Secession.[72] As a result, a new state constitution went into effect (without a public vote) on November 7, 1865. The advent of Reconstruction in 1867 made this document a legal nullity, leading to the promulgation of a new state constitution on February 25, 1868. Following its ratification by the people on May 4, 1868, Florida officially rejoined the Union and resumed civilian government on July 4, 1868.[73]

Notes

1. Florida's legislative body has been known at different points in history as the Legislative Council, the General Assembly, and the State Legislature.

2. Ch. 1094, 1860–61 Fla. Laws 15.

3. Florida's three principal cities during this period were Jacksonville, Key West, and Pensacola. *See* Michael Gannon, Florida: A Short History 2, 285 (1993).

4. At this time, Florida's judicial system was composed (at the trial level) of circuit courts and probate courts. Each county had a probate judge, with various counties grouped into circuits. *See* Fla. Const., art. V, §§ 1–3, 9 (1845).

5. Ch. 1172, 1860–61 Fla. Laws 165–66. *See* John E. Johns, *Florida in the Confederacy* 27 (unpublished Ph.D. dissertation, University of North Carolina, 1958).

6. Ralph A. Wooster, *The Florida Secession Convention*, 36 Fla. Hist. Q. 373, 375, 383–85 (1958); Donald R. Hadd, *The Irony of Secession*, 41 Fla. Hist. Q. 22, 25 (1962).

7. Clifton Paisley, The Red Hills of Florida 1528–1865, at 153 (1989).

8. Michael G. Schene, *A History of Volusia County, Florida* 196 (unpublished Ph.D. dissertation, Florida State University, 1976).

9. Charles H. Hildreth, *A History of Gainesville, Florida* 35 (unpublished Ph.D. dissertation, University of Florida, 1954).

10. Luther Wesley Barnhardt, *The Secession Conventions of the Cotton South* 49–50 (1922) (unpublished M.A. dissertation, University of Wisconsin).

11. Johns, *supra* note 5, at 35–36.

12. Gannon, *supra* note 3, at 4.

13. Johns, *supra* note 5, at 43.

14. Walter W. Manley, II et al., The Supreme Court of Florida and Its Predecessor Courts, 1821–1917, at 189 (1997).

15. Barnhardt, *supra* note 10, at 53.

16. The text of the 1861 constitution can be viewed at http://archive.law.fsu.edu/crc/conhist/1861con.html.

17. Gannon, *supra* note 3, at 41–42. In the interim, work had begun on a "Declaration of Causes" to more precisely set out Florida's grievances. On March 1, 1861, this task was aban-

doned, even though a detailed draft had been completed. *See further Florida Declaration of Causes*, *at* http://www.civilwarcauses.org/florida-dec.htm.

18. 5 Stat. 788 (Mar. 3, 1845) (organizing Florida into one judicial district with one federal judge), and 9 Stat. 131 (Feb. 23, 1847) (dividing Florida into two judicial districts, with one judge authorized in each, and assigning the judge of the District of Florida to the Northern District).

19. Johns, *supra* note 5, at 53; Kevin E. Kearney, *Autobiography of William Marvin*, 36 Fla. Hist. Q. 179, 213–14 (1958).

20. Manley, *supra* note 14, at 193, 229. In Jones v. Pensacola, 13 F. Cas. 1004 (C.C.N.D. Fla. 1873), Fraser held that the City of Pensacola, which had reorganized itself after the end of the Civil War, was not liable for its previously issued bonds.

21. *See, e.g.*, Ritchie Williams, *Flotsam and Jetsam: Admiralty Cases in Confederate Georgia*, 28 J. Mar. L. & Com. 617 (1997).

22. The text of the CSA's constitution can be viewed at http://avalon.law.yale.edu/19th_century/csa_csa.asp. For a line-by-line comparison with the U.S. constitution, see http://jjmccullough.com/CSA.htm.

23. Manley, *supra* note 14, at 225. James D. Westcott Jr., a future justice of the Florida Supreme Court, served as one of the clerks of the Confederate District Court for the District of Florida.

24. As has been pointed out elsewhere, "The establishing Act of March 11, 1861, chap. XXXIX, authorized the holding of court at other points in Southern Florida than the place named in the title of the court." William M. Robinson Jr., *Legal System of the Confederate States*, 2 J. S. Hist. 453, 463 n.16 (1936).

25. Williams, *supra* note 21, at 623 n.27.

26. J.G. de Roulhac Hamilton, *The State Courts and the Confederate Constitution*, 4 J. S. Hist. 425, 433 (1938).

27. Jim Piecuch & Angela D. Tooley, *Finley, Jesse Johnson*, *in* American Civil War: The Definitive Encyclopedia and Document Collection 634–35 (2013).

28. William M. Robinson Jr., Justice in Grey: A History of the Judicial System of Confederate States of America 642 (1941).

29. Johns, *supra* note 5, at 316.

30. Florence Fritz, Unknown Florida 69 (1963).

31. Ch. 1108, § 1, 1860–61 Fla. Laws 56. *See* Johns, *supra* note 5, at 158; Williams, *supra* note 21, at 619.

32. Ch. 1113, § 1, 1860–61 Fla. Laws 61 (altering and changing the time of holding the several terms of the Supreme Court).

33. Ch. 1124, § 2, 1860–61 Fla. Laws 71.

34. Johns, *supra* note 5, at 191 n.102, 241.

35. Hildreth, *supra* note 9, at 47.

36. Ch. 1337, § 4, 1862–63 Fla. Laws 19–20.

37. Johns, *supra* note 5, at ii.

38. *Id.* at 158–59, 203; Ch. 1129, 1860–61 Fla. Laws 76.

39. Johns, *supra* note 5, at 121.

40. *Id.* at 128.

41. *Id.* at 159.

42. Ch. 1261, 1861–62 Fla. Laws 10–11.

43. *Id.*

44. Ch. 1323, 1862–63 Fla. Laws 11.

45. Res. 8, § 3, 13th Leg., 1st Sess., 1864–65 Fla. Laws 38 (relating to the rights of states).

46. Ch. 1166, 1860–61 Fla. Laws 157.

47. Ch. 1287, 1860–61 Fla. Laws 35.

48. Ch. 1302, 1861–62 Fla. Laws 54.

49. Johns, *supra* note 5, at 160, 382.

50. *Id.* at 161, 302.

51. Ch. 1430, 1864–65 Fla. Laws 7.

52. Johns, *supra* note 5, at 303–04.

53. Ch. 1185, 1860–61 Fla. Laws 179; Ch. 1201, 1860–61 Fla. Laws 192; Dig. Fla. Laws ch. 45, §§ 23, 38 (James F. McClellan ed. 1881).

54. Ch. 1300, 1861–62 Fla. Laws 53.

55. Florida Atl. & Gulf Cent. R.R. Co. v. Pensacola & Ga. R.R. Co., 10 Fla. 145, 167 (1862) (emphasis added).

56. In Yulee v. Canova, 11 Fla. 9, 46–47 (1864), for example, the Florida Supreme Court observed, in interpreting a statute enacted by the Confederate Congress, that a particular legal issue was a "well settled rule of law" and cited as authority decisions of the U.S. Supreme Court. *See also id.* at 51–52; Stephens v. Orman, 10 Fla. 9, 100 (1862); Trustees of the Internal Improvement Fund v. Bailey, 10 Fla. 112, 130 (1862); *Florida Atl.*, 10 Fla. at 167.

57. *See, e.g.*, Trustees of the Internal Improvement Fund v. Bailey, 10 Fla. 213, 230, 254–55 (1863) (citing precedents from Connecticut, Maryland, and Massachusetts); Towles v. Roundtree, 10 Fla. 299, 307 (1863) (Pennsylvania); Cook v. Fernandez, 11 Fla. 100, 103–04 (1864) (Massachusetts and New Hampshire); Hunt v. Finegan, 11 Fla. 105, 109–10 (1864) (Indiana).

58. *Bailey*, 10 Fla. at 252.

59. Res. 10, 12th Leg., 2d Sess., 1863–64 Fla. Laws 55 (relating to the state's civil authority).

60. Manley, *supra* note 14, at 239.

61. Johns, *supra* note 5, at 244–45, 283; Paisley, *supra* note 7, at 203–04.

62. Clement Eaton, A History of the Southern Confederacy 150 (1954).

63. John M. Eriksen, Brevard County: A History to 1955, at 55 (1994).

64. Hildreth, *supra* note 9, at 54–56.

65. Kathleen Montpelier, Florida's Heritage 52–53 (1982).

66. Gannon, *supra* note 3, at 46.

67. Manley, *supra* note 14, at 202.

68. Johns, *supra* note 5, at 422–25.

69. Manley, *supra* note 14, at 202.

70. *Id.*

71. Hildreth, *supra* note 9, at 66.

72. Samuel S. Cox, Three Decades of Federal Legislation, 1855 to 1885, at 420 (1885) (explaining that while Governor Marvin asked the delegates to make the secession ordinance "null and void," they opted only to declare it "void").

73. Merlin G. Cox, *Military Reconstruction in Florida*, 46 Fla. Hist. Q. 219, 232 (1968). *See also* Joe M. Richardson, *Florida Black Codes*, 47 Fla. Hist. Q. 365 (1969) (explaining how white supremacy was maintained under the 1868 constitution).

PART II

Special Jurisdiction Courts

5

Military Courts

DAVID J.R. FRAKT

Although all residents of Florida are subject to criminal prosecution in both state and federal courts, a small group of inhabitants—amounting to less than 0.5% of the population—also are subject to prosecution in a third forum: the courts of the armed forces. These tribunals, which follow their own laws, have their own procedures, and are guided by their own ethos, represent an important but little-known branch of the criminal justice system.

Florida's Military Presence

The U.S. armed forces consist of the Air Force, Army, Coast Guard, Marine Corps, and Navy;[1] their respective reserve components; and the two National Guard commands (one for the Air Force and the other for the Army) that in Florida jointly constitute the Florida National Guard.[2]

There are 57,807 active duty military personnel and 36,481 reservists stationed in Florida.[3] As a result, the state has one of the largest concentrations of military bases in the country. At present, there are more than a dozen military installations in Florida, including several major Air Force and Navy bases.[4]

By number of assigned personnel, Florida's biggest air bases are Hurlburt Air Force Base in Pensacola (7,683); Eglin Air Force Base, also in Pensacola (7,648); MacDill Air Force Base in Tampa (5,646); Tyndall Air Force Base in Panama City (3,383); and Patrick Air Force Base near Cape Canaveral (1,446).[5] In addition, Homestead Air Force Base, just outside Miami, continues to be operational, although it now is used primarily by reservists.

The biggest (again by assigned personnel) naval bases in Florida are Naval Air Station Pensacola (8,011); Naval Air Station Jacksonville (5,748); and Naval Station Mayport in Jacksonville (9,844).[6]

Somewhat surprisingly, the Army has no major bases in Florida, although it does host the U.S. Southern Command Headquarters in Miami. There also are a variety of smaller Army units, such as recruiting stations and Reserve Officers' Training Corps units (led by active duty personnel), scattered throughout the state.

The Coast Guard is particularly conspicuous in Florida, with 4,572 active duty personnel stationed across the state.[7] Most of Florida sits in the Coast Guard's Seventh District, whose headquarters are in Miami (the far western panhandle is in the Eighth District). Air stations are located in Clearwater and Miami Beach; the latter city also is home to the District's Integrated Support Command office.

The Marine Corps is represented in Florida by the Marine Corps Support Facility on Blount Island in Jacksonville. From this busy depot supplies are prepositioned for transport to units all over the world.

Lastly, Camp Blanding near Gainesville is the Florida National Guard's primary training facility. At various points in its history, it also has accommodated active duty troops. The headquarters of the Florida National Guard is in St. Augustine, in the historic St. Francis barracks.

Famous Military Trials

Although military trials have a long history, only in rare instances do they attract much public attention.[8] Four such cases, each with a Florida connection, are discussed below.[9]

Robert C. Ambrister and Alexander G. Arbuthnot

Florida's most notorious military trial occurred in 1818, near the end of the second Spanish period (1783–1821). During the First Seminole War, General Andrew Jackson convened a military tribunal to try civilians Robert C. Ambrister and Alexander G. Arbuthnot.[10] According to Jackson, Ambrister, a twenty-one-year-old English mercenary, and Arbuthnot, a seventy-year-old Scottish merchant, had actively assisted the Creeks and Seminoles in opposing Jackson's invasion of Spanish Florida.

The two men appeared before a panel of twelve officers (handpicked by Jackson and headed by General Edmund P. Gaines) at a site near Panama City now known as Court Martial Lake. After a brief hearing, the pair was found guilty and sentenced to death.[11] Subsequently, the panel members changed their minds and decided to commute Ambrister's sentence to one year at hard labor. Finding this lesser punishment to be insufficient, Jackson had a firing squad shoot Ambrister on April 29, 1818; Arbuthnot was hung from the yardarm of his schooner (although some sources claim that he, too, was shot).

The executions were roundly denounced as barbaric and outside the laws of war, particularly by Great Britain (which protested the harsh treatment of its subjects) and Spain (which objected to Jackson's violation of its sovereignty). A Congressional investigation faulted Jackson for his handling of the affair but did not censure the popular war hero.[12] Although Jackson insisted he had done nothing wrong, most historians view his actions as unlawful (and believe he used Ambrister and Arbuthnot as scapegoats to help justify his military campaign).[13]

Dr. Samuel A. Mudd

The assassination of President Abraham Lincoln by John Wilkes Booth on April 14, 1865 (coincidentally Good Friday) shocked the nation; in its immediate aftermath, dozens of suspects were imprisoned. Eventually, however, a military board in Washington, D.C., determined that just eight individuals (seven men and one woman) had taken part in the plot. Four of the accused were put to death (by hanging), one died in prison, and three were later released after receiving presidential pardons.[14]

The guilt of one of the conspirators—Dr. Samuel A. Mudd—has long been a subject of intense debate.[15] Following the assassination, Booth had appeared at Mudd's home in Maryland. After Mudd set Booth's fractured left leg (which he had injured while making his escape), Booth continued on to Virginia (where he later died in a shootout with Union troops). Mudd waited a day before disclosing Booth's nocturnal visit and later repeatedly changed his story while under interrogation. At trial, Mudd avoided the death penalty by a single vote (being sentenced instead to life imprisonment), due to the government's inability to prove that he had been a knowing participant in Wilkes's plan (despite evidence that the pair had been seen together in the capital in the year leading up to the assassination).[16]

Mudd was ordered to serve his sentence in the federal prison at Fort Jefferson in the Dry Tortugas, a remote island chain approximately seventy miles west of Key West (now preserved as a national park). Joining Mudd there were three of his co-conspirators, all of whom also had received life sentences.

The group arrived at Fort Jefferson in July 1865. Because of his medical training, Mudd was assigned to work in the base's clinic. Two months later, Mudd tried to escape by stowing away on a visiting transport ship. The attempt failed, and Mudd was punished by being reassigned to the prison's carpentry shop.

In the summer of 1867 the island was swept by yellow fever. When the epidemic claimed the life of the fort's physician, Mudd agreed to take his place.

Despite also contracting the disease, Mudd recovered and managed to quell the outbreak. In recognition of his efforts, the island's soldiers called on President Andrew Johnson to pardon Mudd. Although Johnson did so in 1869 (just before leaving office), Mudd, who steadfastly insisted he was innocent, lived the rest of his life under a shadow (contrary to popular belief, however, his name did not give rise to the well-known smear "your name is mud"[17]). In 1990, Mudd's relatives began an effort to have the Army's Board for Correction of Military Records clear him. After years of litigation, the Army decided that no change was warranted.[18]

Wallace M. Wheeler Jr.

In the early hours of October 20, 1957, while in Wiesbaden, West Germany, Airman Third Class Wallace M. Wheeler Jr. met up with a female acquaintance named Felicitas Georg at a nightclub. After several drinks, the pair went back to her place and had sex. Upon finishing, Wheeler, in a sudden rage, killed Georg by plunging his switchblade into her neck. After ransacking her apartment, he left with $325 and an heirloom Dutch gold coin.

When Georg's blood-soaked body was discovered, a worldwide manhunt for her killer began (aided only by a pencil-sketch description provided by a witness who saw a man leaving the premises).[19] In the meantime, Wheeler returned to the United States, was discharged from the Air Force, and obtained a job operating machinery in Washington, D.C. Acting on a tip, a federal agent obtained a search warrant for Wheeler's home and found both the switchblade and the gold coin. A short time later, Wheeler was arrested while visiting his parents in Pensacola. After taking a lie detector test, Wheeler gave a full confession to both an Air Force investigator and a local police officer.

At the time of his arrest, Wheeler was an Air Force reservist. This raised the question of whether the military could try him. Wheeler contended it could not and filed a *habeas corpus* petition with the local federal court. In a detailed opinion, it held that the military could try Wheeler because he had been on active duty when he murdered Georg.[20]

With this procedural roadblock cleared, Wheeler was placed on trial at Eglin Air Force Base in Pensacola. On November 4, 1958, he was found guilty of murder, ordered confined for life, given a dishonorable discharge, and forced to forfeit all pay and allowances. However, due to a pretrial agreement (the military's equivalent of a plea bargain), his sentence was reduced to twenty years.[21] On appeal, Wheeler renewed his lack-of-jurisdiction argument, which again was rejected.[22]

Walter T. Perkins

Master Sergeant Walter T. Perkins worked at the Air Defense Weapons Center at Tyndall Air Force Base in Panama City. On October 18, 1971, while waiting to board a commercial flight to Mexico City, he was arrested on suspicion of stealing classified documents with the intent of giving them to the Soviet Union. Through his military attorney, Captain Clyde W. Russell Jr., Perkins vigorously denied the charges: "I guess you'd be upset, too, if somebody accused you of all these things and you found yourself in a confinement facility."[23] Russell also insisted that the idea that Perkins, a married father of four and a nineteen-year Air Force veteran, was in contact with the Russians was ludicrous: "I get more a smile out of it than anything. If it weren't the Russians, it would be China or Cuba or maybe the Bronx in New York."[24]

As the ranking non-commissioned officer at the Weapons Center's intelligence division, Perkins had ready access to critical information. During the trial, Lieutenant Colonel Schuyler Crowell informed the court (which sat without a jury at Perkins's request) that if Perkins had managed to carry out his scheme "the stolen documents would have told the Russians what kind of radar equipment American jets would carry for the next eight years, its capability against Soviet equipment, and would have revealed to the Soviets what we know and didn't know about Soviet missile systems and Eastern European and Russian defense systems."[25]

Perkins was charged with possession of defense secrets, attempting to pass such secrets to foreign agents (the purpose of his attempted flight to Mexico City), filling out false reports that he had disposed of the documents, and falsifying two sets of leave papers.[26] To defend himself, Perkins hired Henry B. Rothblatt, a civilian attorney from New York City. Rothblatt did not try to deny what Perkins had done. Instead, he had Perkins plead not guilty by reason of temporary insanity. According to Rothblatt, Perkins was a chronic alcoholic who had convinced himself that if he gave information to the Russians, they would help free American prisoners of war in Southeast Asia. Rothblatt described Perkins as having a "sick mind" and claimed he had become an alcoholic because of the stress of his job.[27]

Following a week-long trial, Perkins was found guilty. As punishment, he was given three years of confinement, a dishonorable discharge, a reduction in rank (to airman basic), and a $150-a-month fine (which was deducted from his $288-a-month salary). Upon being led out of the courtroom, Perkins turned to his mother and said, "It's a light sentence, isn't it?"[28]

In a post-trial interview, Rothblatt told reporters that he was "delighted by the sentence—it amounts to a little more than a slap on the wrist."[29] However, Rothblatt also announced that he intended to appeal the sentence "because of the importance of the issues involved."[30] Although Rothblatt made good on his promise, Perkins's sentence was affirmed.[31]

The Military Justice System

Trials in the military are known as "courts-martial" and proceed according to strict rules. This always has been true. On September 13, 1822, for example, the Florida Territorial Council passed an act that prescribed, in minute detail, how courts-martial were to be handled.[32]

Since 1951, the armed forces have been guided by the Uniform Code of Military Justice ("UCMJ").[33] Together with the Rules for Courts-Martial (the equivalent of the Federal Rules of Criminal Procedure) and the Military Rules of Evidence (the equivalent of the Federal Rules of Evidence), the UCMJ establishes a comprehensive criminal justice system.[34]

The UCMJ applies to active duty personnel, military reservists while on active duty, and Florida National Guard members performing federal service.[35] Courts-martial under the UCMJ are classified as summary, special, or general. They are called, when necessary, by designated senior military commanders (as will be seen, such officers, who are referred to as the "convening authority," exercise significant control over all stages of the proceedings).

Every major military installation is outfitted with a permanent courtroom for holding courts-martial.[36] On either side of a court-martial will be found a military lawyer, formally known as a "judge advocate."[37] In very serious cases, the defendant may decide to also hire a civilian attorney.

The current process used to hear military cases is briefly described below.[38] Although the military justice system has many similarities to the civilian criminal justice system, it is important to keep in mind that the former's primary purpose is to maintain good order and discipline in the military. This fact often causes the two systems to diverge at critical points, particularly during sentencing.[39]

Courts-Martial Basics

As noted above, there are three kinds of courts-martial: summary, special, and general. Summary courts-martial, which hear minor offenses, may impose a maximum confinement sentence of thirty days. In contrast, special courts-martial may order confinement for up to one year (or the statutory maximum, whichever is less) and a bad-conduct discharge (for enlisted members convicted of certain offenses).

General courts-martial are used to try serious crimes (felonies); in murder cases, a guilty party may be sentenced to death or confined without the possibility of parole. A general court-martial also may decide that the defendant should be given a bad-conduct or dishonorable discharge (enlistees) or be dismissed (officers).

All courts-martial may reduce an enlisted member's rank ("grade") to the lowest enlisted grade (E-1; i.e., airman basic, private, or seaman recruit). In contrast, an officer cannot be demoted by court-martial. Because of the higher potential punishments, the due process afforded to the service member increases with each type of court-martial.

Summary Courts-Martial

A summary court-martial is a simplified procedure for the resolution of charges involving minor incidents of misconduct, such as a brief absence without leave, petty theft, or a single use of illegal drugs. Such proceedings utilize one hearing officer, who acts as both judge and jury. The hearing officer is not required to be a judge advocate.

Commissioned officers may not be tried by a summary court-martial, and the punishment options for non-commissioned officers are quite limited.[40] As a result, summary courts-martial generally are used to punish junior enlisted personnel. The accused (the military's term for defendant) is not entitled to legal counsel in a summary court-martial, although as a practical matter an attorney often is provided.

Because a summary court-martial proceeds without a jury, and there is no right to counsel, the accused must consent to be tried in this forum. Such consent normally is given because the range of available punishments is light[41] and a finding of guilt does *not* result in a federal criminal conviction.

Special Courts-Martial

A special court-martial is the military's intermediate-level trial court. It consists of a military judge, one or more prosecutors (known as trial counsel), at least one defense counsel, and a panel of members (the jury). A special court-martial panel must have at least three members. By default, all panel members are officers. However, an enlisted accused may request that enlisted members be appointed as members and is entitled to have a court composed of at least one-third enlisted personnel. If enlisted members are requested, the convening authority will either add enlisted members to the panel or, more often, substitute enlisted members for one or more of the previously appointed officers. In all circumstances, however, the panel members must be senior in grade (or at least in time of service) to the accused.[42]

The accused may request a trial by a judge alone and often is required to do so as a condition of a pretrial agreement. Regardless of the offenses involved, a special court-martial may not impose a sentence greater than one year of confinement (or the statutory maximum, whichever is less). A special court-martial also may impose up to forty-five days of hard labor without confinement, forfeiture of two-thirds basic pay per month for one year, a reduction in rank to the lowest enlisted grade, and a bad-conduct discharge (for enlisted personnel). An officer accused in a special court-martial cannot be demoted, dismissed from the service, or confined. Thus, officers are rarely tried in special courts-martial.

General Courts-Martial

A general court-martial is the most serious type of military trial. The jury must number at least five (and at least twelve in a capital case). Upon request, an enlisted accused is entitled to a jury of at least one-third enlisted members. Except in capital cases, the accused can waive his or her right to a jury trial and elect trial by judge alone.

The maximum punishment in a general court-martial is the cumulative statutory maximum for each offense of which the accused is convicted, including death (for a small group of offenses); confinement up to life (with or without the possibility of parole); a dishonorable or bad-conduct discharge for enlisted personnel; a dismissal for officers; and various lesser sanctions.

A general court-martial follows the same procedures as a special court-martial. However, unless waived by the accused, a pretrial investigation must be conducted pursuant to Article 32 of the UCMJ before the case can be referred to a general court-martial. Capital general courts-martial have additional procedural requirements.[43]

Article 32 Investigations

The Fifth Amendment to the U.S. Constitution guarantees that "No person shall be held to answer for a capital, or otherwise infamous crime, unless on a presentment or indictment of a Grand Jury, *except in cases arising in the land or naval forces,* or in the Militia, when in actual service in time of War or public danger[.]"[44] Accordingly, military members do not have the right to be indicted by a grand jury. Likewise, they do not have the right to a preliminary or probable cause hearing in front of a judge. Instead, when a general court-martial is contemplated, Article 32 of the UCMJ requires a "thorough and impartial investigation" of the charges and specifications.[45] Even if the accused decides to waive his or her Article 32 rights, the convening authority is free to order such an investigation.

An Article 32 investigation serves several important purposes: (1) it inquires into the matter set forth in the charges; (2) it considers the form of the charges; and (3) it makes a recommendation as to how the case should be resolved "in the interest of justice and discipline." In practice, there often is a fourth aspect to an Article 32 investigation: a consideration of whether additional charges should be filed based on new evidence that has come to light since the original charges. Such evidence often is discovered as a result of the Article 32 investigation.

Thus, an Article 32 Investigating Officer ("IO") is expected to answer the following questions: (1) Is there a reasonable basis (i.e., probable cause) to believe that the accused committed the offenses alleged? (2) Have the offenses been properly charged, or do they need to be amended? (3) Are the offenses serious enough to warrant a trial by a general court-martial, or would some lesser form of court-martial (special or summary), or an alternative to a court-martial (e.g., non-judicial punishment or an administrative discharge), be a more appropriate way to handle the matter?

At the Article 32 hearing, the IO will call witnesses to provide sworn testimony. Although not required, at least one prosecutor normally will be present at the hearing. The prosecutor typically conducts the initial direct examination, but the IO also may ask questions. The defense then is given an opportunity to cross-examine the witness. The prosecutor also frequently introduces documentary evidence.

Formal rules of evidence, such as limitations on hearsay, do not apply at Article 32 hearings (some exceptions do exist, particularly for privileged information). However, the defense may raise, and the IO may comment upon, evidentiary issues that are likely to impact the government's ability to prove its case at trial.[46]

Article 32 hearings generally are open to the public and the media. When circumstances require, however, they will be closed. This most often occurs when a particularly vulnerable type of witness (such as a child) is testifying.

The defense is under no obligation to do anything at an Article 32 hearing. In this sense, an Article 32 investigation serves as a means of pretrial discovery and allows the accused to learn about the government's case. However, the defense may call witnesses, introduce evidence, cross-examine government witnesses, and provide oral or written commentary. The accused has the right to remain silent but can choose to offer sworn testimony (or alternatively an unsworn statement) in defense, mitigation, or extenuation.

Thus, the normal order of events at an Article 32 hearing is as follows:

- The IO announces the opening of the investigation and its purposes.
- The IO advises the accused of his or her right to counsel and ascertains whether the accused is represented by counsel (and if so, by whom).
- The IO reads (or summarizes) the charges filed against the accused.
- The IO advises the accused of his or her right to remain silent under Article 31 of the UCMJ.
- The prosecutor provides the documentary or real evidence to the IO.
- Either the prosecutor or the IO calls any available adverse witnesses.
- The prosecutor provides records from the accused's military personnel file for the IO's review.
- The defense decides whether to call available favorable witnesses.
- The defense decides whether to offer any documentary or other real evidence in defense, extenuation, or mitigation.
- The accused decides whether to testify or offer an unsworn statement.
- The prosecutor and defense counsel decide whether to offer any arguments or commentary regarding the evidence.
- The IO closes the hearing.

Report of Investigation

Following an Article 32 hearing, the IO will prepare a Report of Investigation ("RoI"). Because there is no set formula for an RoI, its length and detail cannot be predicted in advance. However, at a minimum an RoI must contain:

- The names, organizations, and addresses of defense counsel and whether they were present throughout the taking of evidence (and if not, why not).
- The substance (either a verbatim transcript or a summary) of all testimony.
- Any other statements, documents, or matters considered by the IO.
- An explanation (if applicable) of why the IO believes the accused was not mentally responsible at the time of the offense; was incapable of participating in the investigation; or is incompetent to stand trial.
- A statement whether the essential witnesses will be available at the expected time of trial.
- An explanation of any delays in the investigation.
- The IO's conclusions as to whether the charges and specifications are in the proper form.

- The IO's conclusions as to whether reasonable grounds exist to believe that the accused committed the alleged offenses.
- The IO's recommendations regarding disposition of the charges.

Upon completion, the RoI is forwarded to the convening authority. The accused also receives a copy (along with any attachments). Within five days of receipt of the RoI, the defense may submit to the convening authority comments and objections.

It is important to note that the IO's recommendations, no matter how sound, are merely advisory. Thus, even if an IO urges dismissal of the charges, the convening authority has the discretion to refer the case to trial.[47]

Trial Proceedings

In most respects, a general court-martial trial is no different from a criminal trial in state or federal court. Present in the courtroom will be the accused, his or her defense counsel, the trial counsel (prosecutor), a court reporter, a bailiff (typically an enlisted person from the accused's unit), and a judge. Nevertheless, there will be one obvious difference: the accused, the attorneys, and the jurors all will be in uniform.[48]

Each service has a cadre of judges, all of whom are experienced military lawyers. When charges are formally referred to a court-martial, a judge will be detailed to preside over the court.[49] The basic order of the trial also is familiar: jury selection, opening statements, prosecution case in chief, defense case in chief, rebuttal evidence (if any), closing argument, instructions to the jury, jury deliberations, and announcement of the verdict. However, there are a number of differences in trial procedure that will not be immediately apparent to an outside observer.

First, a unanimous jury is not required to obtain a conviction. Rather, only a two-thirds concurrence is required. If the panel number is not divisible by three, the level of concurrence is "rounded up." Thus, for a five-member court-martial panel, four votes are needed to convict.

Second, a two-thirds concurrence is required to agree on a sentence. This number is increased to three-quarters for sentences of confinement of ten years or more. To impose a death sentence, the jury must be unanimous.

A third difference concerns the jury selection process. Initially, the convening authority appoints panel members from among the available officers (typically, those assigned at the installation where the court-martial will take place). If enlisted members are requested by the accused, the convening authority appoints these members as well, often excusing some of the officers previously selected.

The convening authority typically will appoint extra members in the event that some are excused. Thus, for a general court-martial, which requires a minimum of five members, the convening authority is likely to initially appoint as many as ten members.

Under court-martial rules, both the prosecution and the defense are entitled to question (*voir dire*) the panel members, and each side is granted unlimited challenges, or strikes, for cause. However, unlike state or federal courts, each side is permitted to exercise only one peremptory challenge.

The biggest difference between civilian criminal trials and courts-martial concerns sentencing. In most state and federal criminal trials, the jury decides whether the defendant is innocent or guilty and the judge determines the sentence, often utilizing sentencing guidelines that are intended to ensure similar punishments for comparable crimes. Sentencing often occurs weeks, or even months, after the trial (to allow time for the preparation of a presentence report).

In a court-martial, if the accused chooses a trial by members, the members will determine both innocence or guilt *and* the sentence. Moreover, sentencing begins immediately after the findings have been announced. There are no guidelines to ensure consistency in punishment for similar offenses; rather, the members simply are advised by the judge of the authorized range of punishments and then choose whatever punishment they believe is appropriate.

With a few exceptions, offenses under the UCMJ do not have mandatory minimum punishments.[50] Thus, in the majority of cases the members have complete discretion regarding the sentence and are not required to impose any punishment at all.

Courts-martial also offer a broader range of sentencing options than civilian criminal courts, including dismissal (for officers), fines, forfeitures of pay and allowances, hard labor without confinement, punitive discharges (for enlisted personnel), reductions in grade, reprimands, and restriction to base. Another difference is that the UCMJ does not include sentence enhancements or increased punishments for repeat offenders.[51]

Convening Authority Action and Clemency

A final difference between courts-martial and civilian criminal trials is that a guilty verdict, as well as any sentence, is merely a recommendation. Once again, the convening authority has the discretion to approve or disapprove the findings and the sentence; set aside (nullify) any portion of them; and suspend or reduce the sentence.

Figure 5. U.S. Court of Appeals for the Armed Forces visiting Florida International University College of Law. Photograph by Carl-Frederick Francois; courtesy of FIU Division of External Relations.

The convening authority must take action on the findings and sentence. The convening authority cannot increase a sentence, nor convert a "not guilty" finding to "guilty." In other words, the convening authority can only act in a way that benefits the accused.

The convening authority's power to set aside verdicts and mitigate sentences is called the "power of clemency" and is similar to that exercised by presidents and governors.[52] In petitioning the convening authority for clemency, the accused may point to procedural or substantive errors or simply request leniency given his or her personal circumstances.

Post-Conviction Appeals

Once the convening authority has acted, the convicted service member normally will have a right of appeal to his or her service's Court of Criminal Appeals ("CCA").[53] Further appeals, first to the U.S. Court of Appeals for the Armed Forces ("CAAF"), and then to the U.S. Supreme Court, also are possible but normally are available only as a matter of discretion.[54]

Since their creation in 1950, both the CCAs and the CAAF have sat in Washington, D.C.[55] However, as part of a public education initiative dubbed "Project Outreach," the CAAF now occasionally holds hearings in other locations.[56] It has done so in Florida twice: first in February 2006 at Barry University's law school in Orlando,[57] and then again in April 2014 at Florida International University's law school in Miami.[58]

Conclusion

In December 2016, as part of the National Defense Authorization Act for Fiscal Year 2017,[59] Congress passed the Military Justice Act of 2016.[60] While it makes numerous technical changes to the UCMJ, it leaves untouched its most controversial feature: the extraordinary powers given to non-lawyer military commanders acting as convening authorities. As such, Floridians serving in the military, as well as out-of-state service members stationed in Florida, continue to be subject to a separate and distinct system of justice.

Notes

1. The term "armed forces" should not be confused with the term "uniformed services." The latter includes the armed forces as well as the National Oceanic and Atmospheric Administration ("NOAA") Commissioned Officer Corps and the Public Health Service ("PHS") Commissioned Corps. Service in the NOAA or PHS does not qualify as service in the armed forces (except during periods of formal transfer pursuant to 33 U.S.C. § 3061).

2. The Florida National Guard is the oldest military entity in the United States, having been formed at St. Augustine in 1565. For a comprehensive history, see Robert Hawk, Florida's Army: Militia, State Troops, National Guard, 1565–1985 (1987). *See also* George Cassel Bittle, *In the Defense of Florida: The Organized Florida Militia from 1821 to 1920* (unpublished Ph.D. dissertation, Florida State University, 1965).

3. *See* Governing Mag., *Military Active-Duty Personnel [and] Civilians by State, at* http://www.governing.com/gov-data/military-civilian-active-duty-employee-workforce-numbers-by-state.html [hereinafter MADP] (report dated May 31, 2016).

4. U.S. Department of Defense, 2015 Demographics Profile of the Military Community 181 (2016), *available at* http://download.militaryonesource.mil/12038/MOS/Reports/2015-Demographics-Report.pdf.

5. *Id.*

6. *Id.*

7. MADP, *supra* note 3.

8. They also have failed to attract much scholarly attention. As a result, we know very little about Florida's early courts-martial. This is particularly true of the Civil War period, when courts-martial frequently were used to maintain public order and, on at least one occasion, restore a commander's reputation. *See* Boyd Murphree, *Bluff Naked*, Oct. 31, 2012,

at http://www.floridamemory.com/blog/2012/10/31/florida-and-the-civil-war-october-1862/ (brief discussion of Lieutenant Colonel Charles F. Hopkins's request for a court-martial so as to be able to prove that his abandonment of St. Johns Bluff to Union troops was reasonable; although General Joseph Finegan labeled it a "gross military blunder," the panel hearing the case exonerated Hopkins).

9. For a look at other high-profile military cases, see, e.g., William Bradford Huie, The Execution of Private Slovik (1954); Ian Bisset, Trial at Arms: Some Famous Trials by Court Martial (1957); Lawrence A. Frost, Court-Martial of General George Armstrong Custer (1968); Richard Hammer, The Court-Martial of Lt. Calley (1971); Andrew David, Famous Military Trials (1980); John F. Marszalek, Assault at West Point: The Court-Martial of Johnson Whittaker (1994); Douglas Waller, A Question of Loyalty: Gen. Billy Mitchell and the Court-Martial that Gripped the Nation (2004); Kevin Jon Heller, The Nuremberg Military Tribunals and the Origins of International Criminal Law (2011); Michael M. Greenburg, The Court-Martial of Paul Revere: A Son of Liberty and America's Forgotten Military Disaster (2014).

10. The propriety of having the military try civilians has long been controversial. *See, e.g.*, Janet Cooper Alexander, *Military Commissions: A Place Outside the Law's Reach*, 56 St. Louis U. L.J. 1115 (2012). The usual justification given for doing so is that the defendant's acts have made him or her an "enemy combatant" subject to the military's legal authority. This argument has met with mixed success at the U.S. Supreme Court. *See, e.g.*, Ex parte Milligan, 71 U.S. (4 Wall.) 2 (1866) (even in wartime, military cannot try civilians in areas where the civilian courts are open and functioning); Ex parte Quirin, 317 U.S. 1 (1942) (military could try eight Nazi saboteurs, four of whom came ashore near Jacksonville, because they were enemy combatants); Hamdan v. Rumsfeld, 548 U.S. 557 (2006) (military lacked the authority to try detainees at Guantanamo Bay, Cuba). *See also* Hamdi v. Rumsfeld, 542 U.S. 507 (2004) (although government can detain U.S. citizens who are enemy combatants, such detainees must be given an opportunity to challenge their enemy combatant status before a neutral decision-maker).

11. The court's proceedings are reprinted in The Trials of A. Arbuthnot & R. C. Ambrister, Charged with Exciting the Seminole Indians to War Against the United States of America (James L. Ridgway ed. 1819), *available at* https://archive.org/stream/trialsofaarbuthnooarbu#page/n7/mode/2up.

12. *See* Christopher Bates, *The Arbuthnot-Ambrister Incident, in* 1 The Early Republic and Antebellum America: An Encyclopedia of Social, Political, Cultural, and Economic History 25, 25 (Christopher G. Bates ed. 2010) ("[P]ublic opinion ruled the day. The majority of Americans insisted that the 'Hero of New Orleans' had been in the right, especially after it came to light that Arbuthnot and Ambrister had provided arms to the Seminoles, a clear violation of British neutrality. Ultimately, the British backed down, Congress decided to take no action, and Jackson retained his commission.").

13. *See, e.g.*, Deborah A. Rosen, Border Law: The First Seminole War and American Nationhood 140–46 (2015). *But see* Frank L. Owsley Jr., *Ambrister and Arbuthnot: Adventurers or Martyrs for British Honor?*, 5 J. Early Rep. 289 (1985).

14. *See* James L. Swanson & Daniel R. Weinberg, Lincoln's Assassins: Their Trial and Execution (2006).

15. *See* Robert K. Summers, The Assassin's Doctor: The Life and Letters of Dr. Samuel A. Mudd (2014).

16. The evidence for and against Mudd is canvassed in Hal Higdon, The Union vs. Dr. Mudd (1964).

17. *See* Mary Miley Theobald, *Myth #110: The Insult "Your Name Is Mud" Comes from Dr. Samuel Mudd Who Treated Lincoln's Assassin*, History Myths Debunked, *at* https://historymyths.wordpress.com/2013/04/13/myth-110-the-insult-your-name-is-mud-comes-from-dr-samuel-mudd-who-treated-lincolns-assassin/ ("The *Oxford English Dictionary* . . . dates the first written example of the phrase at 1823, more than four decades before Lincoln was assassinated. Moreover, the term appeared in a British book, not an American one. It meant what it appears to mean—that your name is (or will be) dirty as mud if you do such-and-such.").

18. *See* Mudd v. White, 309 F.3d 819 (D.C. Cir. 2002). *See also* Dr. Mudd and the Lincoln Assassination: The Proceedings of a Moot Court of Military Appeal to Hear the Case of Dr. Samuel A. Mudd (John Paul Jones ed. 1995).

19. *See Worldwide Hunt for Killer Ends with Confession*, Rome (Ga.) News-Trib., Mar. 24, 1958, at 1.

20. *See* Wheeler v. Reynolds, 164 F. Supp. 951 (N.D. Fla. 1958).

21. *See Airman's Life Sentence Cut to 20 Years*, Lakeland Ledger, Dec. 4, 1958, at 18B. The deal also allowed Wheeler to avoid being sent back to West Germany, where he would have faced the possibility of a death sentence.

The military has not executed a service member since 1961, when a soldier named John A. Bennett was hanged for the rape and attempted murder of an eleven-year-old Austrian girl. *See* Stephen C. Reyes, *Dusty Gallows: The Execution of Private Bennett and the Modern Capital Court-Martial*, 62 Naval L. Rev. 103 (2013). At present, the military has six prisoners on its death row at Fort Leavenworth in Kansas; the longest-serving such inmate is Ronald A. Gray, who was sentenced to death in 1988 for killing two women and raping a third one. *See* Death Penalty Information Center, *The U.S. Military Death Penalty*, *at* http://www.deathpenaltyinfo.org/us-military-death-penalty. Although born in North Carolina, Gray grew up in a housing project in Miami's impoverished Liberty City, where he regularly was beaten by his stepfather. Gray has based many of his appeals on diminished mental capacity resulting from his brutal childhood. *See further* Gray v. Gray, 2015 WL 5714260 (D. Kan. 2015), *rev'd and remanded*, 645 F. App'x 624 (10th Cir. 2016).

22. *See* United States v. Wheeler, 27 C.M.R. 981, 1959 WL 3708 (Air Force Bd. Rev.), *aff'd*, 28 C.M.R. 212, 1959 WL 3441 (Ct. Mil. App. 1959). The case is discussed in Note, *Reservist Subject to Court-Martial Jurisdiction for Active-Duty Offense*, 73 Harv. L. Rev. 1626 (1960).

23. *See Sergeant Accused of Spying*, Sarasota Herald-Trib., Oct. 22, 1971, at 1A.

24. *Id.*

25. *Crowell Witness in USAF Spy Case*, Waterbury (Conn.) Am., Aug. 10, 1972, at 3.

26. Under Article 107 (now 106a) of the UCMJ ("Espionage"), the maximum punishment for these charges was death.

27. *Sergeant Said Spying for Release of POWS*, Tri-Cities (Ala.) Daily, Aug. 7, 1972, at 2.

28. *Sergeant Gets Three Years on Russian Spy Case Charge*, Chi. Trib., Aug. 12, 1972, at 3.

29. *Id.*

30. *Id.*

31. *See* United States v. Perkins, 47 C.M.R. 259, 1973 WL 14711 (Air Force Ct. Mil. Rev.), *review denied*, 48 C.M.R. 1000, 1973 WL 15080 (Ct. Mil. App. 1973).

32. *See* An Act Organizing the Militia of the Territory, 1822 Fla. Terr. Acts 105 (§§ 17, 19, 22, 25–33, 37, 39, 41–44, 46).

33. The UCMJ is contained in Title 10 of the U.S. Code at §§ 801–946. It is reproduced, along with a brief commentary regarding its history, structure, and purpose, at http://www.ucmj.us/structure-of-the-ucmj. For a further discussion, see Edmund Morgan, *The Background of the Uniform Code of Military Justice*, 6 Vand. L. Rev. 169 (1953). As Professor Morgan explains, the UCMJ replaced the Articles of War, which were promulgated by Congress in 1806. The authority for both the Articles of War and the UCMJ (as well as the Lieber Code, which was used during the Civil War), is found in Article I, § 8 of the U.S. Constitution ("The Congress shall have the power . . . To make Rules for the Government and Regulation of the land and naval Forces").

34. The interplay between the UCMJ and the Rules for Courts-Martials and the Military Rules of Evidence is set out in detail in U.S. Government, United States Manual for Courts-Martial (2012), *available at* http://www.apd.army.mil/pdffiles/mcm.pdf, as supplemented by U.S. Government, 2013, 2014, and 2015 Amendments to the 2012 Edition of the United States Manual for Courts-Martial (2015).

35. When performing state service, Florida National Guard members are subject to the state's code of military justice and may be punished by state courts-martial. *See* Fla. Const. arts. I, § 18, and V, § 1. Florida has adopted the UCMJ, see Fla. Stat. § 250.35, but the maximum punishments under Florida's law are less severe than those under federal law (two hundred days confinement and a $500 fine for a general court-martial and one hundred days confinement and a $300 fine for a special court-martial). Additionally, sentences resulting in confinement are served in Florida county jails rather than in military brigs. *See* Florida National Guard, *1565th Trial Defense Team, at* http://fl.ng.mil/services/Pages/Trial-Defense-Services.aspx.

36. Courts-martial held in the field are known as "drumheads" (the term usually is attributed to the historical practice of using the top of a drum as an improvised desk). They typically occur during times of war in areas experiencing active engagements (making the need for quick action imperative). For an example, see Michael Mueller, Canaris: The Life and Death of Hitler's Spymaster (2007) (describing the drumhead court-martial of Admiral Wilhelm Canaris at the Flossenbürg concentration camp in Bavaria, Germany).

37. The senior military lawyer in each service is the Judge Advocate General; all subordinate military lawyers are judge advocates and are part of the Judge Advocate General's Corps (which also includes enlisted military paralegals and civilian employees). As a result, military lawyers often are referred to as JAG officers or, more simply, JAGs.

To become a judge advocate, an individual must have graduated from an accredited law school and be a licensed attorney in an American state or territory. Specialized training in military law is then provided at the Air Force Judge Advocate General's School at Maxwell Air Force Base in Montgomery, Alabama; the Judge Advocate General's Legal Center and School in Charlottesville, Virginia; and the Naval Justice School in Newport, Rhode Island. It is not uncommon for a JAG officer to attend courses at all three of these schools at some point in his or her career.

In describing what JAG officers do, commentators routinely stress that handling courts-martial are only one aspect of their duties:

Since the Republic's founding, JAG lawyers have been an integral part of the U.S. Armed Forces and have played a role in the development of both a strong military legal practice and international law. Some perceive JAG lawyers in the war context, due to their participation in the highly publicized and often controversial prosecution of war crimes: Major General Benedict Arnold's trial, the Nuremberg tribunal, the My Lai tragedy prosecution, and the military commissions for enemy combatants at Guantanamo Bay. To others, JAG lawyers are simply fighter pilots who happen to practice law. But the modern American military law practice warrants neither the former view's limited perspective nor the latter view's incidental assumption. Today's JAG lawyers practice law in ways that rival their civilian counterparts. Their aptitude not only includes prosecuting and defending criminals but also mediating divorce settlements and filing consumer complaints.

The most visible aspect of military practice is arguably the criminal component, which is governed by the Uniform Code of Military Justice (UCMJ), commonly called the military criminal code. The UCMJ is a comprehensive set of laws that incorporates exclusively military offenses, such as desertion and violation of orders, with most offenses found in civilian criminal statutes, such as murder, rape, and robbery, among others. Under the UCMJ, military cases begin with an Article 32 hearing, which functions like a combined civilian grand jury and preliminary hearing. Military courts-martial, the military equivalent of civilian trials, are governed by the Military Rules of Evidence, which are based on, and amended to coincide with, the Federal Rules of Evidence. Each step of the military criminal-justice process closely parallels the civilian criminal-court system. JAG lawyers prosecute charges like any state or federal prosecutor, defend the accused like any civilian criminal-defense attorney, and oversee and manage the judicial process like any state or federal judge.

JAG lawyers, though, are not limited to conducting criminal work under the UCMJ. Lawyers for the Army JAG Corps, for example, conduct hundreds of administrative and regulatory actions per year; advocate on behalf of roughly 150 clients per year on issues ranging from estate planning and taxes to immigration and naturalization; represent the United States in tort claims []; and recover million[s of dollars] from tortfeasors in actions for injuries to Army personnel and property. Furthermore, they practice environmental law, labor litigation, tax law, and international law.

Michael G. Swansburg Jr., Note, *A Soldier's Heart and a Lawyer's Mind: An Argument for Granting Reciprocity to America's Former JAG Attorneys*, 48 U. Louisville L. Rev. 613, 621–23 (2010) (footnotes omitted).

38. For a more comprehensive treatment, see David A. Schlueter, Military Criminal Justice: Practice and Procedure (9th ed. 2015). As explained *infra* notes 59–60 and accompanying text, numerous technical changes were made to the UCMJ in December 2016. The present discussion does *not* include these changes, which went into effect after the book's research period closed.

39. Hollywood has been particularly active in pointing out the differences to the public. *See, e.g., The Caine Mutiny* (Columbia Pictures 1954), *A Few Good Men* (Columbia Pictures 1992), and *Rules of Engagement* (Paramount Pictures 2000). The television series *JAG* (NBC

1995–96, CBS 1997–2005) likewise often examined the tension between the duty to do justice and the need to maintain an esprit de corps.

40. Non-commissioned officers (*i.e.*, those in the rank of E-5 or above) may only be reduced one rank, or have their pay docked for one month, by a summary court-martial. Neither confinement nor hard labor without confinement is authorized.

41. The maximum sentence that can be adjudged in a summary court-martial is confinement for thirty days, forfeiture of two-thirds pay for one month, and reduction to the lowest enlisted pay grade for grades E-4 and below.

42. This requirement stems from military tradition; it also reflects the reality that junior service members are unlikely to punish senior service members.

43. These additional procedures are set forth in Rule 1004 of the Rules for Courts-Martial, *supra* note 33.

44. U.S. Const. amend. V (emphasis added).

45. *See* 10 U.S.C. § 832. Rule 405 of the Rules for Courts-Martial provides detailed instructions for conducting the investigation. The word "charge" refers to the specific numbered article of the UCMJ that is alleged to have been violated. The word "specification" refers to the facts and circumstances that are claimed to support the charge.

46. For example, if the accused confessed without being advised of his or her rights, his or her statement may be offered at the Article 32 hearing. Almost certainly, however, the IO will point out that the statement is likely to be ruled inadmissible at trial.

47. A convening authority is most likely to reject an IO's recommendations when conflicting advice is received from another legal adviser (such as a staff judge advocate). Unfortunately, political considerations also occasionally convince a convening authority to refer a questionable case to trial.

48. Like civilian criminal judges, Air Force, Army, and Coast Guard judges preside over proceedings wearing a black robe. In contrast, Marine Corps and Navy judges wear just their uniforms. There is no significance to this difference, which is the result of military tradition. *See* Andrew Efaw, *Air Force Court-Martial: A Concerted Effort*, LawWeek Colo., June 4, 2012, *available at* http://www.wtotrial.com/files/LWC%20-%20Efaw%20Deployment%20-%20June%204,%202012.pdf.

49. Although a judge in one service can hear cases arising in another service, this almost never happens:

> Substantively, the Uniform Code of Military Justice controls the conduct of the courts-martial of all services, and appeals ultimately funnel to the same judicial body, the Court of Appeals for the Armed Forces. Court of Appeals' decisions are appealed to the U.S. Supreme Court. Because of this commonality and a memorandum of understanding, each service's judges are authorized to preside over other services' courts-martial. However, in practice the services tend to be proprietary of their own cases.

Id.

50. Article 118 of the UCMJ does require a mandatory life sentence (with the possibility of parole) for premeditated murder and felony murder. Even these theoretical mandatory minimums may be disregarded by the convening authority during the clemency process.

51. This almost certainly is due to the fact that there are very few repeat offenders in the

military, as anyone who commits a serious offense typically is discharged (administratively or punitively), thereby making it impossible for them to commit another serious offense.

52. In Florida, of course, the clemency power is shared by the governor, the cabinet, and the legislature. *See* Fla. Const. art. IV, § 8.

53. Appeals are automatic in cases in which significant punishment has been imposed (*e.g.*, bad-conduct discharge, dishonorable discharge, dismissal, or one year or more in confinement).

54. The appeal route is a little different for courts-martial conducted by the Florida National Guard. Appeals as of right are heard by the Florida First District Court of Appeal in Tallahassee. *See* Fla. Const. art. V, § 1. Discretionary appeals are heard by the Florida Supreme Court and then the U.S. Supreme Court.

In an effort to harmonize federal and state military jurisprudence, the Florida Constitution authorizes the Florida Supreme Court and the Florida District Courts of Appeal to request advisory opinions from the CAAF. *See* Fla. Const. art. V, § 2. This is the only instance in which Florida state courts are permitted to seek advisory opinions.

55. Unlike their locations, the names of the CCAs and CAAF have varied over time:

> Congress enacted the Uniform Code of Military Justice (UCMJ) in 1950 to establish uniform procedures among the service branches. The UCMJ provided for one or more Boards of Review for each of the armed forces. . . .
>
> The Boards were granted broad power to review court-martial records of trial, determine questions of law and fact, weigh evidence, and reduce sentences. Each Board of Review was comprised of three lawyers; typically senior judge advocates. The UCMJ also established the Court of Military Appeals, comprised entirely of civilian judges, to hear appeals from decisions of the respective Boards of Review.
>
> The Boards of Review were renamed the Courts of Military Review in 1968, and again renamed the Courts of Criminal Appeals in 1994. The Court of Military Appeals was renamed the United States Court of Appeals for the Armed Forces in 1994. The decisions of the Courts of Criminal Appeals and the United States Court of Appeals for the Armed Forces have been subject to review by the United States Supreme Court since 1984.

United States Air Force Court of Criminal Appeals, *Brief History*, *at* http://afcca.law.af.mil/content/afcca_data/cp/history.pdf.

56. *See* U.S. Court of Appeals for the Armed Forces, *Practice and Procedure*, *at* http://www.armfor.uscourts.gov/newcaaf/practice_procedure.htm ("Most of the Court's oral arguments are held at its courthouse in Washington, D.C. On occasion, as part of the Court's judicial outreach program, the Court will hold arguments at law schools, military bases, and other public facilities. This practice, known as Project Outreach, was developed as part of a public awareness program to demonstrate the operation of a federal court of appeals and the military criminal justice system.").

57. *See* Barry University School of Law, *US Court of Appeals for the Armed Forces*, *at* http://lawalumni.barry.edu/newsletter/index.asp?id=6/ (explaining that "the five-judge appellate panel heard oral arguments in *United States v. Long*[, 64 M.J. 57, 2006 WL 2788563 (Armed Forces 2006)]. The court also permitted second year law student, Stephanie Knott, to submit and argue an amicus brief before the court.").

58. *See* Florida International University College of Law, *FIU Law Third-Year Evening Student Argues in Front of Judges of the U.S. Court of Appeals for the Armed Forces*, *at* https://law.fiu.edu/fiu-law-third-year-evening-student-argues-front-judges-u-s-court-appeals-armed-forces/ (explaining that the court heard the case of United States v. Jones, 73 M.J. 357, 2014 WL 3583817 (Armed Forces 2014) and that third-year evening law student Rey Martinez argued an amicus brief).

59. Pub. L. No. 114–328 (Dec. 23, 2016), *available at* https://www.congress.gov/bill/114th-congress/senate-bill/2943.

60. *Id.* (§§ 6001–7202).

6 ~

Religious Courts

DONNA LITMAN

In Florida, 76% of adults belong to a specific religious faith, with the three largest groups being Protestants (46%), Catholics (21%), and Jews (3%).[1] Each of these religions has a long tradition of operating its own judicial system.[2]

Religious courts exist for two purposes. The first is to hear and decide "religious issues." Some of these involve purely religious precepts that have no secular counterpart, such as religious sins. Others concern matters that are subject to both religious and secular laws, such as marriage and divorce. Still others focus on questions that have religious and secular counterparts, such as termination of employees, control of organizations, and ownership of property.

The second task of religious courts is to provide adherents with a means of settling disputes consistent with their personal beliefs and values. These disagreements often arise in a commercial or family context and frequently are resolved using alternate methods of dispute resolution (i.e., mediation and arbitration).[3]

The cases handled by religious courts normally are not publicly reported, particularly at the initial or trial stages. Some appellate decisions, as well as some arbitration awards, are published and a few are available electronically. Others become public when one party seeks help from a secular court.

This chapter examines the decision-making processes of Florida's religious courts. It also discusses cases in which a Florida secular court has been asked to decide a religious issue.

Governance Structure of Religious Organizations

Some religious organizations have a hierarchical governance structure, with local, regional, and national or international levels. A religious organization or society is part of a hierarchy when it is "one of a number of such societies, united to form a more general body of churches, with ecclesiastical control in the general association over the members and societies of which it is composed[.]"[4] Catholic, Episcopal, Lutheran, Methodist, and Presbyterian churches are included in the hierarchical category.[5]

Other religious organizations have a "strictly congregational or independent form of church government, owing no submission to any organization outside the congregation[.]"[6] Baptist churches and Jewish synagogues are included in the congregational category.[7] Whether governance is hierarchical or congregational affects how and by whom disputes involving religious issues with secular overtones are resolved. It also affects the role of Florida's secular courts and the deference these courts accord the decisions of religious courts.

A Florida religious court may include an ecclesiastical tribunal that determines issues of fact to which it applies religious law as well as one that hears appeals. In some instances, a Florida religious court may include individuals or panels that arbitrate or mediate civil disputes. Although secular law may involve civil or criminal law, this chapter focuses on civil secular law.

Hierarchical Religious Organizations with Florida-Based Courts

There are a number of different hierarchical religious organizations with Florida courts. This section highlights two of them: the judicial systems of the Roman Catholic Church and the Presbyterian Church (U.S.A.). It also considers how these two systems have been viewed by Florida's secular courts and then briefly discusses other hierarchical systems. To the limited extent that Florida's secular courts have jurisdiction over matters involving hierarchical religious organizations, they generally defer to the decision of the highest ecclesiastical court that has decided the matter in issue.[8]

Before continuing, it should be noted that the First Amendment to the U.S. Constitution significantly limits the number of hierarchical cases that Florida's secular courts can hear. This is because the First Amendment generally precludes secular courts from deciding issues of religious law,[9] including those involving "questions of discipline, or of faith, or ecclesiastical rule, custom, or law."[10]

Roman Catholic Church

The Roman (or Latin or Western) Catholic Church is governed by the 1983 *Codex Iuris Canonici*, or Code of Canon Law ("CCL"),[11] as amended from time to time,[12] at the local, regional, national, and international levels. The CCL contains detailed rules regarding the Church's hierarchical judicial system, including the jurisdiction of tribunals, qualification of judges, and rules regarding evidence and procedure. The CCL provides that the Church has the exclusive right to adjudicate "cases which regard spiritual matters or those connected to spiritual matters" and "the violation of ecclesiastical laws and all those matters in which there is a question of sin, in what pertains to the determination of culpability and the imposition of ecclesiastical penalties."[13] By way of explanation, the Diocese of Palm Beach's website states:

> The Office of Tribunal/Canonical Affairs is established by Canon Law as the judicial arm of the Bishop's government of the diocese. As such, it is the court system of the Church and the canonical forum for the resolution of legal questions arising from the activity of the Church, its entities and of the faithful.
>
> Through a judicial process, the Tribunal also works in conjunction with the Ministry of Marriage and Family in all matters of permission when couples prepare for marriage and in dispensations/annulments.[14]

At the base of the Catholic judicial system are "tribunals of the first instance," which are trial courts.[15] A tribunal of the first instance may consist of one, three, or five judges, depending upon the case being heard.[16] Each diocese is to have "a judicial vicar, or *officialis*, with ordinary power to judge," appointed by the bishop; and the judicial vicar "may be given assistants who are called adjutant judicial vicars, or vice-*officiales*."[17] The judicial vicar and any adjutants must be "priests, of unimpaired reputation, doctors or at least licenses in canon law, and not less than thirty years of age."[18] Judges include the diocesan bishop and clerics appointed as diocesan judges by the bishop. Lay persons may be appointed as judges when permitted by the conference of bishops, and all judges "are to be of unimpaired reputation and doctors or at least licenses in canon law."[19] Cases before a tribunal also may involve an assessor, auditor, defender of the bond, notary, promoter of justice, and relator.[20]

Tribunals of the first instance regularly hear annulment cases, that is, requests to declare the nullity of a marriage.[21] As of September 2015, the Archdiocese of Miami was handling "between 240 and 250 annulment cases annually."[22] If a petition is filed by both spouses, or by one of them with the consent of the other, a streamlined "briefer" process may be used and the matter heard by one judge.[23] Otherwise, the ordinary process applies before three judges, at least one of whom is a cleric.[24] In most cases, the judges and tribunal personnel are "bound to observe secrecy" concerning the trial and the discussions and votes of the judges;[25] and a judge "can bind the witnesses, the experts, the parties, and their advocates or procurators by oath to observe secrecy" when "disclosure of the acts or proofs will endanger the reputation of others, provide opportunity for discord, or give rise to scandal or some other disadvantage."[26]

Appeals of first instance decisions are heard by tribunals of the second instance.[27] The appellate tribunal of the Archdiocese of Miami[28] handles the appeals of cases originating in any of Florida's six dioceses: Orlando, Palm Beach, Pensacola-Tallahassee, St. Augustine, St. Petersburg, and Venice.[29] The Archdiocese of Miami (Florida's only archdiocese) does not hear appeals from its own first instance tribunal, which instead go to the appellate tribunal of the Diocese of Pittsburgh.[30]

The CCL also encourages alternative methods to resolve disputes outside of the tribunal system. First, it encourages peaceful resolution of disputes without litigation.[31] Second, it permits mediation and arbitration of certain disputes.[32]

Typically, the disputes covered by the tribunals in the hierarchical Catholic system are not litigated in Florida's secular courts. These include intra-church disputes regarding the relationships between churches and their pastors or other ministerial employees. Occasionally, however, a party seeks to bring an intra-

Figure 6. Reverend Monsignor Gregory C. Wielunski, Judicial Vicar of the Metropolitan Tribunal of the Archdiocese of Miami. Photograph by Ana Rodriguez-Soto; courtesy of *The Florida Catholic.*

church dispute before a Florida secular court and encounters First Amendment issues. For example, the First District Court of Appeal held that "civil courts lack subject-matter jurisdiction, as a matter of law," to consider an associate pastor's workers' compensation claim because the "church autonomy doctrine, also known as the ecclesiastical abstention doctrine, protects the Archdiocese from state interference in its internal employment disputes" and because permitting a priest "to litigate his claim as a purported 'employee' would violate the Free Exercise Clause of the First Amendment to the United States Constitution by entangling the civil courts in the Catholic Church's internal governance."[33]

Similarly, the Third District Court of Appeal held that a trial court lacked jurisdiction to hear a claim under Florida's Private Sector Whistleblower Act by a former principal of a Catholic school because of the "First Amendment's bar against secular court review of religious policy and administration" and, more specifically, because the "ecclesiastical abstention doctrine precludes courts from exercising jurisdiction where an employment decision concerns a member of the clergy or an employee in a ministerial position[.]"[34]

In contrast, the Florida Supreme Court distinguished third-party actions, holding that the First Amendment does not bar "a third-party tort action against a religious institution grounded on the alleged tortious act by one of its clergy," when the tortious conduct was not "governed by sincerely held religious beliefs or practices" and the cause of action was "based on neutral application of principles of tort law."[35]

Presbyterian Church (U.S.A.)

The Presbyterian Church (U.S.A.) is governed by a constitution, which from time to time is amended.[36] Currently, Part II of the constitution is the 2015–2017 Book of Order ("BoO"), which details the church's hierarchical system of governance and judicial process, including its trial and appellate rules and procedures.[37] The BoO defines the "judicial process" as

> the means by which church discipline is implemented within the context of pastoral care and oversight. It is the exercise of authority by the councils of the church for: (a) the prevention and correction of irregularities and delinquencies by councils or an entity of the General Assembly (Remedial Cases); [and] (b) the prevention and corrections of offenses by persons (Disciplinary Cases).[38]

The religious and spiritual nature of the church's disciplinary system is evident in the preamble to the Rules of Discipline in the BoO:

> The church's disciplinary process exists not as a substitute for the secular judicial system, but to do what the secular judicial system cannot do. The purpose of discipline is . . . to preserve the purity of the church by nourishing the individual within the life of the believing community; to achieve justice and compassion for all participants involved; to correct or restrain wrongdoing in order to bring members to repentance and restoration; to uphold the dignity of those who have been harmed by disciplinary offenses; to restore the unity of the church by removing the causes of discord and division; and to secure the just, speedy, and economical determination of proceedings. In all respects, all participants are to be accorded procedural safeguards and due process, and it is the intention of these rules so to provide.[39]

The BoO acknowledges the "traditional biblical obligation to conciliate, mediate, and adjust differences without strife" and "the duty of every church member to try (prayerfully and seriously) to bring about an adjustment or settlement of the quarrel, complaint, delinquency, or irregularity asserted, and to avoid formal proceedings under the Rules of Discipline unless, after prayerful deliberation, they are determined to be necessary to preserve the purity and purposes of the church."[40] It also provides opportunities for "alternative forms of resolution," such as mediation, arbitration, and settlement, prior to or during the judicial process.[41]

The Presbyterian Church (U.S.A.) has a hierarchical system of governance at the local, district, regional, and national levels. It is

> governed by councils composed of presbyters elected by the people. These councils are called the session, the presbytery, the synod, and the General Assembly. . . . The jurisdiction of each council is limited by the express provisions of the constitution, with the acts of each subject to review by the next higher council.[42]

A session is formed by a local church, and sessions are part of a presbytery or "district governing bod[y]."[43] Florida has six presbyteries: Central Florida (headquartered in Orlando), Florida (Chipley), Peace River (North Port), St. Augustine, Tampa Bay, and Tropical Florida (Deerfield Beach).[44] Presbyteries are part of a synod or a "regional governing bod[y]."[45] There are sixteen synods, and Florida is part of the Synod of the South Atlantic, which also includes Georgia and South Carolina.[46] The General Assembly is the national "council of the whole church" and is "representative of the unity of the synods, presbyteries, sessions, and congregations of the Presbyterian Church (U.S.A.)."[47]

A session conducts its own trials and is comprised of elected ruling elders as well as the installed pastors and associate pastors of the local church.[48] The other councils—the presbytery, synod, and General Assembly—"conduct trials and hearings through permanent judicial commissions."[49] Members of the permanent judicial commissions must be teaching elders or ruling elders.[50] The permanent judicial commission for a presbytery must have a minimum of seven members; for a synod, generally a minimum of eleven; and for the General Assembly, one from each synod.[51] Most disciplinary cases begin at the session level, while remedial cases and some disciplinary cases begin at the presbytery level; all appeals are to the next level.[52]

The appellate process requires that certain preliminary questions be answered with respect to jurisdiction, standing, timely filing, and permitted grounds for appeal.[53] Thereafter, the appeal proceeds, with provisions being made for a pre-hearing conference, the introduction of new evidence, a hearing, deliberation, and a vote by the permanent judicial commission on each "specification of error."[54] The commission may decide whether to affirm or "correct, modify, set aside, or reverse the [appealed] decision."[55] The appellate decision is to be rendered in writing, delivered to the parties, and filed with the stated clerk of the respective council.[56] Additional publicity of an opinion depends on the directions of the commission, except that decisions of the Permanent Judicial Commission of the General Assembly dating back to 1983 are available on the website of the Office of the General Assembly.[57]

Some of the published appellate decisions from the General Assembly's Permanent Judicial Commission involve Florida cases. Although individual decisions differ in style and content, they normally include: a statement that each of the preliminary questions was answered satisfactorily, a history of the case, a list of each specification of error and whether it was sustained, and the specific orders of the commission.[58]

Several remedial cases in Florida have involved the potential closing of a church or the dissolution of a pastoral relationship.[59] One disciplinary case in Florida concerned the censure of a candidate for the ministry because of misconduct.[60] Others were decided on procedural grounds, such as where a party improperly attempted to use a remedial case to contest the ordination of a minister after it had become effective.[61]

Some of the decisions address future issues, including language that would be deemed *dicta* in a Florida secular court opinion, such as providing a suggestion "to avoid misunderstanding in the future"[62] or "admonishing the Session to refrain from future irregular ordinations."[63] Some also add religious aspects, such as "exhort[ing] the church not to . . . initiate disciplinary actions . . . without prayerful consideration."[64]

The published cases also mention churches that have formed Florida not-for-profit corporations or have created Florida trusts to own property.[65] If a schism arises within a church, a majority may choose to leave the parent church and an issue then may arise as to who has the right to the church's property. In such instances, the U.S. Supreme Court has held that states have a "legitimate interest in the peaceful resolution of property disputes, and in providing a civil forum where the ownership of church property can be determined conclusively."[66]

If a church has a hierarchical governance structure (such as the Presbyterian Church (U.S.A.), Florida defers to the decision of the highest ecclesiastical court that has addressed the issue.[67] In this regard, the Florida Supreme Court has observed:

> When the church is representative, republican or episcopal in government, the authorities uniformly hold that the church property[,] whether held by an express or an implied trust[,] cannot be diverted from the parent church by those who withdraw from it and form a separate denomination. It matters not whether those who withdraw from the mother church constitute a majority or a minority faction, the church property remains with the mother church. . . . [I]n churches bound together by associated ecclesiastical government[, where] the local church is obedient to a larger or more important religious organization and is governed by it, such as [in] the Presbyterian, Catholic, Episcopal, Methodist and Lutheran [faiths], [there appears to be] no exception to this rule. They could not function under any other rule.[68]

The BoO provides:

> If there is a schism within the membership of a congregation and the presbytery is unable to effect a reconciliation or a division into separate congregations within the Presbyterian Church (U.S.A.), the presbytery shall determine if one of the factions is entitled to the property because it is identified by the presbytery as the true church within the Presbyterian Church (U.S.A.). This determination does not depend upon which faction received the majority vote within the congregation at the time of the schism.[69]

Other Hierarchical Churches in Florida

Other hierarchical churches exist in Florida with rules for internal governance and resolution of disputes. For example, the Church of Jesus Christ of Latter-day Saints (Mormons) has published detailed handbooks to guide both leaders and members.[70]

The Episcopal Church has a constitution with provisions for courts (for trials of bishops as well as presbyters or deacons) and for courts of review (for appeals).[71] It also has canons that provide for ownership of church property in trust for the benefit of the Church and the diocese in which the congregation is located.[72]

Occasionally, a church or other party seeks help from a Florida court to resolve an employment or property dispute. For example, the Third District Court of Appeal, after determining that the Evangelical Lutheran Church in America is hierarchically organized—with a national church, regional synods and conferences, and local churches and their church councils—held that it should not intervene in a case involving the discharge of a minister. In explaining why, it wrote that the Florida "judiciary is obliged to defer to the hierarchical church's internal decisional processes on matters of internal church discipline," which included the bishop's "ground rules for determining . . . who under the Church and Synod Constitution . . . would be eligible to vote" to discharge the minister.[73]

Likewise, in a property dispute case, the First District Court of Appeal held that a trial court was required to accept the New Jerusalem Church's "self-characterization" as a hierarchical church and defer to the provisions of the church's Book of Rules regarding property ownership of affiliates and the mother church so long as the local church was affiliated with the mother church "such that it was a part of, and subordinate to, the hierarchical structure."[74]

In a lawsuit involving the Polish National Catholic Church and one of its affiliate churches, the Florida Supreme Court prevented the affiliate from using Florida corporate law to avoid complying with hierarchical decisions regarding church governance and property.[75] The original corporate charter of the affiliate recognized the jurisdiction of the national church and its constitution.[76] The bishop of the diocese suspended the minister and the members of the church committee and appointed a new minister; however, the suspended minister and committee members refused to relinquish their powers or deliver the church's assets to their successors. When the diocese sought injunctive relief from the circuit court, the suspended minister and three-fourths of the congregation amended the corporate charter to grant the corporation the "right to affiliate with any national church upon a two-thirds vote of its entire membership."[77] By affirming the permanent injunction, the Florida Supreme Court gave effect to the actions of the bishop of the diocese and disregarded the attempted corporate changes.

Congregational Governance

Congregational churches differ in structure from hierarchical ones because authoritative governance is at the local level only. Congregations within a denomination, such as Baptist churches, may share the same beliefs and scriptures and may receive guidance from regional or national conventions or organizations; however, individual congregations usually are independent.[78] Thus, such congregations generally operate separately from each other and the regional and national groups.

In some instances, the governance structure of a congregation resembles the governance structure of a non-religious, non-profit corporation, with officers, directors, and members, and with corporate documents, such as articles of incorporation and by-laws.[79] These documents may include provisions regarding membership and voting rights; election of directors and officers; hiring of clergy; and potential dissolution of the corporation.[80] Although these documents comply with state law, they often contain significant religious aspects.[81] Other religions (such as Buddhism) include methods for settling disputes in their religious texts but may need to resort to Florida's secular courts in corporate governance or property ownership cases.[82]

A number of Florida cases illustrate the governance structures of various congregations, the disputes that may arise, and the role, if any, of Florida secular courts in resolving matters. These disputes largely have concerned the employment of clergy, control of corporations, and ownership of property. Florida secular courts generally lack jurisdiction over ecclesiastic disputes, including ministerial employment disputes, because of the First Amendment.[83] In other cases, such as property disputes, Florida secular courts are permitted to apply neutral principles of law without running afoul of the prohibition against entanglement in religious doctrine.[84]

Baptist Congregations

Individual Baptist congregations are independent;[85] however, some of them may have representatives in a Baptist convention, such as the American Baptist Convention or the Southern Baptist Convention.[86] In 1985 a dispute arose at the Southern Baptist Convention regarding whether its Committee on Committees had the sole authority to present a slate of nominations for the Committee on Boards, Commissions, and Standing Boards or whether individual delegates ("messengers") could amend the slate. The procedures at the Convention included a motion by a messenger, a ruling from the chair, an appeal to the floor, an explanation of the by-law provision by the parliamentarian, a second ruling from the chair, an appeal to the Executive Committee, and then a lawsuit in federal court which was dismissed on summary judgment.

On appeal, the Eleventh Circuit held that the district court had correctly concluded that it lacked jurisdiction because "the First Amendment bars civil court resolution of this controversy concerning a matter of ecclesiastical government."[87] As previously explained, this sometimes is referred to as the "ecclesiastical abstention doctrine."[88] In a footnote, the Eleventh Circuit explained that its holding would have been the same whether the governance was hierarchical or congregational, with the difference being "the ecclesiastical body to which the civil court must defer in determining rights."[89]

In another case, the First District Court of Appeal held that it lacked jurisdiction over how a specific Baptist church should be governed—by the congregation or by the elders—because it was an "ecclesiastical dispute."[90] The court reached this conclusion even though the complaint was framed in neutral terms regarding whether the defendants had "acted unlawfully by failing to follow the procedures set forth in the Church's Articles of Incorporation and Bylaws for removing individuals as members and officers of the Church, electing directors, and amending the Articles and Bylaws."[91] The court held that "any inquiry into whether the Church adhered to its bylaws in excluding members necessarily entangles the court in religious matters protected by the First Amendment," in part because membership in the corporation was tied to membership in the church.[92]

On different facts, the Third District Court of Appeal held that a trial court was not barred by the abstention doctrine from "applying neutral principles" of Florida corporate law regarding the procedure to remove directors if it could do so "without inquiry into religious doctrine and without requiring the court to interpret the policies or practices of the Bible Baptist Church."[93] In this case, the statute applied by default when the by-laws did not "address the composition of the board, the removal of board members, or any similar aspect of corporate management" and only addressed temporary removal of an officer pending church action.[94] Instead of complying with the notice provisions and other requirements of the statute, one of the directors removed the names of four directors and added the names of three new ones when he filed the corporation's annual report.[95]

The Florida Supreme Court resolved a dispute based on "recognized rules of church order" for a Baptist congregation in determining whether the pastor's services had been terminated by the trustees and whether the actions taken thereafter were at valid meetings of the church or only a faction of the church.[96]

The Court upheld the decision of the "duly elected and qualified trustees" to terminate the services of the pastor and invalidated subsequent meetings where a faction of the church purported to replace trustees and suspend members of the church.[97]

In yet another case, the First District Court of Appeal held that the trial court had jurisdiction to determine whether a "minister's discharge was accomplished in accordance with the corporate charter" because "ecclesiastic matters do not come into play."[98] In this dispute, the church sought an injunction to restrain a minister it had discharged from "assuming or exerting any authority as pastor" and for an accounting, having "alleged that the discharge was accomplished in accordance with the articles and bylaws of the corporation."[99] This case differed from most employment cases because the pastor was not appealing the church's decision on the merits. Instead, he was relying on procedural rules and the church was seeking the court's help to enforce its decision.[100]

Florida's secular courts also have applied neutral principles of law in property dispute cases involving congregational churches, such as in determining whether a quorum existed when certain actions were taken[101] and whether to "apply and enforce principles of parliamentary procedure" for amending bylaws.[102] With respect to "a church of a strictly congregational or independent organization, governed solely within itself, either by a majority of its members or by such other local organization as it may have instituted for the purpose of ecclesiastical government," and its property held "for the use of that congregation as a religious society," the Florida Supreme Court has quoted the U.S. Supreme Court:

> In such cases where there is a schism which leads to a separation into distinct and conflicting bodies, the rights of such bodies to the use of property must be determined by the ordinary principles which govern voluntary associations. If the principle of government in such cases is that the majority rules, then the numerical majority of members must control the right to the use of the property. If there be within the congregation officers in whom are vested the powers of such control, then those who adhere to the acknowledged organism by which the body is governed are entitled to the use of the property. The minority in choosing to separate themselves into a distinct body, and refusing to recognize the authority of the governing body, can claim no rights in the property from the fact that they had once been members of the church or congregation. This ruling admits of no inquiry into the existing religious opinions of those who comprise the legal or regular organization; for, if such was permitted, a very small

> minority, without any officers of the church among them, might be found to be the only faithful supporters of the religious dogmas of the founders of the church. There being no such trust imposed upon the property when purchased or given, the court will not imply one for the purpose of expelling from its use those who by regular succession and order constitute the church, because they may have changed in some respect their views of religious truth.[103]

Thus, in the case of a congregational church, the majority may determine property ownership,[104] whereas the converse may be true of a hierarchical church when a minority remains with the mother church.[105]

Jewish Congregations

Jewish synagogues often choose to be affiliated with national organizations that provide them with guidance and resources, including model documents and agreements.[106] Some of these samples include provisions for mediation or arbitration of employment disputes in accordance with the standards of a specific national organization.[107] Thus, they provide a method for resolving contractual disputes between the synagogue and its present or former rabbis and cantors. This is important given that Florida's secular courts generally lack jurisdiction over these disputes because they are "ecclesiastical in nature."[108]

Jewish courts exist in Florida to address religious issues, such as conversion, divorce, and status.[109] A Jewish court sometimes is referred to in English as a "rabbinical court" and in transliterated Hebrew as a *bet din*.[110] It usually consists of three members. These Jewish courts also may be asked to resolve other matters, such as business disputes or family matters involving alimony or property settlement.[111] Of course, these are the types of issues over which a Florida secular court generally will have jurisdiction, and a Florida secular court may be asked to enforce the decisions of these Jewish courts. A Florida secular court may characterize this type of dispute resolution as arbitration and the parties may be asked to sign an arbitration agreement that references both Jewish and Florida law.[112] In some cases, the parties may agree to have the arbitration decided based on the "Jewish law (*din*)," which may defer to Florida law, based on "compromise or settlement related to Jewish law principles (*p'shara krova l'din*)" where "the relative equities of the party's claims are considered in determining the award," or based on compromise alone (*p'shara*).[113] Generally, decisions of a *bet din* are not published; however, some redacted decisions can be found online.[114]

Alternative Dispute Resolution

Religious organizations may provide for religious disputes to be resolved without resort to their tribunals.[115] These alternative methods of resolving disputes may include mediation and arbitration. In addition, some religious courts, such as a Jewish *bet din*, may be treated as arbitration panels under Florida secular law.[116] Additionally, religious organizations may provide in their corporate documents or agreements for binding arbitration of disputes with members, directors, officers, employees, or others.[117]

Individuals also may agree to submit their business and personal disputes to mediation or binding arbitration based on their religious beliefs. This sometimes is referred to as "faith-based" dispute resolution.[118] The parties may cite scripture in an arbitration agreement and may include religious aspects, such as prayer, as part of the proceedings.[119] The First District Court of Appeal considered an arbitration agreement that provided that disputes that could not be resolved privately by the parties would "be settled by biblically based mediation and, if necessary, legally binding arbitration, in accordance with the Rule[s] of Procedure for Christian Conciliation . . . of the Association of Christian Conciliation Services."[120] The court acknowledged both "private religious arbitration, which is exceedingly common in our pluralistic religious society[,]" and the existence of "valid and enforceable religiously-based arbitration agreement[s,]" with rules providing that "[c]onciliators take into consideration any state, federal, or local laws that the parties bring to their attention, but the Holy Scripture (the Bible) shall be the supreme authority governing every aspect of the conciliation *process*."[121]

Conclusion

For many Floridians, the existence of religious courts and arbitration panels play an important role in their faiths. Nevertheless, in 2012 Florida House Bill 1209, entitled "Application of Foreign Law in Certain Cases," was proposed to void court decisions or arbitration awards in marital or family rights' proceedings based partially or wholly on a "foreign law, legal code, or system" that did "not grant the parties affected by the ruling or decision the same fundamental liberties, rights, and privileges guaranteed by the State Constitution or the United States Constitution."[122] The bill also voided any "contract or contractual provision" calling for the application of such law with the same effect.[123]

Commentators were quick to question whether the bill would make it difficult, if not impossible, for religious courts and arbitration panels to issue religious divorces in Florida.[124] Despite this concern, the bill overwhelmingly passed the House of Representatives (92–24) but later died in the Senate.[125]

Notes

1. *See* Pew Research Center–Religious & Public Life Project, *Religious Landscape Project—Adults in Florida* (2014), *available at* http://www.pewforum.org/religious-landscape-study/state/florida/. The remaining 6 percent of Florida's affiliated religious adults include Jehovah's Witnesses, Mormons, and Orthodox Christians (1 percent each); a small number of Buddhists, Hindus, and Muslims (less than 1 percent each); and an even smaller number of adherents of various other faiths. *Id.* Of Florida's unaffiliated adults, 3 percent are atheists and 4 percent are agnostics. *Id.*

2. *See, e.g., Amici Curiae Brief of Religious Tribunal Experts in Support of Petitioner*, Hosanna-Tabor Evangelical Lutheran Church and Sch. v. Equal Emp. Opportunity Comm'n, No. 10–553 (June 20, 2011) (132 S. Ct. 694 (2012)), *available at* 2011 WL 2470843 (describing Episcopalian, Jewish, Methodist, Presbyterian, and Roman Catholic courts in the United States); Marie Ashe & Anissa Hélie, *Realities of Religio-Legalism: Religious Courts and Women's Rights in Canada, the United Kingdom, and the United States*, 20 U.C. Davis J. Int'l L. & Pol'y 139 (2014); Pew Research Center–Religious & Public Life Project, *Applying God's Law: Religious Courts and Mediation in the U.S.* (Apr. 8, 2013), *available at* http://www.pewforum.org/2013/04/08/applying-gods-law-religious-courts-and-mediation-in-the-us/ (survey of the disciplinary systems of fifteen major religions).

3. *See, e.g.*, Michael A. Helfand, *Arbitration's Counter-Narrative: The Religious Arbitration Paradigm*, 124 Yale L.J. 2994 (2015); Michael A. Helfand, *Between Law and Religion: Procedural Challenges to Religious Arbitration Awards*, 90 Chi.-Kent L. Rev. 141 (2015); Nicholas Walter, *Religious Arbitration in the United States and Canada*, 52 Santa Clara L. Rev. 501 (2012); Lee Ann Bambach, *The Enforceability of Arbitration Decisions Made by Muslim Religious Tribunals: Examining the Beth Din Precedent*, 25 J.L. & Religion 379 (2009–2010); Evan M. Lowry, Note, *Where Angels Fear to Tread: Islamic Arbitration in Probate and Family Law, A Practical Perspective*, 46 Suffolk U. L. Rev. 159 (2013).

4. Watson v. Jones, 80 U.S. (13 Wall.) 679, 680 (1871) (the term "hierarchical" is not used in the opinion). For later cases using and defining the term, see, e.g., Kedroff v. St. Nicholas Cathedral of Russian Orthodox Church in N. Am., 344 U.S. 94, 110 (1952) ("Hierarchical churches may be defined as those organized as a body with other churches having similar faith and doctrine with a common ruling convocation or ecclesiastical head."); Jones v. Wolf, 443 U.S. 595, 619 (1979) (church governance is "hierarchical" when "local church is but an integral and subordinate part of a larger church and is under the authority of the general church"). *See also* Guide to Representing Religious Organizations 24 (Lisa A. Runquist & Jeannie Carmedelle Frey eds. 2009) ("hierarchical type of church government exists when there is a 'higher authority' that exercises authority over all of the local churches, especially with respect to decisions that can affect the ongoing operations of the church").

5. Mills v. Baldwin, 362 So. 2d 2, 6 (Fla. 1978), *vacated and remanded*, 443 U.S. 914, *reinstated*, 377 So. 2d 971 (Fla. 1979), *cert. denied*, 446 U.S. 983 (1980) (quoting St. John's Presbytery v. Central Presbyterian Church of St. Petersburg, 102 So. 2d 714, 718 (Fla. 1958)).

6. *Watson*, 80 U.S. (13 Wall.) at 680. *See also Jones*, 443 U.S. at 619 (church governance is

"congregational" when "authority over questions of church doctrine, practice, and administration rests entirely in the local congregation or some body within it.").

7. *Mills*, 362 So. 2d at 6.

8. *See, e.g.*, Serbian Eastern Orthodox Diocese for the U.S.A. and Canada v. Milivojevich, 426 U.S. 696, 724–25, *reh'g denied*, 429 U.S. 873 (1976):

> [The] First and Fourteenth Amendments permit hierarchical religious organizations to establish their own rules and regulations for internal discipline and government, and to create tribunals for adjudicating disputes over these matters. When this choice is exercised and ecclesiastical tribunals are created to decide disputes over the government and direction of subordinate bodies, the Constitution requires that civil courts accept their decisions as binding upon them.

See also Watson, 80 U.S. (13 Wall.) at 727 ("[W]henever the questions of discipline, or of faith, or ecclesiastical rule, custom, or law have been decided by the highest of these church judicatories to which the matter has been carried, the legal tribunals must accept such decisions as final, and as binding on them, in their application to the case before them."); Malicki v. Doe, 814 So. 2d 347, 352 (Fla. 2002) (quoting *Milivojevich*, 426 U.S. at 709: "[The] First Amendment prevents courts from resolving internal church disputes that would require adjudication of questions of religious doctrine. . . . Instead, civil courts must defer to the interpretations of religious doctrine made by the 'highest ecclesiastical tribunal.'").

9. *See* U.S. Const. amend. I. In pertinent part, the First Amendment provides: "Congress shall make no law respecting an establishment of religion, or prohibiting the free exercise thereof." The Florida Constitution contains nearly identical language: "There shall be no law respecting the establishment of religion or prohibiting or penalizing the free exercise thereof." Fla. Const. art. I, § 3.

In Meltzer v. Board of Pub. Instruction of Orange Cnty., Fla., 548 F.2d 559, 578–79 (5th Cir. 1977), *aff'd*, 577 F.2d 311 (5th Cir. 1978) (en banc), *cert. denied*, 439 U.S. 1089 (1979), the court declared unconstitutional Fla. Stat. § 231.09(2), which mandated that public school teachers, as one of their functions, "embrace every opportunity to inculcate, by precept and example . . . the practice of every Christian virtue," thereby "advancing [the] Protestant religion and inhibiting other religions." However, in Freeman v. Department of Highway Safety and Motor Vehicles, 924 So. 2d 48 (Fla. 5th Dist. Ct. App.), *review denied*, 940 So. 2d 1124 (Fla. 2006), the court upheld a state requirement that motorists have their driver license photographs taken without head coverings. The plaintiff, a Muslim woman, argued that requiring her to take off her veil violated her religious beliefs. In finding no violation, the court wrote:

> In this case, the trial court concluded that Freeman had not shown that the photo requirement substantially burdened her free exercise of religion. This conclusion is supported by expert testimony of Dr. Kahaled Abou El Fadl. Dr. El Fadl testified that in Islamic countries there are exceptions to the practice of veiling. Consistent with Islamic law, women are required to unveil for medical needs and for certain photo ID cards. Examples include photo ID cards to be displayed to police, to enter and take professional exams, and for passports. The only qualification is that the taking of the photograph accommodate Freeman's beliefs. Here, the Department's existing procedure would accommodate Freeman's veiling beliefs by using a female photographer with no other person present.

Id. at 56 (footnote omitted).

For a further look at when secular courts in Florida may hear cases involving religious organizations, see, e.g., Midrash Sephardi, Inc. v. Town of Surfside, 366 F.3d 1214, 1219 (11th Cir. 2004), *cert. denied*, 543 U.S. 1146 (2005) (municipal zoning ordinance "excluding churches and synagogues from locations where private clubs and lodges are permitted violates" federal law); First Baptist Church of Cape Coral, Fla., Inc. v. Compass Constr., Inc., 115 So. 3d 978 (Fla. 2013) (calculation of attorneys' fees due on church's indemnity claim against general contractor); Robbins v. Florida Conf. Ass'n of Seventh Day Adventists, 641 So. 2d 893, 895 (Fla. 3d Dist. Ct. App. 1994), *review denied*, 651 So. 2d 1195 (Fla. 1995) (affirming property tax exemption for vacant land "used exclusively for religious purposes").

10. *See, e.g., Watson*, 80 U.S. (13 Wall.) at 727, cited by *St. John's Presbytery*, 102 So. 2d at 717, and Baldwin v. Mills, 344 So. 2d at 268 (Fla. 1st Dist. Ct. App. 1977) (Smith, J., dissenting), *dissenting opinion adopted* 362 So. 2d at 7. In some cases, such as property disputes, a state may apply neutral principles of law. *See infra* note 66.

11. The text of the CCL can be found at http://www.vatican.va/archive/ENG1104/_INDEX.HTM. *See also* c. 1 ("The canons of this Code regard only the Latin Church."). For a further discussion, see, e.g., Marianne Perciaccante, Note, *The Courts and Canon Law*, 6 Cornell J.L. & Pub. Pol'y 171 (1996).

12. *See, e.g., Apostolic Letter Motu Proprio of the Supreme Pontif Francis Mitis Iudex Dominus Iesus by which the Canons of the Code of Canon Law Pertaining to Cases Regarding the Nullity of Marriage are Reformed, available at* http://w2.vatican.va/content/francesco/en/motu_proprio/documents/papa-francesco-motu-proprio_20150815_mitis-iudex-dominus-iesus.html (effective Dec. 8, 2015). For a further look at how the CCL is amended, see, e.g., Ladislas Orsy, *Stability and Development in Canon Law and the Case of "Definitive" Teaching*, 76 Notre Dame L. Rev. 865 (2001).

13. CCL, *supra* note 11, at c. 1401. *See also* Rachel Zoll, *Catholic Church's Canon-Law Courts Come out of Obscurity as Internal Litigation Grows*, AP, Jan. 16, 2012, *available at* http://www.cleveland.com/nation/index.ssf/2012/01/catholic_churchs_canon-law_cou.html.

14. *See* Diocese of Palm Beach, *Office of Tribunal/Canonical Affairs*, *at* http://www.diocesepb.org/tribunalcanonical-affairs.

15. *See* CCL, *supra* note 11, bk. VII, pt. I, tit. II, c. 1, entitled "The Tribunal of First Instance."

16. *Id.* cc. 1419, 1425 ("penal cases" which can result in "dismissal from the clerical state" or "excommunication" require a "collegial tribunal of three judges"; "[a] bishop can entrust more difficult cases or those of greater importance to the judgment of three or five judges").

17. *Id.* c. 1420, §§ 1, 3.

18. *Id.* § 4.

19. *Id.* c. 1421, §§ 2–3.

20. *Id.* cc. 1424, 1428–32, 1434, 1437.

21. *See Apostolic Letter*, *supra* note 12, at c. 1673. *See also* U.S. Conference of Catholic Bishops, *Annulment*, *at* http://www.usccb.org/issues-and-action/marriage-and-family/marriage/annulment/index.cfm and its link to "Annulment FAQs."

22. *See* Archdiocese of Miami, *Annulment Reforms Seen as Beneficial to Local Catholics*, Sept. 9, 2015, *at* http://www.miamiarch.org/CatholicDiocese.php?op=Article_Annulment+reforms+seen+as+beneficial+to+local+Catholics. *See also* Ana Rodriguez Soto, *Saving Souls through Canon Law*, Fla. Catholic, Feb. 20, 2016, *at* http://www.miamiarch.org/Catholic

Diocese.php?op=Article_145574206430095 ("Most of the time, the [Miami] tribunal handles marriage annulment cases. As judicial vicar, Msgr. [Gregory] Wielunski oversees an office of more than a dozen canon lawyers, six administrative staff and a broad network of trained advocates, people at the parish level who guide Catholics through the annulment process.").

23. *See Apostolic Letter*, *supra* note 12, at c. 1683 ("*libellus* [petition], introducing the briefer process, . . . must: 1° set forth briefly, fully, and clearly the facts on which the petition is based; 2° indicate the proofs, which can be immediately collected by the judge; 3° exhibit the documents in an attachment, upon which the petition is based"). *See also id.* c. 1684.

24. *Id.* c. 1676, § 3.

25. CCL, *supra* note 11, at c. 1455. "Judges and tribunal personnel are always bound to observe secrecy of office in a penal trial, as well as in a contentious trial if the revelation of some procedural act could bring disadvantage to the parties." *Id.* § 1.

26. *Id.* § 3.

27. Appeals also can be taken to the *Tribunal Apostolicum Rotae Romanae*, commonly referred to as the Roman Rota, the Church's highest appellate body. *See* Archdiocese of Miami, *Second Instance Tribunal*, *at* http://tribunal.miamiarch.org/Second_Instance_Tribunal.htm. *See also* CCL, *supra* note 11, at cc. 1405 ("Roman Pontiff"), 1416 ("Apostolic Signature"), 1442–45 ("The Tribunals of the Apostolic See"), 1443–44 ("Roman Rota"), and 1445 ("supreme tribunal of the Apostolic Signatura").

28. In the United States, Latin rite churches are grouped into 33 archdioceses and 145 dioceses. *See* U.S. Conference of Catholic Bishops, *Bishops and Dioceses*, *at* http://www.usccb.org/about/bishops-and-dioceses/index.cfm.

29. *See Second Instance Tribunal*, *supra* note 27.

30. *Id.* ("The Tribunal of Second Instance for the hearing [of] appeals of cases resolved on the First Instance Tribunal of the Archdiocese of Miami is St. Pittsburgh, Pennsylvania.").

31. See CCL, *supra* note 11, at c. 1446, § 1 ("All the Christian faithful, and especially bishops, are to strive diligently to avoid litigation among the people of God as much as possible, without prejudice to justice, and to resolve litigation peacefully as soon as possible.").

32. See id. c. 1446, § 2 ("Whenever the judge perceives some hope of a favorable outcome at the start of litigation or even at any other time, the judge is not to neglect to encourage and assist the parties to collaborate in seeking an equitable solution to the controversy and to indicate to them suitable means to this end, even by using reputable persons for mediation."); § 3 ("If the litigation concerns the private good of the parties, the judge is to discern whether the controversy can be concluded advantageously by an agreement or the judgment of arbitrators according to the norm of [canons] 1713–1716."). See also *id.* c. 1713 ("In order to avoid judicial contentions an agreement or reconciliation is employed usefully, or the controversy can be committed to the judgment of one or more arbitrators."); c. 1715, § 1 ("An agreement or compromise cannot be made validly concerning matters which pertain to the public good and other matters about which the parties cannot make disposition freely.").

33. Malichi v. Archdiocese of Miami, 945 So. 2d 527, 528 (Fla. 1st Dist. Ct. App.), *review denied*, 965 So. 2d 122 (Fla. 2007). *See also id.* at 530 ("Because the Archdiocese maintains an absolute ecclesiastical right to control and direct Appellant's duties and functions, any inquiry into this subject required the JCC [Judge of Compensation Claims] to inquire into internal matters of church governance. This is constitutionally impermissible.").

34. Archdiocese of Miami, Inc. v. Miñagorri, 954 So. 2d 640, 641 (Fla. 3d Dist. Ct. App.

2007), *review dismissed*, 985 So. 2d 1086 (Fla. 2008), *cert. denied*, 555 U.S. 1102 (2009). Of particular significance was the fact that "allowing the whistleblower claim to proceed would especially run afoul of the First Amendment because the requested remedy of reinstatement would require the Archdiocese to employ Miñagorri, a concededly ministerial employee." *Id.* at 644.

35. *Malicki*, 814 So. 2d at 351, 361. The Court further stated:

> We recognize that the Free Exercise Clause and the Establishment Clause require constant vigilance to prevent the government from either stifling the free exercise of religion or excessively and impermissibly entangling itself with interpreting religious doctrine on matters solely within the purview of religious institutions. However, with regard to a third party tort claim against a religious institution, we conclude that the First Amendment does not provide a shield behind [which] a church may avoid liability for harm arising from an alleged sexual assault and battery by one of its clergy members.

Id. at 365.

36. *See generally* https://www.pcusa.org/news/2015/6/21/new-book-order-20152017-now-available/ ("[A]mendments [were] approved by the Presbyterian Church (U.S.A.)'s 221st General Assembly (2014) and a majority of the presbyteries.").

37. The BoO is available at http://store.pcusa.org/OGA15001 (quotations from the BoO in the text of this chapter exclude internal cross-references to title and number, unless otherwise noted). The BoO has four parts: "The Foundations of Presbyterian Polity" (Part F), "Form of Government" (Part G), "Directory for Worship" (Part W), and "Rules of Discipline" (Part D). *See* BoO at 9.

38. BoO, *supra* note **37**, at D-2.0100. "A remedial case is one in which an irregularity or a delinquency of a lower council or an entity of the General Assembly may be corrected by a higher council," while a "disciplinary case is one in which a church member or a person in an ordered ministry [teaching elders, ruling elders, and deacons] may be censured for an offense," including "any act or omission by a member or a person in an ordered ministry of the church that is contrary to the Scriptures or the Constitution of the Presbyterian Church (U.S.A.)." *Id.*, D-2.0202, D-2.0203. *See also* Association of Stated Clerks' Guide for Judicial Process at I-1 (6th ed. 2011), *available at* https://www.pcusa.org/resource/guide-judicial-process/:

> These processes look and sound similar to the secular judicial processes that individuals may be familiar with such as criminal and civil litigation. However, . . . [t]here is no concept of punishment or retaliation within the PC(USA) judicial process and thus it is usually not appropriate to transport secular procedures into the church procedures.

See also Advisory Opinion Note 13: Duties of a Stated Clerk (under "Letter 11.094") (Apr. 2004, updated May 2009), *available at* http://oga.pcusa.org/media/uploads/oga/pdf/advisory-opinion13.pdf ("inappropriate influences from secular law must be resisted," such as motions for summary dismissal; "motions for such dismissals have become commonplace in the records before us, and judicial commissions need to be reminded that a dismissal is only appropriate after thorough examination of the record and opportunity for all parties to be heard.").

39. BoO, *supra* note **37**, at D-1.10101 ("Church Discipline").

40. *Id.* D-1.10103 ("Conciliate and Mediate").

41. *Id.* D-2.0103 ("Alternative Forms of Resolution"); D-6.0310, D-8.0307, D-10.0405, D-13.0307 ("Pretrial Conference").

42. *Id.* G-3.0101 ("Councils as an Expression of Unity of the Church"). See *infra* note 52 for the jurisdiction of the councils.

43. See http://oga.pcusa.org/section/mid-council-ministries/mid-councils/links/. In 2015 there were 9,642 churches and 171 presbyteries in the Presbyterian Church (U.S.A.). *See 2015 Summaries of Statistics—Comparative Summaries, available at* http://www.pcusa.org/resource/2015-summaries-statistics-comparative-summaries/.

44. *See* http://oga.pcusa.org/section/mid-council-ministries/mid-councils/links/.

45. *Id.*

46. See *id.* and http://oga.pcusa.org/section/departments/mid-councils/south-atlantic/.

47. BoO, *supra* note 37, at G-3.0501. The Florida Supreme Court has described the church's hierarchical structure as follows:

> A Church Session is the governing body of a local church. A Presbytery is composed of several churches in a geographical area; a Synod is generally composed of all Presbyteries within a state or other designated geographical area and the General Assembly is the highest governing body in the hierarchical spiritual structure of the Presbyterian Church.

Mills, 362 So. 2d at 3.

48. BoO, *supra* note 37, at D-2.0102, G-3.0201.

49. *Id.* D-2.0102.

50. *Id.* D-5.0101.

51. *Id.* D-5–0100.

52. *Id.* D-3.0101: "In judicial process"

> a. The session of a church has original jurisdiction in disciplinary cases involving members of that church.
>
> b. (1) The presbytery has original jurisdiction in disciplinary cases involving teaching elder members of that presbytery and ruling elders commissioned to pastoral service in congregations in the presbytery. . . .
>
> c. The presbytery, the synod, and the General Assembly have jurisdiction in remedial cases and in appeals.

See also *supra* text accompanying note 42.

53. BoO, *supra* note 37, at D-8.0301 (remedial case); D-13.0301 (disciplinary case). *See also id.* D-6.0305 (requiring similar questions to be asked in remedial cases regarding jurisdiction, standing, timely filing, and whether the "complaint states a claim upon which relief can be granted"). Grounds for appeal include:

> a. irregularity in the proceedings;
>
> b. refusing a party reasonable opportunity to be heard or to obtain or present evidence;
>
> c. receiving improper, or declining to receive proper, evidence or testimony;
>
> d. hastening to a decision before the evidence or testimony is fully received;

e. manifestation of prejudice in the conduct of the case;
f. injustice in the process or decision; and,
g. error in constitutional interpretation.

Id. D-8.0105 (remedial case); D-13.0106 (disciplinary case) ("undue severity of censure" is an additional ground of appeal in a disciplinary case).

54. *Id.* D-8.0307, 8.0403, 8.0404 (remedial case); D-13.0307, 13.0403, 13.0404 (disciplinary case).

55. *Id.* D-8.0101 (remedial case); D-13.0101 (disciplinary case).

56. *Id.* D-8.0404 (remedial case); D-13.0404 (disciplinary case).

57. The decisions of the Permanent Judicial Commission of the General Assembly are included in its minutes and can be found individually at http://oga.pcusa.org/section/committees/gapjc/permanent-judicial-commission-decisions/. With respect to its policy on open meetings, see http://www.pcusa.org/openmeeting/. For trials, see generally BoO, *supra* note 37, at D-7.0303 (open sessions); D-11.0306 (closed sessions).

58. The decisions also state which members were not present or did not participate. *See id.* D-7.0303 (remedial case); D-11.0304 (disciplinary case) (requiring the recording of the "absence of any member . . . after a trial has commenced").

59. *See, e.g.*, Cubbin-Will v. Presbytery of Tropical Fla., Remedial Case 220–12 (Perm. Jud. Comm'n Gen. Assemb. 2012) ("Judicial economy and other practicalities dictate that in limited circumstances, such as those in this case, it is appropriate to allow evidence of events subsequent to the filing of a remedial complaint"; the relevant events included a change in the need to close the church and the curing of procedural defects by the presbytery regarding the providing of notice and an opportunity for discussion), *available at* http://oga.pcusa.org/media/uploads/oga/pdf/pjc22012.pdf; Anderson v. Presbytery of Central Fla., Remedial Case 203–2 (Perm. Jud. Comm'n Gen. Assemb. 1990) (after Administrative Commission issued settlement order on behalf of presbytery dissolving pastoral relationship between church and appellant and forbidding appellant from attending worship services at church, synod's permanent judicial commission found that the Administrative Commission had acted within the scope of its authority except with respect to forbidding attendance, and the General Assembly's permanent judicial commission affirmed the "decisions of [the] synod's judicial commission," unanimously voting that it "did not commit any prejudicial error on any of the specifications of error advanced by the Appellant"), *available at* http://oga.pcusa.org/media/uploads/oga/pdf/pjc20302.pdf; Hoy v. Presbytery of Tropical Fla., Remedial Case 203–1 (Perm. Jud. Comm'n Gen. Assemb. 1990) (stating clerk of presbytery failed to refer appellant's complaint to presbytery's permanent judicial commission, which "prevented proper adjudication of the issues" and "Synod's Permanent Judicial Commission erred in dismissing the complaints against presbytery relating to its Administrative Commission in exceeding its mandate in executing its duties," resulting in an order stating "that the proper disposition of this matter requires that the Presbytery of Tropical Florida take pastoral oversight to counsel with the former members of the Calusa Presbyterian Church"), *available at* http://oga.pcusa.org/media/uploads/oga/pdf/pjc20301.pdf. *See also* Larson v. Presbytery of S. Fla., Remedial Case 194–5 (Perm. Jud. Comm'n Gen. Assemb. 1983–84) (complaint of irregularity properly dismissed for lack of jurisdiction to review dissolution of pastoral relationship where complaint was filed more than 30

days after irregularity occurred), *available at* http://oga.pcusa.org/media/uploads/oga/pdf/pjc19505.pdf.

60. *See* Presbyterian Church (USA) by Presbytery of Central Fla. v. Herrero, Disciplinary Case 207–12 (Perm. Jud. Comm'n Gen. Assemb. 1995) (affirming the "decision of the Synod Permanent Judicial Commission finding Appellant guilty beyond a reasonable doubt of Amended Charge III" because of "unacceptable behavior for a candidate for the ministry of the Word and Sacraments in the Presbyterian Church (U.S.A.) [in] violation of her covenant relationship and her candidate's promises and vows and Holy Scriptures"; setting aside "one year exclusion from candidacy" because it was "not a permissible censure under the Book of Order"; and "modifying the decision of the Synod by imposing a censure of temporary exclusion from membership for a period of one year"), *available at* http://oga.pcusa.org/media/uploads/oga/pdf/pjc20712.pdf.

61. *See, e.g.*, Wier v. Session, Second Presbyterian Church of Fort Lauderdale, Fla., Remedial Case 211–2 (Perm. Jud. Comm'n Gen. Assemb. 1998), *available at* http://oga.pcusa.org/media/uploads/oga/pdf/pjc21102.pdf ("[D]isciplinary action affords individuals specific rights of due process (*e.g.*, facing accusers and speaking in one's own defense) and requires standards of proof that are more stringent than remedial action. Pursuing what are effectively disciplinary ends through remedial action subverts the intent of our polity to safeguard these rights."). *See also* Wier v. Session, Second Presbyterian Church of Ft. Lauderdale, Fla., Remedial Case 214–5 (Perm. Jud. Comm'n Gen. Assemb. 2002) ("As a remedial complaint, it seeks to prosecute a disciplinary case"; it "alleges a violation of constitutional standard that may have extreme consequences to a person's reputation, career, or friendships," and therefore needs "a greater degree of pleading specificity," but it "fails to meet the specificity" required; and it "violates the doctrine of total depravity" when it "single[s] out a category of persons above and beyond other persons as more likely to sin"), *available at* http://oga.pcusa.org/media/uploads/oga/pdf/pjc21405.pdf.

62. *See Anderson*, Remedial Case 203–2 ("The Commission suggests that in order to avoid misunderstanding in the future, a presbytery, in appointing an administrative commission to inquire into and to settle difficulties in a church, state with particularity in the order of appointment, any limitations or restrictions on the powers delegated to the administrative commission. If a presbytery intends or does not intend that an administrative commission have the power to dissolve a pastoral relationship, it should so indicate in clear and express language.").

63. *See Wier*, Remedial Case 211–2 (holding that the order of the Permanent Judicial Commission of Presbytery "admonishing the Session to refrain from future irregular ordinations is, in itself, an appropriate and constitutional action").

64. *Id.*

65. *See generally* Fla. Stat. chs. 617 (not-for-profit corporations) and 736 (trusts). *See also* Full Gospel Temple of Tallahassee v. Redd, 82 So. 2d 589, 589, 590 (Fla. 1955) (Spec. Div. A) (property held in trust "for the use and benefit of the ministry and membership of the Pentecostal Holiness Church" was "vested for that purpose" and "[s]o long as used for the purpose of the trust, there was no authority to convey"; thus, "deed of conveyance executed by those who withdrew from the First Pentecostal Holiness Church of Tallahassee to The Full Gospel Temple" without consideration was void; further issue of whether church polity was "episcopal or congregational in form" was not material because of trust).

66. *See Jones*, 443 U.S. at 602; *Baldwin*, 443 U.S. at 914 ("Judgment vacated and case remanded to the Supreme Court of Florida for further consideration in light of *Jones v. Wolf*, 443 U.S. 595, 99 S.Ct. 3020, 61 L.Ed.2d 775 (1979).").

67. *See, e.g., Mills*, 362 So. 2d at 6. *See also* Townsend v. Teagle, 467 So. 2d 772, 775 (Fla. 1st Dist. Ct. App.), *review denied*, 479 So. 2d 118 (Fla. 1985) ("Civil courts which apply the deference approach are precluded from rejecting the decisions of ecclesiastical tribunals of hierarchical churches, substituting their own inquiry into church policy, and then resolving the dispute based on their own interpretations of church law.").

Florida's deference approach is one of the methods permitted by the First Amendment. *See, e.g., Jones*, 443 U.S. at 602 (quoting Maryland & Va. Eldership of Churches of God v. Church of God at Sharpsburg, Inc., 396 U.S. 367, 368 (1970) ("[A] State may adopt any one of various approaches for settling church property disputes so long as it involves no consideration of doctrinal matters, whether the ritual and liturgy of worship or the tenets of faith."); Jones v. Wolf, 260 S.E.2d 84, 85 (Ga. 1979), *cert. denied*, 444 U.S. 1080 (1980) ("The Supreme Court of the United States has permitted Georgia to apply the principle of presumptive majority rule to local schism cases, provided only that this court shall articulate the method by which the presumption may be overcome. The presumption may be overcome by reliance upon neutral statutes, corporate charters, relevant deeds, and the organizational constitutions of the denomination.").

68. *Mills*, 362 So. 2d at 6–7 (quoting *St. John's Presbytery*, 102 So. 2d at 718).

69. BoO, *supra* note 37, at G-4.0207 (general rule); G-4.0208 (exception for certain congregations that timely voted to be exempt and therefore are permitted to "hold title to [their] property and exercise [their] privileges of incorporation and property ownership under the provisions of the Constitution to which [they were] subject immediately prior to the establishment of the Presbyterian Church (U.S.A.)."). The BoO also provides:

> All property held by or for a congregation, a presbytery, a synod, the General Assembly, or the Presbyterian Church (U.S.A.), whether legal title is lodged in a corporation, a trustee or trustees, or an unincorporated association, and whether the property is used in programs of a congregation or of a higher council or retained for the production of income, is held in trust nevertheless for the use and benefit of the Presbyterian Church (U.S.A.).

Id. G-4.0203 ("Church Property Held in Trust").

70. See Handbook 1: Stake Presidents and Bishops (2010) (not publicly available) and Handbook 2: Administering the Church (2010), *available at* https://www.lds.org/handbook/handbook-2-administering-the-church/?lang=eng&_r=1. *See also* M. Russell Ballard, *A Chance to Start Over: Church Disciplinary Councils and the Restoration of Blessings* (Sept. 1990), *at* https://www.lds.org/ensign/1990/09/a-chance-to-start-over-church-disciplinary-councils-and-the-restoration-of-blessings?lang=eng (explaining when disciplinary councils must be held (*e.g.*, in cases of "apostacy"), may be held (*e.g.*, "to consider a member's standing in the Church following serious transgression," such as "child abuse," "false swearing," or "theft"), and will not be held (*e.g.*, to "try civil or criminal cases" or for "failure to pay tithing")).

71. *See* 2015 Constitution of General Convention art. IX, *available at* http://www.episcopalchurch.org/library/document/2015-constitution-and-canons. *See also Canon of the Dio-*

cese of Florida, c. 26, § 2(a) (regarding "Judicial System of Diocese," "Disciplinary Structure," and "Disciplinary Board"), *available at* http://diocesefl.org/media/106754/canons_with_revisions_from_2016_convention.pdf.

72. *See* 2015 Canons of General Convention tit. 1, c. 7, § 4. *See also* Mary Frances Schjonberg, *FLORIDA: Judge Orders Breakaway Congregation to Return Property to Diocese*, Episcopal News Serv., May 7, 2007, *available at* http://www.episcopalchurch.org/library/article/florida-judge-orders-breakaway-congregation-return-property-diocese-0; *Bishop Inhibits Priests, Pledges to be Responsible Steward*, Episcopal News Serv., Jan. 19, 2006, *available at* http://www.episcopalchurch.org/library/article/diocesan-digest-january-19–2006#FLORIDA.

73. Franzen v. Poulos, 604 So. 2d 1260, 1261, 1263 (Fla. 3d Dist. Ct. App. 1992). The court further observed: "While the trial court is ordinarily empowered to adjudicate questions of Florida corporate law, a First Amendment exception applies to matters of internal governance of a hierarchical religious organization" and the "complaint and prayer for injunctive relief in this case sought to inject the court into the internal governance of the Lutheran Church, a hierarchical religious organization." *Id.* at 1262–63.

For another such case, see Southeastern Conf. Ass'n of Seventh-Day Adventists, Inc. v. Dennis, 862 So. 2d 842, 844 (Fla. 4th Dist. Ct. App. 2003) (citing Lewis v. Seventh Day Adventists Lake Regional Conf., 978 F.2d 940, 942 (6th Cir. 1992)) ("[C]ivil courts must abstain from deciding ministerial employment disputes or reviewing decisions of religious judicatory bodies concerning the employment of clergy, 'because such state intervention would excessively inhibit religious liberty.'").

74. New Jerusalem Church of God, Inc. v. Sneads Cmty. Church, Inc., 147 So. 3d 25, 29–30 (Fla. 1st Dist. Ct. App. 2013), *review denied*, 148 So. 3d 772 (Fla. 2014) (after "determining, as a matter of law, that NJC, Inc. is a hierarchical church, . . . a second layer of inquiry is relevant[: . . . W]hether NJC, Sneads was affiliated with NJC, Inc., such that it was a part of, and subordinate to, the hierarchical structure"). *See also* Bethel AME Church v. Domingo, 654 So. 2d 233 (Fla. 1st Dist. Ct. App.), *review denied*, 662 So. 2d 931 (Fla. 1995) (The "principle of church structure which governs church property disputes . . . requires that church property remain with the parent church where, as here, the church is hierarchical in structure."). For the current governance and leadership structure of the African Methodist Episcopal Church, including its Judicial Council, see http://ame-church.com/our-church/our-structure/ and http://ame-church.com/leadership/.

75. *See* Rekas v. Polish Nat'l Catholic Church, W. Diocese, 102 So. 2d 705 (Fla. 1958). For the Church's current structure, see http://www.pncc.org/?page_id=15; for its 2010 Constitution, which provides in Article XXII ("Judiciary") for Parish, Diocesan, and Supreme Tribunals as well as a General Synod, see http://www.pncc.org/wp-content/uploads/2010/08/PNCC-Constitution-2010-final_1.pdf.

76. In pertinent part, the corporate charter provided:

> The general nature of the objects of said corporation will be for the purpose of religious worship, and for carrying on of such other church functions that the congregation may deem necessary and proper; to acquire, mortgage and sell property or properties in connection with its functions as a religious corporation; *all of the above in accordance with and subject to the jurisdiction of the Polish National Catholic Church as set forth in the Constitution and By-Laws of the Polish National Catholic Church as adopted by various synods of said church.*

Rekas, 102 So. 2d at 706 (emphasis added).

77. *Id.*

78. *See supra* note 6 and accompanying text. See also Runquist & Frey, *supra* note 4, at 25 ("A congregational type of church government . . . exists when the local body is a self-governing, independent organization and those in authority are elected by the local congregation to that position.").

79. *See, e.g.*, 2016 Bylaws of First Congregational United Church of Christ of Sarasota, Inc., *available at* http://uccsarasota.com/wp-content/uploads/2016/01/2016-Proposed-Church-Bylaws-March-Final.pdf ("The government of this church is vested in its members who exercise the right of control in all its affairs. The final authority in all matters shall rest in the membership. It shall be a part of the United Church of Christ cooperating through the Florida Conference."). *See also* Constitution of United Church of Christ art. V, § 18, *available at* http://www.ucc.org/ucc_constitution_and_bylaws#bylaws:

> The autonomy of the Local Church is inherent and modifiable only by its own action. Nothing in this Constitution and the Bylaws of the United Church of Christ shall destroy or limit the right of each Local Church to continue to operate in the way customary to it; nor shall be construed as giving to the General Synod, or to any Conference or Association now, or at any future time, the power to abridge or impair the autonomy of any Local Church in the management of its own affairs, which affairs include, but are not limited to, the right to retain or adopt its own methods of organization, worship and education; to retain or secure its own charter and name; to adopt its own constitution and bylaws; to formulate its own covenants and confessions of faith; to admit members in its own way and to provide for their discipline or dismissal; to call or dismiss its pastor or pastors by such procedure as it shall determine; to acquire, own, manage and dispose of property and funds; to control its own benevolences; and to withdraw by its own decision from the United Church of Christ at any time without forfeiture of ownership or control of any real or personal property owned by it.

80. As has been pointed out elsewhere:

> To protect the religious organization's ability to resolve disputes internally within the tenets of the organization's faith, the bylaws should provide an arbitration procedure. A provision in the bylaws that sets forth an arbitration council or other non[-]judicial dispute resolution mechanism to be used to resolve a controversy pertaining to an internal religious matter that cannot be settled locally, allows the church or other religious organization to avoid having a court decide the matter.

Runquist & Frey, *supra* note 4, at 41.

81. *See, e.g.*, New Testament Baptist Church, Incorporated of Miami, Florida By-Laws art. II, §§ 1.1, 4.1, *available at* http://www.ntbcfl.org/#!by-laws/c23fb (requiring profession of faith for membership in corporation and for "voting privileges in matters of church business" and citing specific biblical verses as part of its disciplinary procedures, which are "for the purpose of reclaiming the individual, expulsion coming only after all other measures have failed.").

82. *See further* Rebecca Redwood French, *What Is Buddhist Law? Opening Ideas*, 63 Buff. L. Rev. 833, 854–59 (2015).

83. *See, e.g.*, Goodman v. Temple Shir Ami, Inc., 712 So. 2d 775, 777 (Fla. 3d Dist. Ct. App.

1998), *appeal dismissed*, 737 So. 2d 1077 (Fla. 1999), *cert. denied*, 528 U.S. 1075 (2000) (court lacked jurisdiction over "ecclesiastical" matters regarding temple's decision not to renew rabbi's employment agreement).

84. *See, e.g.*, Word of Life Ministry, Inc. v. Miller, 778 So. 2d 360, 362, 366 (Fla. 1st Dist. Ct. App.), *review denied*, 792 So. 2d 1214 (Fla. 2001) ("Since the present case implicates neutral legal principles only, precedent supports judicial resolution of the parties' dispute over corporate assets, the corporation's religious purposes notwithstanding" and "we hold that the original members and directors of the corporation remain in control of the Church, absent resignation or removal in accordance with the original articles of incorporation and bylaws, until and unless amended as provided therein.").

85. *See* Carroll v. Fellure, 185 So. 2d 768, 769–70 (Fla. 1st Dist. Ct. App. 1966) (quoting a policy statement adopted by the Association of Free Will Baptists advising: "One of the distinguishing characteristics of all Baptist groups has been their democratic form of government. Almost without exception Baptist bodies have adhered to [a democratic] form of church government. Free Will Baptists are no exception."). In determining that the church's government was congregational, the "chancellor properly considered and construed the rules, by-laws, and resolutions adopted by the church, by the [West Florida Association of Free Will Baptists] Association, and by the National Association of Free Will Baptists." *Id.* at 769. *But see* First Free Will Baptist Church of Blountstown v. Franklin, 4 So. 2d 390, 393 (Fla. 1941) (regional association's resolution of local church's dispute was binding "in light of the provisions of Article 5 of the Constitution adopted by the church [by which] the entire membership, inclusive of appellants, submitted themselves to the ecclesiastical jurisdiction of the church[.]").

86. *See generally* http://www.abc-usa.org/resources/abcusa-resources/board-of-general-ministries-documents/; http://www.sbc.net/aboutus/; http://flbaptist.org/right-beside-you/ (stating that the Florida Baptist Convention is "part of [the] Southern Baptist Convention"). With respect to the independence of individual churches, see Bylaws of American Baptist Churches in the U.S.A., *Prologue Declaration, available at* http://www.abc-usa.org/wp-content/uploads/2012/06/abcACbylawsrevised.2.1.13.pdf ("[The] Northern Baptist Convention declares its belief in the independence of the local church, and in the purely advisory nature of all denominational organizations composed of representatives of churches"); Constitution [of the] Southern Baptist Convention art. IV, *available at* http://www.sbc.net/aboutus/legal/constitution.asp ("While independent and sovereign in its own sphere, the [Southern Baptist] Convention does not claim and will never attempt to exercise any authority over any other Baptist body, whether church, auxiliary organizations, associations, or convention."). *See also Carroll*, 185 So. 2d at 770 ("'[T]he local church is an independent body, so far as it relates to its own government, the transaction of its business, the choice of its officers, and the discipline of its members,' and these rights cannot be denied the local church by any other organization within or without the denomination.").

87. Crowder v. Southern Baptist Convention, 828 F.2d 718, 727 (11th Cir. 1987), *cert. denied*, 484 U.S. 1066 (1988). The Eleventh Circuit also pointed out:

> The [U.S. Supreme] Court [in *Watson*, 80 U.S. (13 Wall.) at 773] reasoned that, although courts could resolve certain types of property disputes and set aside any punishment for crimes imposed by ecclesiastical tribunals,
>
> [I]t is a very different thing where a subject-matter of dispute, strictly and purely

> ecclesiastical in its character—a matter over which civil courts exercise no jurisdiction—a matter which concerns theological controversy, church discipline, ecclesiastical government, or the conformity of the members of the church to the standard of morals required of them—becomes the subject of [an] action. . . . [I]t is easy to see that if the civil courts are to inquire into all these matters, the whole subject of the doctrinal theology, the usages and customs, the written laws, and fundamental organization of every religious denomination may, and must, be examined into with minuteness and care, for they would become, in almost every case, the criteria by which the validity of the ecclesiastical decree would be determined in the civil court.

Crowder, 828 F.2d at 722.

88. Bendross v. Readon, 89 So. 3d 258, 259 (Fla. 3d Dist. Ct. App. 2012). *See also Malichi*, 945 So. 2d at 528, and *Miñagorri*, 954 So. 2d at 641 (both applying the doctrine in the context of a hierarchical church).

89. *Crowder*, 828 F.2d at 726–27 n.20 (quoting *Watson*, 80 U.S. (13 Wall.) at 679). The Eleventh Circuit further quoted *Watson* for the proposition that:

> If a congregational form of government is involved and the will of a majority of church members is to control, then the court will enforce the right of a majority of members to use the church property. If the congregational church has officers "in whom are vested the powers of such control, then those who adhere to the acknowledged organism by which the body is governed are entitled to the use of the property."

Crowder, 828 F.2d at 726–27 n.20.

90. Rosenberger v. Jamison, 72 So. 3d 199, 201 (Fla. 1st Dist. Ct. App. 2011), *review denied*, 92 So. 3d 214 (Fla. 2012).

91. *Id.* at 201.

92. *Id.* at 201, 204. The court stated: "[E]xercising jurisdiction in this instance would be tantamount to 'intervening on behalf of [a group] espousing particular doctrinal beliefs.' We can discern no way under the facts of this case to draw a clean line between essentially religious matters protected by the First Amendment and matters of corporate law." *Id.* at 204–05. Pursuant to the 1995 articles of incorporation, only active members were members of the corporation, and the applicable 1994 by-laws permitted the exclusion of those members who "had become an offense to the church and to its good name by reason of immoral or unchristian conduct, or by persistent breach of his or her covenant vows." *Id.* at 203. Under the 2008 amended and restated articles, only the Board of Directors/Elders were members of the corporation. *See* http://search.sunbiz.org/Inquiry/CorporationSearch/ConvertTiffToPDF?storagePath=COR\2008\0501\24999127.Tif&documentNumber=704293.

This case is consistent with the Florida property ownership cases based on majority rule discussed *infra* text accompanying notes 101–04. As the trial court observed, the appellants constituted an outnumbered "rump faction" who "ultimately withdrew from the church and started a new congregation" and felt "they should still control the Church building." Rosenberg v. Jamison, 2010 WL 9449938, at *1 (Fla. 8th Cir. Ct. 2010).

93. *Bendross*, 89 So. 3d at 261.

94. *Id.* at 260 n.1, 261.

95. *Id.* at 259.

96. *See* Epperson v. Myers, 58 So. 2d 150, 152 (Fla. 1952) (Spec. Div. A) (suit by 114 church members against six persons purporting to be church trustees). According to the Court:

> The Baptist Church is congregational in government and conducts its proceedings by well-established rules of church order. . . . There is no theory under which the affairs of the Baptist Church can be administered by a "rump faction" in the manner found to have been done in this case. It must be accomplished by the Church organization under recognized rules of church order. When a "faction" of the church arrogates authority to itself, disrupts the organization and sets at naught well-defined rules of church order, there is no course left for those who desire their rights settled through orderly processes but resort to the courts.

Id. at 152.

97. In reaching its decision, the Court acknowledged the general rule that "the matter of calling a pastor, excluding members from the church, electing church officers and the conduct of other routine church business [are] purely ecclesiastical" but acknowledged "the exception that when there is a showing of fraud, collusion or arbitrary conduct on the church authorities, the courts will interfere to protect the rights of those imposed on." *Id.* at 151–52.

With respect to hierarchical churches, see *Jones*, 443 U.S. at 609 n.8 (limiting the exception to fraud or collusion based on *Milivojevich*, 426 U.S. at 713). In *Milivojevich* the Court explained:

> [W]hether or not there is room for "marginal civil court review" under the narrow rubrics of "fraud" or "collusion" when church tribunals act in bad faith for secular purposes, no "arbitrariness" exception in the sense of an inquiry whether the decisions of the highest ecclesiastical tribunal of a hierarchical church complied with church laws and regulations is consistent with the constitutional mandate that civil courts are bound to accept the decisions of the highest judicatories of a religious organization of hierarchical polity on matters of discipline, faith, internal organization, or ecclesiastical rule, custom, or law.

Id.

98. Hemphill v. Zion Hope Primitive Baptist Church of Pensacola, Inc., 447 So. 2d 976, 977 (Fla. 1st Dist. Ct. App. 1984).

99. *Id.* ("Copies of those articles and bylaws are included in appellant's appendix, and reveal that no interpretation of church doctrine is required to effect a judicial construction of those provisions pertaining to the discharge of corporate employees. Therefore, the trial court's acceptance of jurisdiction and resulting orders do not violate the constitutional requirement of separation of church and state.").

100. *Compare* Covington v. Bowers, 442 So. 2d 1068 (Fla. 1st Dist. Ct. App. 1983), a case in which the parties each sought an injunction to prevent interference with the operations of the Macedonia Missionary Baptist Church. Both sides agreed that "church custom governs church procedures," leading the court to find: "If the meeting at which Covington [the pastor] was fired was duly assembled according to church custom, and if those assembled had the authority according to church custom to terminate the pastor, the trial court acted properly by refusing to interfere with the actions taken by the group." *Id.* at 1069.

101. *See* Rolle v. Judge, 310 So. 2d 42, 42 (Fla. 1st Dist. Ct. App.), *cert. denied*, 324 So. 2d 633 (Fla. 1975) ("[T]here was competent substantial evidence to support the trial court's determination that a quorum did *not* exist on August 6, 1971, the date on which action was taken by the appellant to change the name of the church[;] withdrawing its association from the Primitive Baptist congregation[;] and diverting the use of church property.") (emphasis added).

102. Umberger v. Johns, 363 So. 2d 63, 64–65 (Fla. 1st Dist. Ct. App. 1978) (amended complaint, seeking "to have the [trial] court apply and enforce principles of parliamentary procedure" contained in "adopted rules of church order (the by-laws) applicable to San Souci Baptist Church," stated cause of action alleging that "appellees effected a change in the church by-laws without complying with the notice requirement of the by-laws"; action was not filed "for purpose or effect of involving a court of law in an ecclesiastical matter.").

103. Partin v. Tucker, 172 So. 89, 90 (Fla. 1937) (quoting *Watson*, 80 U.S. (13 Wall.) at 725). *See also* Presbyterian Church in the U.S. v. Mary Elizabeth Blue Hull Mem. Presbyterian Church, 393 U.S. 440, 449–50 (1969) (state could not resolve church property disputes using a "departure-from-doctrine element of the implied trust theory" because doing so "requires the civil judiciary to determine whether actions of the general church constitute such a 'substantial departure' from the tenets of faith and practice existing at the time of the local churches' affiliation that the trust in favor of the general church must be declared to have terminated." The Court further warned: "States, religious organizations, and individuals must structure relationships involving church property so as not to require the civil courts to resolve ecclesiastical questions." *Id.* at 449.).

104. *See, e.g.*, Austin v. Mt. Zion Primitive Baptist Church of W. Palm Beach, 165 So. 2d 412, 413 (Fla. 2d Dist. Ct. App. 1964) (quiet title action based on prior possessory action in which the trial court found that "under the government of this church the majority of the congregation controls" and that majority owned, and never abandoned, old church building that was used by minority after majority moved to new facility); First Indep. Missionary Baptist Church of Chosen v. McMillan, 153 So. 2d 337, 342 (Fla. 2d Dist. Ct. App. 1963) (because majority abandoned building but not church, property owned by church "at the time of the abandonment by the majority of the church building, belongs to the majority group").

105. *See, e.g.*, *supra* note 68 and accompanying text.

106. *See generally* Orthodox Union (www.ou.org) and Rabbinical Council of America (www.rabbis.org); National Council of Young Israel (www.youngisrael.org) and Young Israel Council of Rabbis (no separate web site); United Synagogue of Conservative Judaism (www.uscj.org) and Rabbinical Assembly (www.rabbinicalassembly.org); Union for Reform Judaism (www.urj.org) and Central Conference of American Rabbis (www.ccarnet.org); Jewish Reconstructionist Communities in Association with the Reconstructionist Rabbinical College (www.Jewishrecon.org). *See also* Hearken to the Statutes—Synagogue Articles of Incorporation, Bylaws and Policy Manuals (2007), *available at* http://uscj.org/images/GuidetoWritingBylawsConstitution_1008.pdf; http://www.urjbooksandmusic.com/download/resources/HearkenToStatutes_Incorporation.pdf.

107. *See, e.g.*, http://www.uscj.org/Objects/Documents/guide_contractual_relations.pdf ("A Guide to Contractual Relations") (providing, *id.* at 26, that disputes involving rabbis are to be resolved with the help of the "professionals of the United Synagogue of Conservative Judaism and the Rabbinical Assembly" and, if that is not successful, "such dispute shall be settled by arbitration in accordance with the rules of the United Synagogue of Conservative

Judaism Committee on Congregational Standards and any award rendered may be enforced in the manner provided for the enforcement of arbitration awards in accordance with the laws of this state."). The model cantorial agreement contains the same provision except that it provides for settlement by "mediation or arbitration." *Id.* at 38.

See also The Kehilla Affiliations and Standards Committee Rules for Settling Disputes, at http://www.uscj.org/LeadingKehilla/ProgramsServices/MediationArbitration/CommitteeonCongregationalStandards.aspx (providing, *id.* at 3, that its dispute resolution process is available "to all employees of synagogues, Schechter Day Schools and other affiliates of the Conservative Movement, as well as to disputes concerning or between institutions within our movement, provided all parties have agreed in a contract or voluntarily agree at the time the dispute arises to use our process.").

See also http://www.ccarnet.org/rabbis-communities/professional-resources/rabbis-contract-checklist/ and http://www.ccarnet.org/media/filer_public/2016/03/10/guidelines_for_rabbinical-ongregational_relationships.pdf ("Rabbi's Contract Checklist and Guidelines for Rabbinical-Congregational Relationships") (providing, for Reform-affiliated congregations, dispute resolution, including mediation, arbitration, and an option for the National Commission on Rabbinical Congregational Relationships to conciliate or arbitrate disputes).

See also http://www.reconplacement.org/guidelines.php ("Placement Guidelines") (providing model contracts calling for the parties first to "attempt to negotiate or mediate the dispute internally using any mutually agreed-upon mechanism"; otherwise "the parties agree to submit to arbitration by the Reconstructionist Placement Commission (as described in Sec. 22 of the Placement Guidelines) in accordance with its established procedures," using a three-person arbitration panel).

108. *Goodman*, 712 So. 2d at 777 (rabbi's claims for breach of employment contract and tortious interference were "constitutionally-barred" and decision to not renew rabbi's contract was "ecclesiastical in nature, involving the selection of the Temple's spiritual leader, and for this reason the Court has no jurisdiction over the claims against" temple; trial court could, however, consider rabbi's claim under contract for unpaid compensation and unreimbursed expenses, because "[t]his claim does not create excessive entanglements with religious beliefs, and thus does not preclude civil court intervention.").

109. *See, e.g.*, http://www.beisdinofsouthflorida.com (Orthodox *beis din*) ("Beis Din of South Florida was established by local Rabbis in Miami . . . to serve the entire South Florida area" and "offer synagogues, Rabbis, and individuals the services of Halachic Geirus—conversion to Judaism, Get—Jewish divorce, and certification of personal Jewish status."); https://bethdin.org/gps and http://www.judaismconversion.org/batei.din.html (Orthodox *batei din*); https://jjcjax.org/conversion (Conservative congregation—Jacksonville) ("One of the final steps in the conversion process includes an appearance before a Beit Din (usually a panel of the candidate's sponsor and two rabbis). . . ."); http://www.tbeboca.org/convert-to-judaism (Reform congregation—Boca Raton) ("Prior to conversion, individuals must meet with a bet din, which is a Jewish court that is made up of three rabbis.").

While Florida civil courts cannot require a party to appear before a *bet din* to give or receive a Jewish divorce document (known as a "*get*"), they may determine or re-determine the parties' economic rights based on whether a *get* has been given and received. *See, e.g.*, Bloch v. Bloch, 688 So. 2d 945, 946 (Fla. 3d Dist. Ct. App. 1997) (circuit court could reserve jurisdiction to change economic terms of a final judgment dissolving marriage "to make them more equitable" for former wife if former husband failed "within fifteen (15) days . . . [to] initiate and cooperate in the obtaining of a GETT' [*sic*][.]"); Fleischer v. Fleischer, 586 So. 2d 1253, 1254 (Fla. 4th Dist. Ct. App. 1991) (affirming trial judge's order requiring "husband to give his approval to the wife's application for a 'get'" and allowing "wife to withhold money she owes the husband under the final decree until he gives such approval," where husband stated "he would agree to it if he got the property he wanted"); Turner v. Turner, 192 So. 2d 787, 788 (Fla. 3d Dist. Ct. App. 1966), *cert. denied*, 201 So. 2d 233 (Fla. 1967) ("circuit judge had no authority to order the appellee to participate in a religious ceremony" for "a religious divorce").

110. The Hebrew term is sometimes translated literally as "house of judgment." *See, e.g.*, The Principles of Jewish Law 561 (Menachem Elon ed. 1975). *Bet din* also can be transliterated in the singular, as *beth din* or *beis din*, and in the plural as *batei din*. *See further* Ainsworth v. Schoen, 606 So. 2d 1275, 1276 & n.1 (Fla. 3d Dist. Ct. App. 1992) ("The terms 'Bais Din' and 'Beth Din' appear to be used interchangeably and refer to 'a religious tribunal that adjudicates disputes according to Jewish law and custom.' *Meisels v. Uhr*, 79 N.Y.2d 526, 593 N.E.2d 1359, 583 N.Y.S.2d 951 (1992).").

111. *See* https://bethdin.org/dintorah (cases heard by "arbitration judges" include "commercial (such as employer-employee, landlord-tenant, real property, business interference, breach of contract, breach of fiduciary duty, investor mismanagement, defective merchandise and unfair competition disputes), communal (such as rabbinic contract disputes and other congregational issues) and familial (such as family business, inheritance and matrimonial) disputes."). The Beth Din of America's *Layman's Guide to Dinei Torah (Beth Din Arbitration Proceedings)* defines a "Beth Din" as a "Jewish court" and "Din Torah" as "Arbitration in a Jewish Court" and notes: "There are many Batei Din in the United States, with no particular hierarchy." *See* http://s589827416.onlinehome.us/wp-content/uploads/2015/07/Laymans-Guide.pdf.

112. *See, e.g.*, https://bethdin.org/forms for a form agreement to arbitrate before Beth Din of America. *See also Ainsworth*, 606 So. 2d at 1275 (agreement to arbitrate commercial dispute before a *Bais Din* provided "decisions of this Arbitration will be legally binding upon us with no recourse to any other authority whatsoever.").

113. *See, e.g.*, Beth Din of America's Rules and Procedures § 3, at 4, *available at* http://s589827416.onlinehome.us/wp-content/uploads/2015/07/Rules.pdf ("[I]n compromise or settlement related to Jewish law principles (*p'shara krova l'din*)," the award may depend on a "party's conduct throughout the matter under dispute" and additional remedies, such as public apology, may be available). *See also* Steven H. Resnicoff, Understanding Jewish Law 209 (2012) (providing that "p'sharah kerovah ledin (a compromise close to the strict din) can vary from the strict din by one-third.").

114. *See* https://bethdin.org/decisions (selected decisions have been published "to familiarize litigants and their attorneys with the types of decisions typically rendered in cases heard by the Beth Din of America," with consent of the parties and with their names, dates, and other identifying information changed). Reported decisions include (1) "claims relating to the sale of allegedly defective merchandise," (2) "hasagat gevul [unfair business competition] case involving the opening of a confectionary store," (3) "case regarding a claim for reimbursement of fees paid to a Pesach [Passover] program," (4) "decision upholding limited liability of a corporation under Jewish law," (5A, B) "interim decision" and "final decision regarding landlord tenant dispute," (6) "case relating to claims for the failed sale of a pizza store," (7) "case

of apartment mate seeking reimbursement under a rent sharing agreement," and (8) "claim by a utility cost savings consultant for reimbursement of amounts owed under contract." *Id.*

115. *See supra* notes 31–32 and 41 and accompanying text. *See also* supra note 107 and accompanying text.

116. *See supra* notes 110–14 and accompanying text. Florida does not permit child custody, support, or visitation disputes to be arbitrated. *See* Fla. Stat. §§ 682.25, 682.014(3)(k).

117. *See, e.g.*, Charter and ByLaws [of] Islamic Center of Baymeadow, Inc. art. XIV.E, *available at* http://www.bicjax.org (under "Useful Links: BIC By-Laws"):

> Arbitration shall be the sole means to reach resolution for all otherwise litigable conflicts that may arise among the Baymeadows Islamic Center members, directors, officers, employees, the persons served by the Baymeadows Islamic Center and all members of the committees or subcommittees. . . . The decision of the Arbitrator(s) is final and binding and cannot be appealed in court. . . . This arbitration clause shall be integrated, as appropriate, in the employment contracts, membership application forms, and all other contracts in which Baymeadows Islamic Center is a party.

See also Garcia v. Church of Scientology Flag Serv. Org., Inc., 2015 WL 10844160, at *4 (M.D. Fla.), *reconsideration denied*, 2015 WL 2356732 (M.D. Fla. 2015) (quoting representative arbitration clause).

118. *See* R. Seth Shippee, Comment, *"Blessed are the Peacemakers": Faith-Based Approaches to Dispute Resolution*, 9 ILSA J. Int'l & Comp. L. 237, 238 (2002).

119. *See, e.g.*, Spivey v. Teen Challenge of Fla., Inc., 122 So. 3d 986 (Fla. 1st Dist. Ct. App. 2013).

120. *Id.* at 988. For the rules regarding Christian Conciliation, see http://peacemaker.net/wp-content/uploads/2015/06/Guidelines-version-4-6-1.pdf.

121. *Spivey*, 122 So. 3d at 989, 992, 993 (emphasis in original).

122. H.B. 1209, § 1, ¶ 3, *available at* http://www.flsenate.gov/Session/Bill/2012/1209/BillText/Filed/PDF. The bill was filed by Representative Larry Metz (R-Eustis). A companion bill (S.B. 1360) was sponsored by Senator Alan Hays (R-Umatilla). *See* https://www.flsenate.gov/Session/Bill/2012/1360 (applying only to chapters 61 and 88 matters).

The bills were preceded by a Tampa circuit court's decision "to determine whether Islamic dispute resolution procedures have been followed." *See* Mansour v. Islamic Educ. Ctr., No. 08-CA-3497 (Fla. 13th Cir. Ct. Mar. 22, 2011), *available at* http://www.fljud13.org/Portals/0/Forms/pdfs/genciv/Mansour_v_Islamic_EducCenter-Opinion_of_Court.pdf?ver=2011-03-22-085723-377, *writ denied*, 75 So. 3d 279 (Fla. 2d Dist. Ct. App. 2011). *See also* Justin Elliott, *Debunking the Latest Sharia Scare*, Salon, Apr. 2, 2011, *at* http://www.salon.com/2011/04/02/sharia_florida_case/ (explaining that the dispute involved "two factions of . . . the Islamic Education Center of Tampa" and concerned "control of [$2.2 million] that was given to them by the government through an eminent domain taking. . . .").

Upon further consideration, the court dismissed the lawsuit after deciding that the First Amendment prohibited it from becoming involved. *See* William R. Levesque, *Ruling Tosses Islamic Law Case*, St. Petersburg Times, Dec. 13, 2011, at 1B. For a further discussion, see Katherine A. Sanoja, *The Impact of "Anti-Sharia" Legislation on Arbitration and Why Judge Nielsen in Florida Got It Right*, 8 FIU L. Rev. 181 (2012).

123. H.B. 1209, *supra* note 122, at § 1, ¶ 4.

124. *See, e.g.*, Paul Berger, *Jewish Divorce Caught in Sharia Law Fight*, Forward, Mar. 7, 2012, *at* http://forward.com/news/152534/jewish-divorce-caught-in-sharia-law-fight/. *See also* Brad Hirschfield, *Florida's Anti-Sharia Law Problematic, and Not Only for Muslims*, On Faith, Apr. 29, 2013, *at* http://www.faithstreet.com/onfaith/2013/04/29/floridas-anti-sharia-law-problematic-and-not-only-for-muslims/11408 ("[The] law would strip people of their constitutional rights to voluntarily participate in communities and/or contracts which should not be governed by secular law.").

125. *See* Marcy Oster, *Bill Banning Application of Religious Law Dies in Florida Senate*, Jewish Telegraphic Agency, Mar. 11, 2012, *at* http://www.jta.org/2012/03/11/news-opinion/united-states/bill-banning-application-of-religious-law-dies-in-florida-senate.

In 2014 an entirely different bill, approving existing case law and also limited to marital disputes and child custody matters, was signed by Governor Rick Scott. *See* http://flsenate.gov/Session/Bill/2014/0386/BillText/er/PDF, codified at Fla. Stat. § 61.0401. *See also* The Florida Bar International Law Section, *Florida Avoids Passage of Foreign Law Ban through Rational Compromise that Codifies Existing Case Law*, May 12, 2014, *at* http://internationallawsection.org/florida-avoids-passage-foreign-law-ban-rational-compromise-codifies-existing-case-law/.

7

Black Courts

ERNESTO A. LONGA

Miami's Negro Municipal Court ("NMC") was the only U.S. court ever set up as a purely black court.[1] Its creation in 1950 had been urged for years by some of Miami's most prominent black businessmen and professionals, who argued that their community's contempt for law and order, and even human life, was the product of the disdainful and humiliating treatment that black defendants received in the city's existing courts.[2] In particular, they pointed to the white judiciary's view of black-on-black offenses, which were deemed both less serious than crimes involving whites[3] and the result of blacks being naturally disorderly, irresponsible, and lacking in moral traits.[4]

Figure 7. Lawson E. Thomas, Judge, Miami Negro Municipal Court (*second from left*), with black police officers. Courtesy of the State Library and Archives of Florida.

According to the NMC's proponents, these ills could be ameliorated, at least in part, by forming an all-black court to hear cases involving black defendants arrested in black neighborhoods[5] by black police officers.[6] Not only would a black judge be more capable of adjudging a black lawbreaker, it was claimed that such a judge would be less inclined than a white one to treat black offenders leniently.[7] Dr. Ira P. Davis, a local dentist and one of the court's staunchest supporters, insisted, "When the judge starts cracking down on the boys carrying switchblade knives and guns and the people learn that it is going to go hard with them when they are caught, then major crimes will drop, too."[8]

By August 1949, white officials in Miami had been won over. As a result, they appropriated $60,000 for the construction of a two-story building at 480 Northwest 11th Street to house both the city's growing black police unit (on the first floor) and its newly approved black court (on the second floor).[9] In November 1949, the black community gathered in Dixie Park to express its appreciation.[10] When the NMC opened its doors six months later, Lawson E. Thomas was installed as its first judge.[11]

A Pioneering Black Attorney

Lawson Edward Thomas was born on January 28, 1898, in Ocala, Florida, to Hattie (Butler) and Robert J. Thomas.[12] The oldest of seven sons, Thomas earned a B.S. from Florida A & M College in 1919 and a law degree from the University of Michigan in 1923 (the first black to do so).[13] After passing the state bar exam, Thomas began his legal career in Detroit.[14] In 1928, he relocated to Jacksonville and went to work for McGill & McGill, a prominent black law firm.[15]

In 1935, Thomas moved to Miami.[16] Thomas later described his early years in the city as difficult due to the discrimination he encountered at every turn.[17] For example, black lawyers were limited to performing legal work that did not require them to appear in court.[18] If such a trip became necessary, they hired white attorneys to plead their cases.[19] When he asked about this custom, Thomas was told by the Dade County Bar Association not to make waves.[20] Undaunted, Thomas went to the municipal courthouse on Thanksgiving Day 1937.[21] When he slipped into a seat at the front of the courtroom (located on the sixth floor), the bailiff told him that if he did not take a seat in the back "with the rest of the niggers," he would be thrown out the window.[22] Thomas coolly went into the hallway, waited for the judge to take the bench, and then re-entered the chamber, thereby becoming the first black attorney in Miami to present a case.[23]

Throughout the 1940s, Thomas was a key participant in a number of groundbreaking civil rights campaigns and lawsuits. In 1942, for example, with the assistance of Thurgood Marshall and the National Association for the Advancement of Colored People ("NAACP"), Thomas filed and tried the first teacher equalization salary suits in Lake and Marion counties.[24]

In the summer of 1945, Thomas helped the Negro Citizens Service League organize a "wade-in" at Haulover Beach to protest the exclusion of blacks from Miami's beaches.[25] As a result, Virginia Key Beach was designated a "Dade County Park for the exclusive use of Negroes."[26]

In 1946, Thomas, as an *amicus curiae*, took part in a lawsuit that prevented Dade County from formally zoning itself along racial lines.[27] Thomas also filed a declaratory judgment action against the Broward County School Board to end its practice of holding split sessions at Fort Lauderdale's all-black Dillard School (which was done to provide local white farmers with a ready source of cheap labor during harvesting season).[28] And at a two-day meeting in Atlanta, Thomas met with the NAACP's national legal staff and other prominent civil rights attorneys to discuss "the next steps in the fight for equal facilities and curricula for Negroes in the Southern States."[29]

In August 1947, the NAACP asked Thomas to represent Aaron Quince,[30] a 19-year-old black man accused of killing Leona Carter Sparkman, a 29-year-old white housewife, near Holly Hill, Florida.[31] Thomas challenged Quince's indictment for first-degree murder on the ground "that Negroes were unlawfully, arbitrarily and systematically excluded from the grand jury which indicted him solely because of their race."[32] Agreeing with Thomas, Circuit Judge George W. Jackson quashed the indictment.[33] Jackson also "ordered the Spring term Grand Jury discharged and directed the County Commission to purge the entire 1947 jury box and refill it 'as provided by law.'"[34]

In April 1950, Miami Mayor Robert L. Floyd proposed that Thomas be named the NMC's first judge, describing him as a fair, just, and impartial man; a leader among his people; and a lawyer who had earned the respect of courts throughout the state, including the Florida Supreme Court.[35] After his nomination was unanimously approved,[36] Thomas pledged to give his "full consideration for the rights of the people who will come before me and for the rights of the community."[37] In an op-ed in the *Miami Times*, the city's black newspaper, Reverend Lorenzo A. Thompson wrote that Thomas's appointment would be "hailed far and wide as a forward step in practical democracy," showed that "we are coming," and predicted it would "lift the dark clouds of frustration that have hung so long and heavily" over the black community.[38]

Elsewhere, however, the NMC drew ridicule. Lucius C. Harper, the editor of the *Chicago Defender*, another black newspaper, described it as "a compromise on the race issue that is the most asinine and most disgusting spectacle to come to public notice in many, many years."[39] Harper further contended that

> [s]uch an arrangement does not point in the right direction: it is a throwback to the worse sort of Jim Crowism; and is loaded with dynamite, the like of which will cause the Negro citizens of Miami to be "blown" later into the most humiliating patterns of segregation ever conceived in the South.[40]

Another commentator described the NMC as "merely a new pattern of segregation" and called its "Negro Judge" only "half a judge."[41] The NAACP likewise denounced the court.[42]

To these critics Thomas responded forcefully:

> If the only objection to this court is that it does not try white people, then the objection is not to what we do, but that we don't do enough. Of course this court is not the final answer to our problem. But we Negroes must use the tools that are at hand. This tool at least gives us a measure of self-government within the bounds of segregation.[43]

In addition, Thomas believed the court would provide

> a rare opportunity to train a large mass of Negroes, who have no proper schooling, in their general attitude toward law and order. We must remember that our people are no different from others, and that we are no more prone to being criminals than any other people. . . . This is all part of the process of building, on a mass basis, good citizens. Changes are coming fast, faster than most of us realize. Most of the South is going to wake up one morning and find segregation is gone. They won't know how it happened, but it will have vanished for good. I wouldn't have backed the court or taken the job if I thought it was going to be indefinite. A few years will see vast changes.[44]

On May 22, 1950 (three weeks later than originally expected), the NMC held its first session before a packed house of black spectators, many wearing their Sunday best.[45] In addition to Thomas, there was a black bailiff (Clyde Lee, one of Miami's original five black patrolmen), and a black clerk (F.W. Reynolds).[46] After a speech by Floyd (who greeted the crowd as "my fellow citizens of Miami" and hailed the day as striking a blow for fair play and progress), Thomas was sworn in by City Clerk Frank L. Correll and presented with a gavel and flowers.[47] In his first decision on the bench, Thomas fined a man named John Rivers $10 (or eight days in jail) for disturbing the peace.[48]

Miami's All-Black Court

Those who predicted that a black police precinct and a black court would aid Jim Crow quickly were proved right.[49] White commanders were put in charge of the black sub-station and ran it as a fiefdom, making sure that black patrolmen arrested only black suspects within the black community.[50] Likewise, the NMC made sure to only hear cases involving blacks suspected of committing either victimless crimes or crimes against other blacks.[51] If two suspects, one white and one black, were arrested together in a black neighborhood, only the latter would be tried in the NMC.[52] More significantly, the NMC could never handle a case involving a black defendant accused of committing a crime against a white person.[53]

At the same time, however, the black police precinct and the NMC functioned as relatively autonomous entities of the City of Miami's police department and municipal court. It was this limited measure of self-government within the confines of segregation that Thomas recognized as a progressive step for his people.[54] Not only did the black police precinct maintain its own arrest slips, do its own bookings, and draw up its own charges, it also detained suspects in its own cells until trial.[55] Likewise, the NMC kept its own docket and had its own black bailiff, clerk, and judge.[56] Only if a black criminal defendant was found guilty and sentenced to jail would he or she leave the custody of the black precinct and be transferred to the city stockade.[57]

Like the main municipal court, the NMC handled only defendants suspected of municipal ordinance violations.[58] However, this included any state misdemeanor committed within the city's limits.[59] Consequently, the NMC had jurisdiction over cases involving drunk and disorderly conduct; behavior of a lewd and lascivious nature; simple assault; carrying a concealed weapon; and, prior to 1955, assault with a deadly weapon.[60]

On average, the NMC heard 8,000–9,000 cases a year (all without a jury).[61] A remarkable feature that the NMC shared with the main municipal court was that trials rarely involved attorneys.[62] Consequently, patrolmen often served as both prosecutor and chief witness, while the judge often served as both fact-finder and defense counsel.[63]

The NMC was unique because for the first time black defendants experienced both due process and equal protection in a Miami court.[64] Prior to the establishment of the NMC, black defendants received widely divergent sentences based solely on the race of the victim.[65] If the victim was white, white judges would hand out a heavy sentence to punish the black defendant and intimidate the black community.[66] In contrast, if the victim was black, white judges would impose a light sentence that conveyed condescending resignation.[67]

Thus, as long as black disorderliness and violence was confined to the black community, it was of no real consequence to whites. Black violence was considered a problem by white judges only if it affected the white community. In contrast, Thomas recognized the inherent value and dignity of all people and took seriously the problem of violence in the black community. At the same time, black defendants were presumed innocent until proven guilty and were given an opportunity to be heard.[68]

Between 1950 and 1959, Elliott J. Pieze wrote a column for the *Miami Times* entitled "Good Morning Judge" (the title reflected the fact that the job of NMC judge was part-time, with the court holding sessions in the morning six days a week).[69] His reporting provides the only surviving contemporaneous accounts of a typical day at the NMC. In his pieces Pieze discussed the courtroom environment,[70] including the judge's general disposition towards the defendants;[71] the presence of attorneys[72] and visitors;[73] the names of defendants and witnesses; the sentences and fines imposed; and, most revealing, at least one "featured" case.[74]

Nearly half of the cases that came before the NMC involved drunk and disorderly conduct.[75] Simple assault and battery cases also were quite common and typically involved matters of a domestic nature.[76] The NMC frequently heard cases of aggravated assault, with the weapons ranging from guns[77] and knives[78] to potash (a readily available fertilizer with toxic properties).[79] Even after aggravated assault became a felony, the NMC continued to handle such cases.[80]

Pieze regularly mentioned cases involving drunk and reckless drivers,[81] gamblers,[82] petty thieves,[83] and vagrants.[84] Pieze's most sensational columns featured defendants charged with lewd and lascivious behavior, including adultery[85] and sexual assaults,[86] as well as female impersonators,[87] men discovered in "compromising positions,"[88] and women engaged in "unnatural relationships."[89]

Pieze's lewd and lascivious behavior cases never included a white person "living in adultery" with, or "occupying the same room" as, a black person.[90] The reason for this omission is that these cases could not be heard by the NMC due to its inability to try white defendants.[91] Moreover, black patrolmen never enforced the miscegenation laws. Symbolically, of course, such laws served no purpose other than to codify white racist notions of black inferiority. More practically, because black patrolmen could not arrest whites, the apprehension of an interracial couple required the assistance of a white officer.[92]

During his time on the bench, Thomas became known as a tough judge.[93] In an interview with the *Miami Daily News*, he insisted this reputation was "not altogether well-founded," although he conceded that he had been strict with anyone accused of carrying a concealed weapon.[94] Thomas explained he had yet to hear a defendant offer a good reason for being armed,[95] and admitted he had been hard on violent offenders in order "to shock [them] into the idea that everybody has a right to have peace and dignity."[96]

At the same time, Thomas was well known for tempering justice with mercy when it appeared that a stiff fine, or a long jail sentence, would impose an unnecessarily harsh burden on the defendant's family.[97] As Thomas saw things, "[l]ots of judges forget . . . that somebody—maybe the kids—won't eat so good if a man is out a day's pay. I always stop myself and say, 'who are you fining?'"[98]

One case in particular illustrates the softer side of Thomas's judgeship.[99] It involved three families charged with disorderly conduct.[100] The testimony revealed that they paid a combined $25 per week for a three-room shack with an outside bathroom, unprotected from general use.[101] When Thomas learned "of the pathetic condition under which these people were living, and of the exorbitant rent which they were forced to pay," he dismissed all of the charges and pledged to help them find "much needed relief."[102]

Whites in the All-Black Court

Although the jurisdiction of the NMC was limited to hearing cases involving black defendants arrested by black patrolmen inside Miami's black ghettos, many whites participated in the court's proceedings. White lawyers, for example, regularly appeared in the NMC,[103] and despite initial worries to the contrary, were quick to show Thomas their respect:

> [W]hen the court was being discussed before its establishment the newspapers were commenting that no white lawyers would appear before it. It was felt that they would refuse to call me "Your Honor," and it was thought that therefore the Negro lawyers would have a monopoly. But the first case I heard was a white lawyer representing a Negro client, and now white lawyers outnumber Negro lawyers twenty to one in appearing in this court. . . . Complete segregation can't work and won't work [in this court], and thus far we have never had any difficulty over the term "Your Honor."[104]

White police officers also regularly attended the court's sessions. As Thomas pointed out, their presence actually was a necessity: "When this court was established the idea was to keep white officers out of the court room, not to have them appear before a Negro judge. But this led to a series of backfires. [Now, it] is impossible to keep white officers out of court."[105] Black patrolmen C.W. Grimes elaborated on Thomas's comment:

> [I]t was quickly realized that it would be impossible to run a court in such a fashion. It was absolutely essential, in many cases, for the white officers to appear as witnesses. If they had Negro officers appear in their stead it would be hearsay evidence and not useable. Thus, they must appear in the court on complaints from time to time, and no one objects now.[106]

In an early case, a white officer was surprised by the treatment he received at the NMC:

> The arresting officer was white, and the prisoner, a Negro, was charged with speeding. The officer had handcuffed the prisoner, thrown him in jail, and appeared before the court hoping, no doubt, to have the violator of the city ordinance sentenced to prison. . . . However, the Judge, upon listening to the charge, questioned the officer as to why he had handcuffed the prisoner and then proceeded to lecture him on the subject of human dignity[,] pointing out that since this was a traffic violation, his duty was merely to issue a ticket and not to handcuff the citizen and bring him into court, as was the case. In addition, he admonished the arresting officer not to do this sort of thing again after which the charged man was dismissed.[107]

From time to time, white witnesses and white judges also appeared in Miami's all-black court. White employers occasionally testified as character witnesses on behalf of their black employees,[108] while white judges sat on the NMC's bench during periods when the court did not have a black judge[109] or he was on vacation.[110]

Integrating Miami's Courts

In December 1961, the Miami City Commission, increasingly stung by accusations that it was running a Jim Crow court, replaced Thomas, its lone black judge, with a white lawyer named Arthur C. Massey Jr.[111] In response to rumors that this step was a prelude to disbanding the NMC, the Adelphian Club, an association of black businessmen and professionals who favored keeping it open, asked the commission to hold a public hearing to discuss the matter.[112]

On January 5, 1962, the commission met to fill four judicial vacancies.[113] Commissioner Henry L. Balaban read the petition from the Adelphian Club and suggested leaving one judicial post vacant so as not to preclude later consideration of whether to retain or abolish the NMC.[114] Commissioner Joseph X. DuMond Jr. replied that a public hearing was unnecessary because a substantial feeling existed within the black community that a "segregated court . . . [was] not in keeping with the tempo of Miami."[115] Commissioner David T. Kennedy then added that he had received a call from the Reverend Edward T. Graham, of the Greater Miami Ministerial Alliance ("GMMA"), "one of the outstanding spokesmen for the colored citizenry in Miami, and he requested that we do away with second-class justice in the City and have integrated courts. . . ."[116]

Based on these comments, the commission voted to fill all four judicial vacancies with white judges; as for the NMC, the commission neither abolished it nor decided whether there would be a public hearing to discuss its fate.[117] Consequently, the city's five white municipal judges began taking turns presiding over a black-staffed court that continued to be limited to trying black defendants arrested by black patrolmen within the black community.[118]

In the weeks following the vote, the commission found itself paralyzed.[119] Finally, however, on February 23, 1962, it convened a public hearing to consider the future of the NMC.[120] Adelphian president Charles A. Lockhart made it clear that his group was not asking for retention of the NMC as a "Negro or Colored court, but as a branch of the Municipal Court."[121] At the same time, he allowed that the Adelphians would not object to the appointment of a black judge.[122]

Reverend John E. Culmer, the rector of Miami's Saint Agnes Episcopal Church, praised the Adelphians' suggestion as a "painless way of bringing about integration."[123] Culmer pointed out that white judges frequently employed "opprobrious epithets"[124] and recounted an incident in which a prosecutor, having referred to a black defendant as a "Colored lady," was interrupted by the white judge, who told him that "all Colored people in my court are just plain Niggers."[125] Culmer argued that if white judges were forced to preside over a black-staffed court in the black community, they would have to think twice before indulging in such "contemptuous terminology."[126]

Culmer also accused black leaders who opposed the NMC of "speak[ing] out of both sides of their mouths."[127] On the one hand, they wanted to close down a court that was conveniently located, provided ten blacks with good jobs, and had a proven record of service.[128] On the other hand, they were pushing for the establishment of "Negro segregated insurance companies" and "Negro banks."[129] A few days later, Culmer added, "I live in a Negro settlement and I'm a pastor of a Negro church. Until we are ready to abolish the church, I'm not ready to abolish the court."[130]

In contrast, a black police sergeant named Lury F. Bowen unapologetically argued for the retention of a completely segregated court.[131] Bowen insisted that white judges were incapable of effectively serving the black community because they did not understand, nor try to understand, its problems.[132] Bowen also complained about the attitude that white judges displayed towards black defendants:

> I don't want a man to feel sorry for me because my skin is black, and I haven't had an opportunity to get this, that and the other . . . and I don't want the judge to say, "Well, he didn't know any better, and he has had it bad all his life, so I will give him $25.00 or five days["]; where a Colored judge would give a man that much for saying a profane word.[133]

When Mayor Robert King High asked Bowen whether he feared "perpetuating a situation where it could never be any different,"[134] Bowen replied, "I have got a lot of white friends, and all I can do is go by what they tell me. I have lived in the Negro area all my life. I understand my problems better, I feel, than you would."[135]

According to Culmer, the NAACP favored total integration (i.e., a court presided over by white and black judges that would take cases as they came, regardless of race).[136] Nevertheless, not a single NAACP member attended the hearing.[137] Likewise, no one from the GMMA was present.[138]

The most probable explanation for the absence of the GMMA and the NAACP was that they were engaged in a much bigger campaign to compel Miami to desegregate all of its city buildings and public facilities.[139] Whatever the reason, only DuMond made any attempt to refute the NMC's supporters. First, he argued that the opprobrious epithets mentioned by Culmer were a thing of the past.[140] Second, he reported that many people had told him that the NMC had done more harm than good.[141] Finally, he explained that a single, integrated city court would treat all persons equally regardless of race.[142]

Not surprisingly, the hearing failed to break the logjam. As a result, two separate courts continued to exist in Miami. The NMC lost its black judge but continued to be limited to trying only black defendants apprehended in the black community. Meanwhile, the city's main court continued to try white and black defendants but failed to gain a black judge.

Arguably, this state of affairs represented a step back from, rather than a step toward, the fully integrated court envisioned by the NAACP. Certainly, black defendants arrested by black patrolmen within the black community were no closer to the first-class justice advocated by Graham, especially with white judges like Massey describing the black community as a "jungle" and saying of his experience at the NMC, "I never saw anything like this. These people don't know right from wrong."[143]

The End of the All-Black Court

The end of the NMC finally came on July 25, 1963, when Melvin L. Reese, Miami's city manager, ordered all municipal buildings and recreational facilities desegregated.[144] At the same time, the police department announced that the black police precinct was being abolished.[145] The city's seventy-nine black patrolmen were ordered to stop booking suspects, close the precinct jail, and report to police headquarters for integrated roll calls.[146] Colonel Donald D. Pomerleau, the city's director of public safety, assured the public that despite these changes, most black officers would continue to work in the black neighborhoods.[147]

The demise of the black police precinct also meant the demise of the NMC as a separate court. However, Miami did not integrate its courts in the manner envisioned by the NAACP until 1967, when Donald W. Jones, a former president of the NAACP's Miami chapter, became the city's first regularly appointed black municipal court judge.[148]

Conclusion

Following the closing of the black police precinct, the building housing it and the NMC sat vacant for decades and gradually fell into a state of disrepair. In 2000, the City of Miami began to appropriate funds to rehabilitate it.[149] On January 15, 2009, following more than $1 million in renovations and nearly four years of work, the Black Police Precinct and Courthouse Museum officially opened.[150] As many as 9,000 visitors now annually pass through the building, including its fully restored courtroom.[151]

Few museum visitors can fully appreciate what the NMC meant to the black community during its existence. Although the NMC was not a panacea, it did make "the Negro a little larger citizen" within the bounds of segregation.[152] At the NMC, many black defendants experienced due process and equal protection under the law for the first time. Not only were they presumed innocent until proven guilty, they were given an opportunity to be heard and, most importantly, treated with dignity and humanity.

Ironically, the NMC often handed out tougher sentences than white courts. Many observers felt this helped the black community by taking dangerous offenders off the streets. And while the NMC rightly was criticized as second-rate because of the jurisdictional limitations imposed by the white establishment, the justice it rendered to individual black defendants was first-class. Thus, the NMC should not be remembered for what it could not do, but rather for how it served the black community and advanced the cause of individual civil rights.[153]

Notes

1. In 1932, California governor James Rolph Jr. had floated the idea of a black court for his state. It immediately drew widespread opposition from the legal profession and failed to get off the ground. *See Separate Court and Judge Irk California*, Afro-Am., Dec. 3, 1932, at 2 ("Hundreds of lawyers reading the press dispatch and hearing the radio reports of Governor Rolph's monstrous suggestion of Jim Crow courts became flamingly indignant. This indignation resulted in the formation of a committee of white lawyers who called upon Governor Rolph and assured him that there was no place for a Jim Crow court in California, but that there were colored lawyers before the bar in California who were capable of filling any of the positions on the municipal court which he had open for appointment."). *See also Appointment of Negro for L.A. Judge Stirs Trouble*, San Bernardino Daily Sun, Nov. 24, 1932, at 2 ("Negro delegations called on the governor . . . while he was in Los Angeles . . . and demanded that no special courts be established for their race.").

Slave courts, which formally existed in some states (such as Louisiana, South Carolina, and Virginia) and informally in others (including Florida—see chapter 4 of this book), cannot be considered black courts because they were operated by and for the benefit of whites:

> To guard against their entry into the most formal forums of the criminal justice system, whites created special courts for slave defendants charged with assault, theft, or anything short of capital offenses. . . . [T]hese courts often reflected the passions and prejudices of the neighborhood. In such courts a typical case involved a slave caught taking something from some white off his home plantation. (Theft from a slave's own master resulted in non[-]judicial punishment or, if the master chose to overlook it, no punishment at all.) Magistrates often had little knowledge of law and conducted their trials in the presence of the defendant's master. No grand jury protected defendants against unfounded accusations. Mississippi's 1857 code empowered justices to proceed . . . "upon complaint being made to [the justices], or information received upon oath." Slave courts often made no record, allowed no appeal, and assumed the prisoner's guilt.

Christopher Waldrep, *Substituting Law for the Lash: Emancipation and Legal Formalism in a Mississippi County Court*, 82 J. Am. Hist. 1425, 1430 (1996). For a further look at such courts, see, e.g., Judith Kelleher Schafer, *"Under the Present Mode of Trial, Improper Verdicts are Very Often Given": Criminal Procedure in the Trials of Slaves in Antebellum Louisiana*, 18 Cardozo L. Rev. 635 (1996); Alan D. Watson, *North Carolina Slave Courts, 1715–1785*, 60 N. Car. Hist. Rev. 24 (1983); Daniel J. Flanigan, *Criminal Procedure in Slave Trials in the Antebellum South*, 40 J. S. Hist. 537 (1974).

For a modern-day call for all-black criminal courts, see Mark Sabel, Note, *Racing Away from Georgia v. McCollum: The Case for an All-Black System of Criminal Justice*, 13 Nat'l Black L.J. 83, 121–22 (1993) ("Thus, I posit that American courts should play no part and enjoy no role in punishing African-American criminal defendants. This separatist contention flows from the ideology most forcefully announced by Malcolm X. Although it is true that legalistic separation can achieve little without economic empowerment, courts organized and controlled by African-Americans can bestow concrete benefits upon African-American defendants. American courts that presently exist should be divested of their jurisdiction over

African-Americans accused of crimes, such that the new system observes jurisdictional boundaries as if those boundaries were geographical.") (footnotes omitted).

2. *See Possibility of Negro Judge Considered*, Miami Times, Dec. 25, 1948, at 1.

3. Arthur E. Chapman, *The History of the Black Police Force and Court in the City of Miami* 68–73 (unpublished Ph.D. dissertation, University of Miami, 1986).

4. *Id.* at 68; *Negro Judge Will Handle Own Race*, Negro Star (Wichita), May 5, 1950, at 1.

5. During this period, Miami had three black neighborhoods: Coconut Grove, Liberty City, and Overtown (formally called the Central Negro District but colloquially known as "Colored Town"). Miami's black population numbered 50,000 out of a total city population of 249,000. *See Miami Approves All-Negro Court*, Panama City News-Herald, Apr. 21, 1950, at 10.

6. Miami had begun hiring black police officers, who were designated "patrolmen," in 1944. *See* Arva Moore Parks & Laura Pincus, Miami Police Department: A Century of Service 1896–1996, at 45 (1996); *Negro Police Celebrate Birthday*, Miami Herald, Sept. 9, 1945, at 2A. *See also infra* note 146. With no station house of their own, they initially operated out of a local dental office and later a "shack behind a pool hall on N.W. 2nd Avenue." Parks & Pincus, *supra*, at 45–46. During their first year on the job, the black patrolmen made 4,326 arrests, generated $56,321 in fines, and saved the city an estimated $50,000 in hospital expenses by drastically lowering the number of knifings and shootings in Overtown. *See Negro Police Celebrate Birthday, supra*. Taking note of these statistics, Don D. Rosenfelder, Miami's public safety director, declared that the black police unit had earned a permanent place in Miami's law enforcement apparatus. *Id.*

Despite their successes, the patrolmen (a pejorative term intended to make it clear that they were not full police officers), suffered many hardships, including being denied civil service status, membership in the local police union, and admission to the police academy. They also were forced to work their beats on foot. After six months of doing so, they were given bicycles. Squad cars, however, continued to be issued only to white cops.

In 1946, patrolman John Milledge was killed after ordering a group of teenagers to disperse (Leroy "Fats" Strachan, one of the youngsters, returned with a rifle and shot Milledge in the throat). This incident led to the patrolmen being given civil service status. At the same time, the patrolmen formed their own union, which they called the Miami Colored Police Benevolent Association. In 1973, the organization changed its name to the Miami Community Police Benevolent Association (http://mcpba1946.com/). For a further discussion, see Jacob Bernstein, *Black in Blue*, Miami New Times, Nov. 13, 1997, *at* http://www.miaminewtimes.com/news/black-in-blue-6360329.

7. Chapman, *supra* note 3, at 71; *Plan All-Negro Court to Reduce Crime in Miami*, K.C. Plaindealer, Mar. 31, 1950, at 1.

8. *Plan All-Negro Court, supra* note 7.

9. *The Beginning of a Realization of a Dream*, Miami Times, Nov. 5, 1949, at 3. For details about the building's physical appearance, see *infra* note 149.

10. Charles North, *Over 3000 Attend Community Mass Meet*, Miami Times, Nov. 11, 1949, at 3.

11. Many sources at the time described Thomas as the first black judge in the South since Reconstruction. *See, e.g., Att'y Thomas Named Judge*, Miami Times, Apr. 22, 1950, at 1; L.A. Thompson, *The Moving Finger*, Miami Times, June 3, 1950, at 3; *Courier Records Top 1950 Events in Pictures, Stories*, Pitt. Courier, Dec. 30, 1950, at 20. At least one newspaper, however,

correctly reported that Joseph E. Lee had served as a Jacksonville municipal court judge from shortly after the end of Reconstruction until the beginning of the twentieth century. *See* Lucius C. Harper, *Dustin' Off the News: Miami Sacrifices Race Principles to Make One Negro a Jim Crow Judge*, Chi. Defender, May 13, 1950, at 7. For a further discussion, see *Jacksonville's First African-American Lawyer: Joseph E. Lee*, Florida Memory Blog, June 20, 2014, *at* http://www.floridamemory.com/blog/2014/06/20/jacksonvilles-first-african-american-lawyer-joseph-e-lee/ (explaining that "[i]n April 1888, Lee was elected Municipal Judge of Jacksonville, the first African-American to have this honor.").

12. *Att'y Thomas Named Judge, supra* note 11.

13. *Id.*

14. *Id.*

15. *Id.*

16. *Id.*

17. *Lawyers Pay Tribute to Lawson E. Thomas, First Black Judge in Dade County*, Miami Times, Sept. 21, 1989, at 1.

18. Ellyn Ferguson, *To Him, Overtown is Not "Over There,"* Miami Herald, Feb. 16, 1983, at 1B.

19. *Id.*

20. *Id.*

21. *Id.*

22. *Id.*

23. *Id.*

24. *Att'y Thomas Named Judge, supra* note 11, at 13; *Florida Must Pay Same Pay to All Teachers Judge Says*, K.C. Plaindealer, Apr. 10, 1942, at 1.

25. Glenn Garvin et al., *Remembering Protest that Led to Opening First Beach for Black Miamians*, Miami Herald, May 9, 2015, *at* http://www.miamiherald.com/news/local/community/miami-dade/article20608311.html.

26. *Id.*

27. State v. Wilson, 25 So. 2d 860 (Fla. 1946).

28. Walker v. Board of Pub. Instruction for Broward Cnty., Fla., 154 F.2d 726 (5th Cir. 1946).

29. *Legal Minds to Ponder School Equalization*, Atlanta Daily World, Apr. 27, 1946, at 1.

30. *Quince to be Defended by Negro Lawyer: Accused Man to Enter Plea Before Judge on Tuesday*, Daytona Beach Evening News, Aug. 15, 1947, at 1A.

31. Wallace Meyers, *Suspect Held in Woman's Death*, Daytona Beach Morning J., July 26, 1947, at 1A.

32. Bill Finney, *Quince Wins a Brief Technical Delay in Court: His Attorney Objects that No Negroes on Grand Jury*, Daytona Beach Evening News, Aug. 19, 1947, at 1A.

33. Bill Finney, *Grand Jury is Ousted in the Quince Case: Jackson Tells Commission to Put Negro Names in Jury Box*, Daytona Beach Evening News, Sept. 30, 1947, at 1A.

34. *Id.*

35. *Appointment of Judge—Negro Municipal Court,* City of Miami Commission Meeting (Apr. 19, 1950) (statement of Mayor Robert L. Floyd) (microformed on Florida Documents at the Miami Public Library). During this period, the city's charter provided that municipal court judges were to be appointed by the commission, without input or approval by the public. *See* Miami (Fla.) Code, at Part I: The Charter § 59(a) (1945).

The lack of any checks on the commission meant that municipal court judges had very little job security. Thomas learned this hard truth several times. In November 1951, after 18 months on the bench, he was rehired by the new city commission. *See Florida Judge is Reappointed*, Pitt. Courier, Dec. 8, 1951, at 1. In November 1955, however, when a different city commission took office, he was summarily replaced:

> When the traditional Thanksgiving turkey axe fell and political pay-offs were made, Miami found herself with a new colored judge on the Municipal Court bench.
>
> Atty. John D. Johnson was named to succeed Judge L. E. Thomas by the new City Commissioners at their first meeting on Thanksgiving Day.
>
> Judge Johnson [is] a supporter of newly elected Commissioner James W. High. . . .

Miami Gets New Negro Judge, Pitt. Courier, Dec. 3, 1955, at 1. Thomas regained his job in 1959 (when Johnson resigned), but lost it again in 1961, when yet another city commission decided to play racial politics. *See infra* note 109.

36. Miami (Fla.) Res. No. 22403 (Apr. 19, 1950). In full, the resolution read: "That L. E. Thomas be, and he is, hereby appointed and elected a Municipal Judge of the City of Miami, Florida, to preside at sessions of the Negro Municipal Court."

37. *Negro Attorney Named Judge of New Court*, Miami Herald, Apr. 20, 1950, at 1B.

38. Thompson, *supra* note 11.

39. Harper, *supra* note 11.

40. *Id.*

41. Chapman, *supra* note 3, at 73.

42. *See Miami Jim-Crow Court Disapproved by NAACP*, Pitt. Courier, June 3, 1950, at 2.

43. Albert Q. Maisel, *His Court is a Classroom*, Christian Herald, Aug. 1951, at 69.

44. Interview of Judge L.E. Thomas, Municipal Judge, City of Miami, *in* Chapman, *supra* note 3, at 143–44 (Interview No. XVI) [hereinafter Thomas Interview].

45. Stephen Trumbull, *First Session Brings 55 Offenders to Miami's New All-Negro Court*, Miami Herald, May 23, 1950, at 7A. One reason for the delay was the city code, which required all sessions of the municipal court to take place at the main (downtown) courthouse. *See* Miami (Fla.) Code ch. 32, § 2 (1945). It was not until May 17, 1950, that the city commission amended the code by adding a new provision (§ 4) permitting sessions to also be held at the black police precinct's building. *See* Miami (Fla.) Ord. No. 4010 (May 17, 1950).

46. Trumbull, *supra* note 45.

47. *Id. See also Negro Judge*, Daytona Beach Morning J., May 23, 1950, at 2 (an example of the NMC being referred to as the "Negro Police Court," a technically incorrect but sometimes-used alternate name); *First Negro Judge Holds Court Session in Miami*, N.Y. Age, June 10, 1950, at 31.

48. *See Induct First Miami Judge*, Pitt. Courier, May 27, 1950, at 1.

49. Some, however, continued to disagree. *See, e.g., Florida Solving Race Problem without FEPC*, Palm Beach Post, Dec. 2, 1951, at 32 (reporting on a speech by Professor Jesse Walter Dees Jr. of Bethune-Cookman College, who claimed that a "silent bloodless revolution" was taking place in Florida and cited the NMC as proof of its success).

50. Howard Kleinberg, *First Black Policemen Started in 1944*, Miami News, Feb. 10, 1987, at 8BH.

51. Luther Voltz, *New All-Negro Court Expected to Cut Crime*, Miami Herald, Mar. 3, 1950, at 8B.

52. *Precinct Court—Proposed Abolition*, City of Miami Commission Special Meeting (Feb. 23, 1962) (statement of Sergeant Lury F. Bowen) (microformed on Florida Documents at the Miami Public Library) [hereinafter *Proposed Abolition*].

53. *Negro Attorney Named Judge, supra* note 37.

54. Maisel, *supra* note 43.

55. *Proposed Abolition, supra* note 52 (statement of Captain George W. Haller).

56. *Id.*

57. *Id.*

58. Miami (Fla.) Code ch. 32, § 1 (1945).

59. Miami (Fla.) Code ch. 35, § 36 (1945).

60. Vernon W. Clark, *The Significance of Penalty Provisions of the Florida Criminal Statutes*, 9 U. Fla. L. Rev. 289, 294 (1956).

61. J.L. (Dixie) Smith, *Municipal System About to Burst at Seams: City's Judges Labor Under Heavy Load*, Miami Herald, Feb. 14, 1956, at 1C. The use of juries in municipal court was prohibited by the city's charter. *See* Miami (Fla.) Code, at Part I: The Charter § 59(b) (1945). Miami was not alone in this respect; municipal courts in most Florida cities operated in a highly informal manner. Eventually, however, this fact contributed to their demise. *See* Steven Wisotsky, *The Status of Municipal Courts in Florida*, 48 Fla. B.J. 290 (1974).

62. Jack W. Roberts, *Why All the Bickering in Miami's City Court?*, Miami Daily News, Nov. 11, 1954, at 15A.

63. *Id.*

64. *See* Maisel, *supra* note 43.

65. *Id.*

66. *Id.*

67. *Id.*

68. *Id.*

69. *See* Elliott J. Pieze, *Good Morning Judge: News and Views from Miami's Municipal Negro Court*, Miami Times, Aug. 19, 1950-June 6, 1959.

70. *See, e.g., id.* Aug. 19, 1950, at 9 ("[Judge Thomas] brought praise from the capacity-filled courtroom, and obvious approval from the defendants."); Feb. 2, 1952, at 16 ("As usual . . . the courtroom was crowded to capacity, with many spectators standing in the aisles."); Oct. 4, 1952, at 3 ("The case provoked more laughter than any other from the jammed packed courtroom."); Mar. 7, 1953, at 12 ("The crowd in the courtroom went into a great laughter[.]").

71. *See, e.g., id.* Aug. 19, 1950, at 9 ("Monday morning was house-cleaning [as Judge Thomas] rendered judgment after judgment, in a manner that brought praise from the capacity filled courtroom, and obvious approval from the defendants."); Jan. 6, 1951, at 2 ("[A] liberal consideration was given the defendants[.]"); Oct. 20, 1951, at 4 ("[T]he judge 'threw the book' time and again throughout the session, with stern warnings that heavier fines will be levied in the future."); Jan. 5, 1952, at 4 ("Judge Thomas 'threw the book' hard and fast in [the] levying of fines and sentences—in some cases to the limit of the law."); June 27, 1953, at 8 ("[S]traight jail sentences to persons found guilty of using profanity on the public streets"); July 16, 1957, at 10 ("A similar latch was also dropped on habitual vagrants, who were warned to get a job or else.").

72. *See, e.g., id.* Aug. 19, 1950, at 9 (noting that "This was the only case on the docket for the day where the defendants were represented by an attorney"); Jan. 5, 1952, at 4 (stating that a

defendant was represented by attorney Grattan E. Graves Jr.). *See also infra* note 103 (discussing the presence of white attorneys in the courtroom).

73. *See, e.g., id.* Dec. 16, 1950, at 4 ("Among visitors to the court was Miami's newly appointed deputy constable for District 2, Stanley Sweeting, who was invited by Judge Thomas to occupy one of the seats at the Judge's bench, and who was apparently keenly interested in all of the proceedings."); Jan. 6, 1951, at 2 ("Dr. I.P Davis and Attorney William D. Brooks, of Washington D.C., were guests at the session."); May 19, 1951, at 5 ("Among first time visitors to the court was Miss Josephine Bronson . . . a teacher in the Dade County School system, who remained throughout the entire session."); Mar. 14, 1959, at 15 (emphasizing how Judge James E. McCrary of Robbins, Illinois "was a very pleasant visitor to the local court.").

74. *See, e.g., id.* Aug. 26, 1950, at 5 (reporting on Eugene Watkins's case for operating a gambling house and Marian Marshall's case for possessing bolita tickets); Sept. 30, 1950, at 12 (reporting on Lawrence Carroll's case for petty larceny); Oct. 8, 1955, at 10 (reporting on Samuel Charlton's case for disorderly conduct); Apr. 7, 1956, at 16 (reporting on Alvin Lee Chaney's case for assault and battery).

75. *Id.* Aug. 19, 1950–June 6, 1959.

76. *Id.*

77. *See, e.g., id.* Sept. 30, 1950, at 12 (describing a defendant who severely slapped a woman, drew a weapon on her, and threatened to kill her); Apr. 16, 1955, at 3 (discussing a defendant who beat up his girlfriend when she refused to "do as he ordered" and then pulled a gun on her as she attempted to flee).

78. *See, e.g.,* Trumbull, *supra* note 45 (reporting on a defendant sentenced to 30 days for brandishing a razor during a drunken brawl); Pieze, *supra* note 69, Apr. 17, 1956, at 16 (reporting on a defendant who cut a woman several times with a knife for supposedly helping his homosexual lover arrange a date with another man).

79. *See, e.g., id.* Nov. 30, 1957, at 6 (featuring a case in which the defendant threw potash on another woman, causing burns to her eyes and neck, when the victim showed up at the defendant's home looking for her common law husband).

80. *See, e.g., id.* Feb. 25, 1956, at 9 (reporting on a defendant who beat up an alleged prostitute with a gun when she pulled it on him to thwart his unsolicited overtures); May 12, 1956, at 13 (describing a defendant who "exploded" out of the kitchen of the Nasty Man's Café, wildly firing a gun, when he heard that a patron was attempting to borrow a dime to pay his bill).

81. *See, e.g., id.* Dec. 12, 1950, at 3 (reporting on a drunk driver on the wrong side of the road who led the police on a high speed chase that ended when he drove into a dead end).

82. *See, e.g., id.* Aug. 26, 1950, at 5 (describing the seizure by police of a handbag full of bolita tickets); Jan. 21, 1951, at 13 (reporting on the accidental shooting of a suspected gambler); Aug. 14, 1954, at 10 (noting that "Wednesday is usually the day for trials of the bolita boys").

83. *See, e.g., id.* July 5, 1952, at 10 (refusing, for lack of jurisdiction, to hear a case involving the theft of property valued at more than $50); June 21, 1958, at 10 (noting a case in which the defendant allegedly stole two cans of spam and two cans of corned beef from a supermarket); May 30, 1959, at 15 (reporting that the defendant had been arrested for the "theft of an apple, a potato and a tomato, valued at 35 cents").

84. *See, e.g., id.* July 7, 1957, at 10 (noting that the judge warned "habitual vagrants . . . to get a job or else").

85. *See, e.g., id.* Mar. 15, 1952, at 4 (stating that a married woman and a man other than her

husband were charged with lewd and lascivious behavior after they were "clearly observed" together in bed).

86. *See, e.g., id.* Dec. 29, 1951, at 6 (reporting how a daughter discovered an intoxicated, naked man in her invalid mother's bed when she heard her mother pleading with the defendant to "leave her alone"); Feb. 2, 1952, at 16 (featuring the case of a step-father who attempted to compel his step-daughter to "submit" to him).

87. *See, e.g., id.* July 31, 1954, at 12 (describing the case of a well-known transvestite performer arrested for, *inter alia*, leading police on a high speed chase and "dressing in a manner unbecoming his sex"); Mar. 1, 1958, at 12 (reporting on a case involving a defendant who had been apprehended for "dressing in a manner not keeping with his sex").

88. *See, e.g., id.* Oct. 4, 1952, at 3 (describing two defendants who were observed driving early in the morning on a seldom-used street. One of the defendants was completely nude and in a "compromising position" while the other was at the "steering wheel . . . dumb-founded" over his lover's actions).

89. *See, e.g., id.* Oct. 20, 1951, at 4 (sentencing two young women to 30 days in jail after their landlady complained that "something unnatural had been going on for some time").

90. *See* Pieze, *supra* note 69.

91. *See* Voltz, *supra* note 51.

92. *See* Kleinberg, *supra* note 50 (noting that a black patrolman could detain a white suspect until a white officer arrived to arrest the suspect).

93. *Judge Thomas—Hard on Switchblades and Guns*, Miami Daily News, Dec. 11, 1955 (news clipping in "Blacks" file in the Florida Collection at the Miami Public Library).

94. *Id.*

95. *Id.*

96. *Id.*

97. Trumbull, *supra* note 45.

98. Maisel, *supra* note 43.

99. Pieze, *supra* note 69, July 28, 1951, at 12.

100. *Id.*

101. *Id.*

102. *Id.*

103. *See, e.g., id.* Aug. 26, 1950, at 5 (noting that "All of the defendants were represented by an attorney—Robert Slatko (White)"); Sept. 30, 1950, at 12 (reporting that "Jenkins was defended by Atty. Carter, white"); Nov. 11, 1950, at 7 (pointing out that the defendant was represented by a "White council [*sic*], Atty. Rabinowitz, who put up a very formidable [defense]"); June 27, 1953, at 8 (highlighting that the defendant "was represented by Atty. C.C. Crandell, a white lawyer"); July 3, 1954, at 15 (reporting that a "prominent White attorney" threatened to appeal the case); Aug. 14, 1954, at 10 (pointing out that the defendant was represented by "White . . . Atty. Rainwater"); Oct. 16, 1954, at 8 (reporting on the rare presence of Assistant City Attorney Edward J. Fitzpatrick in a gambling case); Oct. 25, 1958, at 15 (stating that the defendant was represented by a "well known white attorney . . . [who] indicated he may appeal the judge's ruling.").

104. Thomas Interview, *supra* note 44, at 143.

105. *Id.*

106. Interview of Policeman First Class C.W. Grimes, Supervisory Personnel, Precinct Patrolmen, *in* Chapman, *supra* note 3, at 129 (Interview No. VIII).

107. Willard Townsend, *Townsend Visits a Different Kind of Court in Miami, Fla.*, Chi. Defender, Feb. 2, 1952, at 11.

108. Interview of Olavi Hendrickson, Esq., Assistant City Attorney, Miami, Fla., *in* Chapman, *supra* note 3, at 133 (Interview No. XI); *see, e.g.*, Pieze, *supra* note 69, Aug. 15, 1953, at 3 (reporting that "In her defense, Mrs. Culmer had as a character witness her White employer, who spoke very highly of her."); Jan. 3, 1959, at 10 (pointing out how the "Victim's white employer was present at the trial and offered a very fine character reference in her behalf.").

109. As explained *supra* note 35, in November 1955 John D. Johnson succeeded Thomas, thereby becoming the NMC's second black judge. *See also Johnson Named Judge; Replaces Thomas*, Miami Times, Nov. 26, 1955, at 1. In May 1959, Johnson resigned and his duties were performed (on a rotating basis) by Miami's white municipal judges. *See, e.g.*, Pieze, *supra* note 69, May 30, 1959, at 15 (noting that Johnson had submitted his resignation and that white Judge Francis A. Sobieski was temporarily presiding over the court). In December 1959, Thomas was reappointed to the NMC and served until December 1961, when he was replaced by the city commission. *See infra* note 111 and accompanying text. Thereafter, white judges again took turns staffing the NMC until its abolition in 1963.

Johnson, a Howard University law school graduate, resigned from the NMC when the job proved too burdensome:

> In Miami, Municipal Judge John D. Johnson, 45, resigned his $8,500-a-year post after a county judge, Frank Dowling, cited him for contempt and ordered him jailed until he paid $500 to an estate for which he acted as attorney. Johnson said he has paid the money, which were rentals collected from the estate, and had delayed payment only because work on the bench kept him too busy. He said he has heard as many as 150 cases in one day since coming to the bench in November 1955. He said the post interrupted his private legal practice.

Miami Negro Judge Resigns After Jail Threat, JET, June 4, 1959, at 5. For a further look at Johnson's life and career, see Robert Beatty, *Pioneer Judge; Civil Rights Activist John D. Johnson Dies*, S. Fla. Times, July 13, 2011, *at* http://www.sfltimes.com/uncategorized/pioneer-judge-civil-rights-activist-john-d-johnson-dies (reporting that during his time at the NMC, Johnson heard approximately 50,000 cases).

110. *See, e.g.*, Pieze, *supra* note 69, July 12, 1958, at 14 (reporting that white Judge Francis A. Sobieski was presiding over the court while Judge Johnson was on vacation); July 19, 1958, at 10 (reporting that white Judge Mitchell Coleman was presiding over the court because Judge Johnson was still on vacation).

111. Haines Colbert, *The Negro in Miami: Why They're Knee Deep in Crime*, Miami Daily News, Mar. 3, 1962, at 3A. *See also People are Talking About*, JET, Dec. 21, 1961, at 43 (explaining that "[w]hile Negroes like the integration idea, they think it ought to start in downtown municipal courts.").

112. *See Municipal Judges—Appointing Milton Friedman, Carlos Fernandez, John Barrett, and Milton Wallace*, City of Miami Commission Meeting (Jan. 5, 1962) (comments by Commissioner Henry L. Balaban, reading from a telegram) (microformed on Florida Documents at the Miami Public Library). Signatories to the petition included Dr. John O. Brown of the Congress of Racial Equality; Otis James of the Crusade for Voters; and Dr. George Simpson of the NAACP.

113. *Id.*

114. *Id.* (comments of Commissioner Henry L. Balaban).

115. *Id.* (comments of Commissioner Joseph X. DuMond Jr.).

116. *Id.* (comments of Commissioner David T. Kennedy).

117. *Id.*

118. *Negro Attorney Named Judge, supra* note 37.

119. Inside the black community, however, the NMC was being talked about at length. On January 20, the *Miami Times* published an editorial that summarized the issues at stake:

> It is not news that the City Commission is planning to close the Precinct at N.W. 11th St. and 5th Ave. However, this news is being discussed by many with regret, while others see it as just doing away with a segregated court.
>
> The opening of the precinct with a Negro judge and his staff was hailed with delight by the whole community. Congratulations came from in and out of the state.
>
> The first Negro judge presiding over a municipal court in Miami was certainly a progressive step. Judge L. E. Thomas presided with dignity and held the respect due his office. After serving two terms he was succeeded by Judge John D. Johnson, and re-appointed following Judge Johnson's resignation.
>
> The precinct and court have become a fixture in our community, and we would like to keep it, whether the judge be a Negro or not.
>
> The court is a convenience to the public and [that fact] should be considered.
>
> We see no reason why any citizen, white or colored, should not be tried in this court.
>
> We should get away from the idea of a Negro court. Let us call it what it is, a municipal court.
>
> If the decision is made to close this court, will the Negro employees be integrated into the main police force?

Keep the Precinct Court, Miami Times, Jan. 20, 1962, at 4.

120. *Proposed Abolition, supra* note 52.

121. *Id.* (comments of Mr. Charles A. Lockhart).

122. *Id.*

123. *Id.* (comments of Reverend John E. Culmer).

124. *Id.*

125. *Id.*

126. *Id.*

127. *Id.*

128. *Id.*

129. *Id.*

130. Haines Colbert, *The Negro in Miami: An Equal Chance Their Top Desire*, Miami News, Feb. 27, 1962, at 3A.

131. *Proposed Abolition, supra* note 52 (comments of Sergeant Lury F. Bowen).

132. *Id.*

133. *Id.*

134. *Id.* (comments of Mayor Robert King High).

135. *Id.* (comments of Sergeant Lury F. Bowen).

136. *Equal Chance, supra* note 130.

137. *See generally Proposed Abolition, supra* note 52 (making no mention of the group in the meeting's minutes).

138. *Id.*

139. By 1962, the Miami chapter of the NAACP, led by Reverend Theodore R. Gibson and represented by attorney Grattan E. Graves Jr., had succeeded in integrating Miami's buses, golf courses, parks, and pools. *See* Ward v. City of Miami, 151 F. Supp. 593 (S.D. Fla. 1957); Cecil Mann, *Edict's Effective Sept. 1st*, Miami Herald, Aug. 9, 1957, at 1B; Phil Meyer, *City's Swimming Pools, Facilities Open to All*, Miami Times, Apr. 8, 1961, at 1. It also had forced Dade County to desegregate its beaches, parks, and public schools. *See* Gibson v. Board of Pub. Instruction of Dade Cnty., 272 F.2d 763 (5th Cir. 1959); *Ervin OKs Gradual Integration*, Miami Herald, Nov. 20, 1959, at 2D; Phil Meyer, *8 Negroes Swim at Crandon Park*, Miami Herald, Nov. 26, 1959, at 1D; *Negro Swims; No Incidents*, Miami Herald, Jan. 18, 1960, at 15A (reporting that no protests occurred when a young black man went for a swim at Dade County's Hammock Beach).

140. *Proposed Abolition, supra* note 52 (comments of Commissioner Joseph X. DuMond Jr.).

141. *Id.*

142. *Id.*

143. *Knee Deep, supra* note 111, at 3A.

144. *Miami Ends Bias in City Employment: Manager Issues Official Order*, Miami Times, July 27, 1963, at 1.

145. *Police Abolish Precinct*, Miami Herald, July 26, 1963, at 1B.

146. *Id. See also* National Organization [of] Black Law Enforcement Executives 10 (Turner Pub. Co. ed. 1998) (pointing out that by the time the black police precinct closed, the number of black patrolmen had grown from the initial five hires in 1944 to 15 in 1945, 19 in 1946, 30 in 1949, 41 in 1950, 71 in 1960, and 79 in 1962 (out of a total city police force of 380)).

147. *Police Abolish Precinct, supra* note 145.

148. *See Atty. Jones is First Negro Judge in Miami*, Pitt. New Courier, Dec. 23, 1967, at 3.

149. *See* Jason T. Smith, *Historic Black Police Precinct Gets New Lease on Life*, Miami Times, Apr. 17–23, 2002, at 1. *See also* Sarah E. Eaton, *Black Police Precinct and Courthouse Designation Report*, Sept. 17, 2002, *available at* http://www.historicpreservationmiami.com/pdfs/Black%20Police%20Precinct.pdf.

Eaton's report contains a wealth of information about the NMC, the history of Miami's black neighborhoods, and the hiring of the black patrolmen. It also includes numerous photographs. Perhaps the most valuable part of her report, however, is its detailed description of the building:

> The Miami City Commission authorized the construction of a "colored police precinct station at NW 11th Street and NW 5th Avenue" in August 1949. The award for the design of the building went to long-time Miami/Coral Gables architect Walter C. DeGarmo.
>
> Walter C. DeGarmo (1876–1952) earned his reputation as an architect of distinction early on as a member of the original team of architects that set the standard for the Mediterranean Revival design of the emerging City of Coral Gables. DeGarmo came to Miami in 1904 from the offices of John Russell Pope in New York. Pope, educated at the Ecole des Beaux Arts, designed the National Gallery and Jefferson Memorial in Washington, D.C.

DeGarmo was immediately sought after and designed significant early Miami buildings, including the 1907 Miami City Hall (demolished), the 1916 McAllister Hotel (demolished), and the 1907 Miami Fire Station No. 1 (demolished). In addition to a prodigious number of designs for private residences, DeGarmo collaborated with Paul Chalfin and Phineas Paist in the design for the Colonnade Building and the Douglas Entrance in Coral Gables, both completed in 1926.

During World War II, DeGarmo resided in Panama City (Florida), where he designed liberty ships. He returned to Coral Gables in 1945 and reopened his practice from offices in the Colonnade Building, a building of his own design. The Black Police Precinct and Courthouse was designed just two years before his death at the age of 76. The building is particularly important in illustrating the evolution of DeGarmo's career, in that it illustrates the architect's range and ability to adapt to then-current architectural trends.

This 1950 building is clearly representative of the era in which it was built, as it departs from the historicism of Miami's previous architectural expressions and sets itself solidly in the genre loosely classified as "Modern." The building relies on its form and the arrangement of its parts for its visual impact; therefore there is an absence of surface ornament. . . .

The original building plan was "L" shaped, with a two-story section at the north end, placed perpendicularly to the one-story block that extended along NW 5th Avenue. In 1957, a one-story addition to the southeast changed the building's plan from an "L" shape to a rectangle.

The Black Police Precinct and Courthouse has a reinforced concrete structural system set on a poured concrete slab foundation. The exterior walls are covered with a smooth stucco finish and the flat roof is covered with built up materials. The primary entry on NW 5th Avenue consists of a two-story block at the north end. A double leafed door with a horizontal roof projection above provided access. Concrete retaining walls flank the sidewalk leading up to the main entrance. A one-story rectangular section then extends to the south, parallel to NW 5th Avenue.

The east or rear elevation, closest to NW 4th Court, features a cantilevered roof that extends across the drive acting as a porte cochere. The cellblocks for both men and women were located in this area. In keeping with the need for heightened security, "concrete fixed louvers and adjustable wood jalousies outside in each cell panel" were used to enclose the openings. . . .

The [1957] addition maintains the stark simplicity of the original building. It continues the use of a flat roof, and the doors and windows follow the same proportions and configuration of those in the original building. While the addition does modify the original plan shape and obscures the first floor of the south elevation, its modest one-story scale and dimensions do not destroy the integrity of the original building.

Id. at 9–13.

150. The museum's web site can be found at http://historicalblackprecinct.org/. It includes photographs from both the 2005 groundbreaking ceremony, see http://historicalblackprecinct.org/galleries/ground-breaking-ceremonies/, and the 2009 ribbon-cutting ceremony. *See* http://historicalblackprecinct.org/galleries/opening-ceremonies/.

151. David Ovalle, *A Badge of Pride: Retired Police Lieutenant Recalls Being One of the*

First Black Officers in Miami, Miami Herald, Feb. 4, 2016, *at* http://www.miamiherald.com/news/local/community/miami-dade/article58801318.html. *See also* Julie Schwietert Collazo, *Must-See in Miami: Black Police Precinct & Courthouse Museum*, May 23, 2013, *at* http://collazoprojects.com/must-see-in-miami-black-police-precinct-courthouse-museum/ (describing the author's visit to the museum); *Best Historic Museum: Black Police Precinct & Courthouse Museum*, Miami New Times, 2012, *at* http://www.miaminewtimes.com/best-of/2012/arts-and-entertainment/best-historic-museum-6403197.

152. Maisel, *supra* note 43, at 69.

153. For a further look at the NMC and its place in local history, see, e.g., Marvin Dunn, Black Miami in the Twentieth Century 174 (1997); N.D.B. Connolly, A World More Concrete: Real Estate and the Remaking of Jim Crow South Florida 127–28 (2014); Chanelle N. Rose, The Struggle for Black Freedom in Miami: Civil Rights and America's Tourist Paradise, 1896–1968, at 89–91 (2015). In February 2001, the City of Miami officially recognized the contributions of the NMC by holding a ceremony at which it issued proclamations to both Johnson and Thomas's widow Eugenia. *See City of Miami Honors its Black Legal Pioneers*, Fla. B. News, May 1, 2001, *available at* https://www.floridabar.org/divcom/jn/jnnews01.nsf/Articles/1B2A66BBB23176A785256AEA006260E6 (explaining that the program was organized by the City Attorney's Office).

8

Indian Courts

TONYA KOWALSKI AND ROBERT M. JARVIS

Florida's population includes 101,000 Native Americans, representing 0.5% of the state's inhabitants.[1] Although a number of tribes call Florida home, only two, both headquartered in South Florida, are officially recognized by the U.S. government: the Miccosukee Tribe of Indians of Florida (600 members; four reservations in Broward and Miami-Dade counties) and the Seminole Tribe of Florida (4,000 members; six reservations in Broward, Collier, Glades, Hendry, Hillsborough, and St. Lucie counties).[2]

Since the 1930s, in an effort to foster greater self-governance, the Bureau of Indian Affairs ("BIA"), an agency of the U.S. Department of the Interior, has encouraged tribes to set up their own court systems. Both the Miccosukees (in 1981) and the Seminoles (in 2015) have taken this step, albeit with significant differences in design, operation, and transparency.[3]

The Miccosukee and Seminole Tribes

Origins

The stories of the Miccosukee and Seminole tribes are epics of resistance and preservation, and those themes continue today in their approaches to government and justice. These two nations are related as (somewhat) separate ethnic and language communities within the larger Muskogee (Creek) culture:

> The Seminole tribe was formed in part by elements of the Creeks, and therefore have part of their history in Alabama. In some treaties with the United States, the Seminoles were included with the Creek Confederacy, at least up until the beginning of the removals to the west. Outlaw and refugee Creeks, along with other Indians groups from Alabama and Georgia, moved into Florida. These groups, along with the survivors of the original Florida tribes, gave rise to the Seminoles.

> Most of the native tribes of Florida were gone by the 1760s. They were killed by European diseases, Spanish suppression, and raids from southern American colonists and their Indian allies. Moving in to fill the void in the now unoccupied Florida lands were various Indian groups. . . . In addition to the aforementioned Creeks, some of these were the Yamasees, Mikasukis, Shawnees, and Yuchis. Joining these various Indian groups to make up what would become the Seminoles were numerous blacks. If escaping black slaves could reach Florida, they were welcomed by the Spanish and were essentially free. Many became members of these various Indian tribes as freedman or slaves. . . .
>
> Today, the Seminoles are broken into the Miccosukee and Seminole tribes. The Miccosukees are politically and linguistically, but not ethnically, separate from the Seminoles. The Miccosukee language is a dialect of Hitchiti and Seminole is a dialect of Creek. However, since both Hitchiti and Creek belong to the Gulf Family, Muskogean Branch, the Miccosukee and Seminole languages are very similar.[4]

Tribes within the Muskogean cultural group once occupied the southeastern United States and Mississippi valley.[5] Following the passage of the 1830 Removal Act, members were forced to march westward on what became known as the "Trail of Tears."[6] As a result, Oklahoma's Indian population includes members of the Seminole Nation of Oklahoma.[7]

Some southeastern Indians defied removal. Among those who did were a small group of Muskogees. To avoid capture, they migrated ever deeper into Florida, eventually settling in the Everglades, whose inhospitable marshy terrain finally forced the U.S. Army to abandon its chase of them in 1842 (thereby marking the end of the Second Seminole War).[8] As a result, the Seminoles never signed a peace treaty with the United States, the only tribe not to do so.[9] Present-day Miccosukees and Seminoles in Florida strongly identify with this fact, referring to themselves as America's only "unconquered" tribes.[10]

Federal Recognition

Following the end of the Second Seminole War, the Seminoles spent almost a century avoiding contact with Florida's white settlers:

> Seminole "aloofness" is best expressed by the phrase, LEAVE US ALONE, a recurrent message to White society aptly proclaimed in those very words by the Seminoles at a 1936 conference between Florida Indians and State-of-Florida officials, the delegation of which was headed by Governor Da-

> vid Sholtz. The meeting took place on the Tamiami Trail, February 22, 1936, and the Seminole reply to an offer of economic assistance was, "JUST LEAVE US ALONE."[11]

The increasing urbanization of South Florida, however, made it impossible for the Seminoles to remain in isolation, and in 1937 the federal government opened the 52,000-acre Big Cypress reservation in Clewiston (just south of Lake Okeechobee).[12] This marked the beginning of a twenty-five-year period that culminated in the splintering of the tribe and the bestowal of federal recognition. Professor Sarah Krakoff has succinctly summarized this turbulent period:

> The Big Cypress Reservation was established in 1937, and the government appointed a white man who spoke Mikasuki to be the agent there. [He] was able to recruit several of the families living nearby to move to the reservation. According to historian James W. Covington, "Those . . . who left their villages to live on the Big Cypress Reservation represented an element of the Indian population undergoing rapid change." One aspect of this was that some Seminoles were converting to Christianity, and in particular becoming members of the Baptist faith. . . .
>
> Other Seminoles remained in villages in and near the Everglades. They maintained a land-based economy and culture, supporting themselves by hunting, fishing, small-scale agriculture, and gathering wild plants. When the Tamiami Trail (U.S. Highway 41) . . . cut through the Everglades [in 1928], some of these Seminole moved to scattered communities along the Highway, and became known as the "Trail Indians." The Seminole from these communities who refused to move to the Big Cypress or other reservations created an identity distinct from the Seminoles who had relocated, and eventually the two groups formed the basis for what would become two distinct federally recognized tribes. To some extent, the divide was cultural. The Trail Indians identified as hewing more closely to indigenous cultural and religious practices than the Seminole who had moved onto reservations. In addition to refusing to relocate, they took pride in their independence from federal assistance and their maintenance of traditional ecological knowledge, which they passed on to the younger generations. Despite these emerging differences in cultural identity, all Seminole, whether reservation-based or not, kept their core traditions alive. The most significant practice was (and remains) the Green Corn Dance, and this "central religious, social, and political focus of tribal life" was maintained by all Seminole, whether on-reservation or not.
>
> Given all that the Trail group and the reservation Seminoles shared, it

seems unlikely that the emerging cultural differences would have been enough on their own to cause the formal split into two tribes. Instead, the catalysts were legal and political. First, the reservation-based Seminoles filed a claim against the United States under the Indian Claims Commission Act for taking Seminole land and other violations during the period of the Seminole Wars. The Seminoles who filed the case had hired a law firm to represent them, but the bands of people living along the Tamiami Trail or otherwise outside of the reservations had not participated in nor authorized the representation. The Trail Indians, most of whom spoke Mikasuki, sought their own legal counsel and began to differentiate themselves from the legal and political strategies of the reservation Seminole. During this process, the Miccosukee emerged as a distinct self-governing political entity.

Second, while the claims case was being pursued, the Federal Government embarked on its short-lived and disastrous policy of terminating the federal relationship with American Indian tribes. The Termination Era (1947–1961), as it is known, began after World War II when various political sentiments converged on the conclusion that the "Indian problem" could be solved once and for all by eliminating the separate political status of American Indian tribes. Federal bureaucrats and politicians hatched the idea, and it had a sufficient veneer of equality and civil rights to gain momentum. . . .

House Concurrent Resolution 108, which outlined the Termination Era's goals, was passed without any meaningful consultation with tribes. . . . For reasons that remain somewhat mysterious, the Florida Seminoles were on H.C.R. 108's list of tribes to be considered for termination. While tribes were afforded virtually no input concerning whether they should be on the list, Congress had to pass a separate termination bill for each tribe. Hearings were conducted on the bills, and this was when the Seminole and other tribes had a brief and vital chance to make their voices heard.

The Senate and the House of Representatives introduced companion Seminole termination bills in January of 1954. Senator [Arthur V.] Watkins [R-Utah] presided over hearings on the bills before a joint subcommittee in March of the same year. The Seminole bills provided that within three years, the Secretary of the Interior would release all tribal lands from protected trust status, transfer them to a tribal corporation or its elected trustees, and then open the lands for sale. Shortly thereafter, the federal trust relationship with the tribe would be formally severed. Two separate groups of Seminoles, one representing the on-reservation and the other the off-reservation, or Trail, group, came to Washington to speak against termination. A delegation of eight people elected by the on-reservation Seminole testified at the hearings and entered a prepared statement into the record requesting "that no action be taken on the termination of Federal supervision over the property of the Seminole Indians for a period of 25 years." Their reasons included that basic services and infrastructure, including, housing, education, and health care, were not yet sufficient to meet the tribe's needs and allow them to manage their own affairs independently. The inadequate services also affected the tribe's ability to manage its land, and a premature release of tribal land from trust status could result in the tribe's inability to make tax payments.

The off-reservation Seminole, who increasingly self-identified as Miccosukee, also opposed Congress's actions, but they used different rhetoric and tactics. George Osceola and Jimmie Billie represented the Miccosukee, and instead of testifying before Congress, sought to meet with President Eisenhower directly. While in Washington, they presented their "Buckskin Declaration," which expressed the Miccosukee intent to maintain their separate cultural and political existence as well as their land. According to historian Harry Kersey Jr., it was in response to President Eisenhower's sympathetic reply that nonetheless urged the Miccosukee to work through existing bureaucratic channels that "the Mikasukis [*sic*] developed a position that they were an independent nation with a political existence separate from other Seminoles."

The Seminole and Miccosukee opposition succeeded in staving off the termination bills in 1954. There was a revival of the idea in 1955, and the House Subcommittee on Indian Affairs held hearings in Florida during April of that year. The Seminole and Miccosukee again spoke out against termination, and their voices were joined by those of several local officials who were concerned about the increased burden on state and local services. Again, the diverging positions of the Seminole and Miccosukee became apparent. The Miccosukee raised the issue of the Seminole claims case during their testimony, with Buffalo Tiger stating "'We don't want a claim for money' . . . 'we want a claim for land.'" In the end, no Seminole termination legislation was introduced that year or ever after, and in retrospect historians have wondered why the Seminole, few in number and persistently outspoken in their desire to remain independent peoples, were on the list at all.

The lasting impact for the Seminole and Miccosukee was the separation into two federally recognized tribes. Shortly after the threat of termination subsided, the on-reservation Seminoles began to consider organizing formally under the Indian Reorganization Act. Having barely escaped involuntary termination of their separate status, they wanted to ensure against any future efforts along those lines. A group of Seminole leaders that included Sam Tommie, Billy Osceola, Frank Billie, and Bill Osceola led the drive toward IRA organization, and federal officials supported them. The Miccosukee group refused to join, and the on-reservation Seminole decided to move forward largely without them. In 1957, an IRA charter was issued to the Seminole Tribe of Florida, and the charter was ratified by a majority of voters, who included at least thirty percent of those eligible to participate in the election. The Tribe then adopted its constitution and by-laws, and the Tribal Council became its governing body. The split between the Seminole Tribe of Florida and the Miccosukee was complete.

The next chapter was for the Miccosukee to obtain separate federally recognized status. They took steps toward formal organization under state law during the same period that the Seminoles were working on their IRA status. In 1957, the Everglades Miccosukee General Council adopted a constitution that was recognized by the State of Florida. Eventually, however, the Miccosukee's efforts to obtain recognition and land from Florida ran into opposition. They began, as the 1960s dawned, to engage in pan-Indian organizing and to reach out to international as well as national agencies to address their concerns. The Miccosukee's outreach included sending a "'buckskin of recognition' to Fidel Castro who had just come to power in Cuba." The Miccosukee succeeded on several fronts with their efforts. Florida set aside 143,400 acres of the Everglades for their use in 1959. Then, with the support of the Bureau of Indian Affairs and no opposition from the Seminole Tribe, the Miccosukee adopted a constitution and bylaws, and achieved federal recognition in 1962 as the Miccosukee Tribe of Indians of Florida.[13]

Economy

The federal government's recognition of the Miccosukees and the Seminoles, while politically important, did little to address their persistent poverty. Historically, the tribes had engaged in subsistence activities (farming, fishing, frogging, and hunting).[14] In the late nineteenth century, they began trading alligator hides, bird feathers, and otter pelts to white settlers.[15] By the 1920s their attention was on Everglades tourists, to whom they sold handicrafts[16] and for whom they staged alligator wrestling exhibitions, conducted airboat rides, and in 1964 opened a gas station, general store, and restaurant along the Tamiami Trail.[17]

In 1976, the U.S. Supreme Court held that Indian tribes had the right to sell cigarettes and other tobacco products on their reservations free of state taxes.[18] This led to a rapid change in the tribes' fortunes:

> [The] Seminoles began to operate tribally regulated tobacco sales operations, known as smoke shops. They negotiated an agreement by which the state of Florida affirmed the tribe's authority to license and operate smoke shops free of state taxation. . . . [The] smoke shops [caused the] Seminoles . . . to realize significant profits, with tribal annual income jumping from $600,000 in 1968 to $4.5 million in 1977. . . . [19]

An even more important development occurred in 1979, when the Seminoles, relying on the precedent that had paved the way for their smoke shops, opened a high-stakes bingo hall in Hollywood. Although objected to by Broward County Sheriff Bob Butterworth on the ground that Florida state law permitted only low-stakes bingo played for charitable purposes, his position was summarily rejected, with the U.S. Court of Appeals for the Fifth Circuit writing:

> This appeal involves a question arising under Public Law 280, the federal law permitting states to exercise civil and criminal jurisdiction over the Indian tribes. All parties agree that the case turns on the determination of whether Florida Statute Section 849.093, which permits bingo games to be played by certain qualified organizations subject to restrictions by the state, is civil/regulatory or criminal/prohibitory in nature. If the statute is civil/regulatory within the meaning of [Public Law 280 as interpreted in] *Bryan v. Itasca County*, 426 U.S. 373, 96 S.Ct. 2102, 48 L.Ed.2d 710 (1976), the statute cannot be enforced against the Seminole Tribe of Florida. . . .
>
> Bingo appears to fall in a category of gambling that the state has chosen to regulate by imposing certain limitations to avoid abuses. Where the state regulates the operation of bingo halls to prevent the game of bingo from becoming a money-making business, the Seminole Indian tribe is not subject to that regulation and cannot be prosecuted for violating the limitations imposed. . . . [20]

The success of the Seminoles' bingo hall caused numerous other Indian tribes to open similar venues. These enterprises received an important boost in 1987, when the U.S. Supreme Court, which had declined to review the Fifth Circuit's decision, placed its imprimatur on them in a similar case called *California v. Cabazon Band of Mission Indians*.[21] In response, Congress passed the Indian

Gaming Regulatory Act of 1988 ("IGRA"),[22] thereby providing a comprehensive framework for such gambling.[23]

Nationally, Indian gambling now is a $28.6 billion-a-year powerhouse.[24] The Seminoles, who universally are credited with being the industry's founders, generate $2.2 billion-a-year from their seven casinos (two in Hollywood (just west of Fort Lauderdale) and one each in Brighton (Okeechobee), Clewiston, Coconut Creek (just north of Fort Lauderdale), Immokalee (near Naples), and Tampa).[25] The Miccosukees have one casino in western Miami; its annual revenue is estimated to be at least $100 million.[26]

Both the Miccosukees and the Seminoles have used their gambling profits (which account for at least 90% of their annual revenues) to provide increased government services, distribute yearly stipends to their members (often worth in excess of $100,000), and diversify their economies.[27] In 2007, for example, the Seminoles purchased the iconic Hard Rock Cafe theme restaurant chain for $965 million.[28] In 2016, the chain purchased the naming rights to the Miami Dolphins' home field. Pursuant to the eighteen-year, $250 million deal, the venue has been renamed Hard Rock Stadium, a reminder to locals and tourists alike that the Seminoles "have made quite the profit with their casinos in the state, including one not 15 minutes from the stadium."[29]

With these enterprises have come numerous patron and vendor lawsuits. In defending themselves, the tribes regularly argue that they cannot be sued because they have sovereign immunity. This strategy has proven very successful.[30]

Tribal Court Practice

Depending on which one of the country's 300 tribal courts an advocate finds herself in,[31] the proceedings may closely resemble what she is used to or be markedly different, with relaxed procedural and evidentiary rules, altered standards of due process, and an emphasis on traditional tribal law. As in any jurisdiction, tribal court practitioners must research the relevant law, including treaties,[32] tribal constitutions and codes, case law, and court rules. Tribal jurisdictions typically also consider state and federal law to be valid sources of persuasive authority for resolving questions of tribal law. As detailed below, this appears to be truer for the new Seminole court than for the existing Miccosukee court.

Written tribal law is easy to obtain in some jurisdictions but very difficult to find in others. The Seminole Tribal Court is making its codes and rules available on the Internet, along with forms, a *pro se* manual, and other litigation aids.[33] The Miccosukees, in line with their traditionally guarded approach, do not release their materials in writing.[34] When cases and codes are not readily available to the larger public in print or online, practitioners must visit the clerk's office to perform legal research and may need the court's permission to obtain copies of previous opinions, which may be considered private matters between the court and the parties. The latter is true of the Miccosukee Tribal Court. The published law of other tribes also may be used as persuasive authority,[35] but as with any such source, the attorney must ensure that the law and policy of the sister jurisdiction is compatible with that of the host.

Tribal customary law plays a crucial role in ensuring that tribal court outcomes reflect the justice priorities of the community and preserve tribal culture. Unwritten customary law does not often deeply affect non-Indian parties; as with Anglo-American courts, in multi-ethnic cases it usually simply plays a role in policy reasoning (to protect community values).[36]

Vitally, lawyers must understand that vast amounts of tribal customary law is passed down not in writing, as in Western culture, but orally. Accordingly, unless the law already is known by the court (and therefore becomes part of the case through judicial notice), such law must be testified to by an expert witness (typically a community elder). The expert may testify in a traditional language, and an interpreter may or may not be available. In the unusual case where a non-speaker is involved, this process can lead to due process concerns, as has happened in Miccosukee Tribal Court proceedings.[37]

Another notable difference are the relaxed rules of evidence and procedure and the less-demanding due process standards.[38] In an effort to increase access to justice for their citizens, many tribes make their court proceedings less technical for litigants, who often appear *pro se* or with just a lay advocate. In contrast, the Seminole Tribal Court, in an effort to gain the acceptance of the non-Indian community, uses the Federal Rules of Civil Procedure for cases in excess of $5,000 and Florida's Small Claims Rules for cases below $5,000.[39]

Outsiders also will notice that tribal proceedings do not always guarantee a jury trial and, even when they do, it rarely is possible to seat a panel that is impartial by state and federal standards. This is because in Native American communities, most jurors either will be related to the participants or will have heard about the case. Of course, strong shared community values may make such juries more reliable. Similarly, misdemeanor criminal defendants are not guaranteed a right to counsel[40] and civil litigants may be prohibited from having lawyers by their side.[41] Finally, observers may be surprised to learn that American Indian defendants potentially can be tried for the same crime by federal, state, and tribal authorities, thereby making them subject to "triple jeopardy."[42]

The Miccosukee Tribal Court

In keeping with its past, the Miccosukee Tribe maintains a traditional, culturally driven governmental design. As with many such societies, political power tends to be vested in a single body rather than in separate branches. In 1971, the Miccosukees negotiated for the devolution of local governmental functions from the BIA to the tribe.[43]

As with many tribal courts, the Miccosukee court has review powers over government action but is not a constitutionally separate branch.[44] Although a number of Indian nations have changed their constitutions in this respect, the use of a unitary system is not always merely a retention of the old BIA model constitution form of government. It also can represent a compromise between the deep need to preserve traditional law versus the pressure to assimilate to Westernized justice standards to increase external legitimacy. In the case of the Miccosukees, legislative power is not vested in an elected tribal council but instead resides in the tribe's members (collectively known as the General Council), with daily affairs managed by the tribe's Business Council.[45]

The Miccosukee Tribal Court began in 1981 and is located at the tribe's headquarters in Miami.[46] Because it carefully adheres to traditional tribal law and procedure and community values limit exposure to outside lawyers and litigants, the court tends to be fairly insular:

> [T]he Miccosukee Tribal Court in Florida has established a system of justice in which two judges sit and preside over cases. One judge is a traditional judge applying customs and traditions of the Miccosukee Tribe in the proceedings. The other judge applies more conventional legal process and law to the case before the court.
>
> On each motion or objection, and throughout the case, both judges consult with one another prior to entering any ruling or decision. Both attorneys and lay representatives may be admitted to practice before the court. Admission to practice is done on a case-by-case basis and requires that the party representing the litigants file an application and take a test demonstrating knowledge and understanding of the tribe and its customs and traditions, as well as the law that will be applied. Tribal laws are not readily available to the general public and cases are rarely, if ever, reported or available for review or research.[47]

Other distinguishing features include the fact that judges can question witnesses and courtroom proceedings normally are closed to all but family members—even attorneys, unless they have special permission to appear.[48]

The Miccosukee Tribal Court disfavors using Anglo-American adversarial and punitive approaches, including trials and jail sentences, and instead favors restorative methods even for serious criminal infractions.[49] In one high-profile case, a tribal member who killed his children was forgiven rather than imprisoned.[50] This emphasis on traditional law and dispute resolution techniques has drawn sharp criticism from parties, victims, and attorneys who do not recognize the validity of this form of justice.[51]

The Miccoskuee justice system does not have a permanent appellate court. Instead, the losing party can "petition[] the Tribe's Business Council for leave to appeal the judgment to the Tribe's General Council, which acts as the Tribal Court of Appeals."[52]

The Seminole Tribal Court

Although normally more willing to engage with outside communities than the Miccosukees, the Seminoles did not establish their court system until 2015. For years, the stumbling block had been the issue of impartiality:

> Since [the advent of] gaming [in 1979], the absence of a court is not for lack of finances. Instead, a major reason is uncertainty about how to establish the court's authority. Who would be the judges? It was unclear to every Seminole I asked how any tribal member could achieve the objectivity and distance sought in judges, since in general is it deemed both moral and inevitable that Seminoles would favor family. Clans have limited authority. The Tribe has solved this problem during clothing contests and the Miss Seminole [beauty] pageant by turning to non-Seminole judges. But there is strong sentiment against hiring outside judges for a court system; as it is, there is unease about the fact that almost all officers in the Seminole Police Department (SPD) are non-Seminole. On the one hand, having a tribal court would strengthen Seminole self-governance. On the other hand, it is feared that a tribal court would not be able to surmount internal differentiation. Older tribal members remembered when Green Corn Dance councils issued sentences as severe as execution, but they did not see the Corn Dance as sufficiently inclusive of today's tribal citizens to serve as a fully functioning court of law. A secondary concern about the legitimacy of tribal courts is whether the Tribe's gaming and other business partners would agree to adjudication by tribal courts. Public ridicule in South Florida of a 2001 Miccosukee court ruling to forgive an accused murderer only reinforced this concern. With some Seminoles incarcerated and with gaming-related legal entanglements growing, the question

Figure 8. Seminole Tribe of Florida Chairman James E. Billie (*left*) swearing in Willie Johns as Chief Justice of the Seminole Tribe of Florida Appellate Court. Photograph by Beverly Bidney; courtesy of *The Seminole Tribune*.

> of whether judicial authority is internal or external is acutely felt, but no answer is forthcoming.[53]

Finally, however, in 2005 a thirty-person Tribal Court Committee was tasked with creating a judicial system that would "give[] teeth and bones to [Seminole] sovereignty."[54] On February 19, 2015, following a decade of fits and starts, the committee's efforts bore fruit when three lay trial judges and three lay appellate justices, drawn from the tribe's various clans and reservations,[55] were sworn in during a ceremony at the Hollywood reservation, just yards from the tribe's famed "Council Oak" tree.[56]

The court operates pursuant to the Seminole Tribal Court Ordinance ("STCO").[57] Its key provisions are summarized on the court's web page:

> The Tribal Council, under the authority of the Constitution of the Seminole Tribe of Florida, at Article X, has established a division of the judicial branch of government to be known as the Seminole Court.
>
> The powers of the Seminole Court are vested in the Seminole Tribe of Florida Appellate Court and the Seminole Tribe of Florida Trial Court. The Seminole Court shall have broad civil jurisdiction to hear cases and controversies that are brought before the Court.
>
> The Tribal Court shall insure the just, efficient and unbiased resolution of conflict for all persons who come before the Court. The Court will respect the customs and traditions of the Seminole Tribe of Florida and will ensure that the rights and powers which are inherent to the Tribe's sovereign status are secure.
>
> The Seminole Trial Court consists of a Chief Judge and two associate judges. All judges of the Seminole Court must be members of the Seminole Tribe of Florida per the Tribal Constitution and must abide by the Seminole Tribal Court Code of Judicial Conduct.
>
> The Chief Judge or one of his associate judges will hear those cases filed with the Trial Court.
>
> The Trial Court has a Judicial Advisor on staff who provides advice and assistance to the Judges on matters of law and procedure.
>
> The Seminole Appellate Court consists of a Chief Justice and two associate justices. All justices of the Seminole Appellate Court must be members of the Seminole Tribe of Florida per the Tribal Constitution and must abide by the Seminole Tribal Court Code of Judicial Conduct.
>
> Appeals from the Trial Court shall be heard by a panel of three Appellate Court Justices. The decisions of the Appellate Court cannot be overturned by [the] Tribal Council.[58]

Further insight into how the court intends to go about deciding cases can be gleaned from a newspaper interview that Associate Justice Amy Johns gave just before her investiture:

> As an Unconquered Tribe, our tribal culture and customs are critically important in maintaining peace and equilibrium within our communities. The establishment of a Tribal Court system is a crucial step towards embracing the uniqueness of our ways, while further promoting our self-reliance and sovereignty. Only when we can fully address our grievances/issues within a Tribal Court system, presided over by Tribal people, can we begin to fully embrace and appreciate the Tribe we have evolved into today. Too often, the state, county and even federal court systems are ill-equipped

> to deal with the various cultural/traditional nuances that accompany Tribal members and their families as they enter those systems. Through the establishment of a Tribal Court system, we are creating an environment that will provide justice, fairness and most importantly, it will be sensitive to the needs of the people it serves, from a Seminole standpoint.[59]

Initially, the court, which has offices on the Big Cypress and Hollywood reservations,[60] will exercise only civil jurisdiction and will focus on child welfare and family law matters.[61] Over time, however, it is expected to take on a broader array of civil matters and expand into criminal cases.[62]

To help the judges (who are not lawyers) carry out their duties, the STCO creates the position of judicial advisor.[63] The STCO does not specify the judicial advisor's duties, but a "want ad" explains what these positions entail:

> The Judicial Advisor is the advisor to the Seminole Trial Court judicial staff, making recommendations on law and procedure to their assigned judge. The Judicial Advisor must follow all policies and procedures of the Seminole Tribal Court and is bound by the ethical standards established by the Seminole Tribal Court. . . .
>
> The applicant must be a law school graduate at the time of appointment and must have a minimum of 7 years legal work experience post law graduation. Experience on law review, moot court and/or publication of noteworthy article and high academic standing is preferred. Florida Bar membership is beneficial, but not a requirement. Must have experience in trial court advocacy, with a tribal court preferably. Experience as a Tribal Court judge preferred. Must possess excellent research, writing and communication skills. Must be proficient in Microsoft software packages and add-ins. Attention to detail, strong organizational and time management skills. Must be able to travel to all STOF Reservations and work flexible hours including evenings, weekends and holidays.[64]

At present, the court's web page does not list any judicial advisors, but it does give the names of the court's director, clerk, deputy clerk, and special projects administrator.[65] The court's director is Stan Wolfe, a graduate of Washburn University's law school in Topeka, Kansas.[66] His extensive resume includes serving as a "project manager for the Justice Research and Statistics Association . . . prosecutor for the Little River Band of Ottawa Indians and . . . magistrate for the Eastern Band of Cherokee."[67]

Attorneys wishing to appear before the court must be members of the Seminole Tribe of Florida Bar Association, which is open to attorneys who are licensed to practice before the courts of any state. In addition to completing an application form, paying an admission fee, and taking an oath of professional responsibility, the attorney must confirm that he or she is familiar with tribal law, including traditional law.[68] The court also allows lay advocates[69] and permits *pro se* representation.[70]

In addition to using (with some modifications) the Federal Rules of Civil Procedure, Federal Rules of Appellate Procedure, and Florida Small Claims Rules, the Seminoles, through their Judicial Commission, have adopted a judicial ethics code patterned after the National Tribal Judicial Center's Sample Tribal Code of Judicial Conduct.[71]

The Seminoles' Judicial Commission, created pursuant to a separate tribal ordinance,[72] is authorized to hear and decide complaints made against a judge. The Judicial Commission is composed of the Chairman of the Tribal Council, the Chief Justice (or the next senior justice if the Chief Justice is the subject of the complaint), and three tribal members chosen from the Judicial Commission's seven-person Selection Panel.[73] Any person may submit a complaint to the Judicial Commission,[74] which must be investigated within six months.[75] Depending on what it finds, the Judicial Commission can dismiss the complaint, hold a hearing, or refer the complaint to the Chief Judge or Chief Justice for further action.[76]

Conclusion

The Miccosukee and Seminole tribal courts represent a crucial means for maintaining the spiritual health of their communities. In addition to deciding disputes in a manner that accords with local standards of justice, these courts help to preserve the cultures, languages, and traditions of the peoples they serve. At the same time, they give voice to the tribes' sovereign powers of self-determination. Lastly, by helping the Miccosukees and Seminoles, they aid the many non-Indian Floridians who benefit from the tribes' economic and social well-being.[77]

Notes

1. *See* U.S. Census Bureau, *American Fact Finder*, *at* http://factfinder.census.gov/faces/tableservices/jsf/pages/productview.xhtml?src=bkmk (under "Florida—July 1, 2015").

2. For additional information about the Miccosukees, see http://www.miccosukee.com/. For additional information about the Seminoles, see http://www.semtribe.com/. For more in-depth studies, see, e.g., Patsy West, Seminole and Miccosukee Tribes of Southern Florida (2003); Brent Richards Weisman, Unconquered People: Florida's Seminole and Miccosukee

Indians (1999); Patsy West, The Enduring Seminoles: From Alligator Wrestling to Ecotourism (1998); Cynthia R. Kasee, *Florida, in* 1 Native America: A State-by-State Historical Encyclopedia 183–226 (Daniel S. Murphree ed. 2012); William C. Sturtevant & Jessica R. Cattelino, *Florida Seminole and Miccosukee, in* 14 Handbook of North American Indians 429–49 (William C. Sturtevant & Raymond D. Fogelson eds. 2004); Dorothy Downs, *Florida Seminole and Miccosukee Indians: Trade, Change, Adaptation and Innovation, at* http://www.kislakfoundation.org/millennium-exhibit/downs1.htm.

3. Despite the passage of more than three decades, the Miccosukee Tribal Court remains insular, largely closed to outsiders, and heavily reliant on customary law. *See* David Ovalle, *Miccosukee Tribal Court a Contrast to Florida's System*, Miami Herald, Mar. 23, 2009, at B1, *available at* 2009 WLNR 5432622 (describing complaints by non-members about the Miccosukee Tribal Court's process, restrictions on attorney representation, and unavailability of translators). In contrast, the newly formed Seminole Court, in an effort to win external legitimacy and recognition, has publicized itself extensively and has adopted procedural rules and due process standards that closely resemble those found in Florida's federal and state courts. *See* Peter Gallagher, *Tribune Q-and-A: Helene Buster—The Seminole Tribal Court*, Seminole Trib., July 29, 2011, at 1A.

4. Don C. East, A Historical Analysis of the Creek Indian Hillabee Towns 12 (2008). As East mentions, prior to the Creeks Florida was home to a number of earlier tribes, including the Ais, Apalachee, Calusa, Chatot, Jeaga, Mayaimi, Ocali, Tequesta, Timucua, and Tocobaga. For accounts of these groups, see Theodore Morris & Jerald T. Milanich, Florida's Lost Tribes (2004); Kevin M. McCarthy, Native Americans in Florida (1999); Jerald T. Milanich, Florida's Indians from Ancient Times to the Present (1998).

As East also mentions, both black freedmen and black slaves joined the Seminoles. For a look at these "Black Seminoles," see Anthony E. Dixon, Florida's Negro War: Black Seminoles and the Second Seminole War 1835–1842 (2014); Bruce Edward Twyman, The Black Seminole Legacy and North American Politics: 1693–1845 (2002); Kenneth W. Porter et al., The Black Seminoles: History of a Freedom-Seeking People (1996); Joyce A. McCray Pearson, *Red and Black—A Divided Seminole Nation: Davis v. U.S.*, 14 Kan. J.L. & Pub. Pol'y 607 (2005) (discussing the Seminole Nation of Oklahoma's exclusion of the Black Seminoles to keep them from sharing in a distribution of federal money).

5. *See generally* Carl Waldman, Encyclopedia of Native American Tribes 83–84 (3d ed. 2006) ("The Native Americans known as the Creek received their tribal name, pronounced as spelled, from early English traders because they built most of their villages on woodland rivers and creeks. . . . Their ancestral territory included what now is most of Georgia and Alabama, as well as small parts of northern Florida, eastern Louisiana, and southern Tennessee. The various bands are discussed as two branches, the Upper Creek, mostly in Alabama, and the Lower Creek, mostly in Georgia. The Native name for the most powerful band of Creek, sometimes applied to other groups as well, is Muskogee."). *See also* James W. Covington, *Migration of the Seminoles into Florida, 1700–1820*, 46 Fla. Hist. Q. 340 (1968); Andrew K. Frank, *Taking the State Out: Seminoles and Creeks in Late Eighteenth-Century Florida*, 84 Fla. Hist. Q. 10 (2005).

6. The complex logistics involved in relocating 100,000 Indians (of whom 15,000 died en route) are examined in Ethan Davis, *An Administrative Trail of Tears: Indian Removal*, 50 Am. J. Legal Hist. 49 (2008–2010).

7. For further commentary on the Trail of Tears and the present-day Oklahoma tribes, see Encyclopedia of American Indian Removal (Daniel F. Littlefield Jr. & James W. Parins eds. 2011). For the relationship between the Seminoles in Florida and those in Oklahoma, see Richard A. Sattler, *Seminole in the West, in* Sturtevant & Fogelson, *supra* note 2, at 450–64.

8. The Second Seminole War (1835–42), also known as "The Florida War," was the longest and most expensive Indian conflict in U.S. history. *See further* John K. Mahon, History of the Second Seminole War, 1835–1842 (rev. ed. 1991). Miami-Dade County is partially named for Major Francis L. Dade, one of the war's earliest casualties. *See* Frank Laumer, Dade's Last Command (1995) (explaining that Dade was ambushed in December 1835 while leading 110 soldiers from Tampa to Ocala to reinforce Fort King).

While the massacre of Dade and his troops came to be the defining moment of the Second Seminole War for Florida's white settlers, for the Seminoles it was the capture of Osceola, the tribe's war chief, under a white flag of truce:

> A general Seminole belief exists "that White men do not keep their promises." The history of the Seminole Wars shows a tendency for the Seminoles to keep their word in negotiations, and it shows the opposite to be true for the Whites. At least two incidents are infamous in which Major General Thomas Jesup captured Seminole leaders under a white flag of truce.
>
> Wildcat and Blue Snake were captured on September 26, 1837 under a white flag when they presented themselves for negotiation, and almost a month later on October 21, 1837 Osceola himself was seized under similar circumstances. While there could have been war objectives in the minds of the Seminoles in agreeing to truce conferences, e.g. as a way of scouting the enemy, clearly they expected the enemy to keep their word—especially under a white flag of truce. According to [Professor John K.] Mahon those Seminoles who continued to resist did so, "more fanatically than before. Any confidence they had felt in the world of the White leaders was utterly shattered."

John C. Paige & Lawrence F. Van Horn, *An Ethnohistory of Big Cypress National Preserve, Florida* 40 (1982) (citations omitted), *available at* https://www.nps.gov/parkhistory/online_books/bicy/ethnohistory.pdf. Although Jesup's behavior did not affect the remainder of his career, it has since come to stain his reputation. *See* Chester L. Kieffer, Maligned General: A Biography of Thomas Sidney Jesup (1979). For a further discussion, see Thom Hatch, Osceola and the Great Seminole War: A Struggle for Justice and Freedom (2012).

9. *See* Seminole Tribe of Florida, *History—Where We Came From: No Surrender!, at* http://www.semtribe.com/History/NoSurrender.aspx ("Unlike their dealings with other Indian tribes, however, the U.S. government could not force a surrender from the Florida Seminoles. Historians estimate there may have been only a few hundred unconquered Seminole men, women and children left—all hiding in the swamps and Everglades of South Florida. No chicanery, no offer of cattle, land, liquor or God, nothing could lure the last few from their perches of ambush deep in the wilderness. The U.S. declared the war ended—though no peace treaty was ever signed—and gave up."). For further discussions, see the sources cited *supra* note 2.

10. *See further* Brent R. Weisman, *Nativism, Resistance, and Ethnogenesis of the Florida*

Seminole Indian Identity, 41:4 Hist. Archaeology 198 (2007). The slogan of the *Seminole Tribune*, the monthly newspaper of the Seminoles, is "Voice of the Unconquered," and this motto appears on the front page of every issue. *See* http://www.semtribe.com/SeminoleTribune/. With permission, Florida State University has appropriated this aspect of the tribes' auto-identification and applied it to its athletic teams. *See* Robert Andrew Powell, *Florida State Can Keep Its Seminoles: Support from Tribe Causes N.C.A.A. to Relent on Ban*, N.Y. Times, Aug. 24, 1995, at D1.

11. Paige & Van Horn, *supra* note 8, at 38 (citations omitted). As a result, relatively little is known about the Seminoles during the period from 1843 to 1934. *See* Mikaëla M. Adams, *Savage Foes, Noble Warriors, and Frail Remnants: Florida Seminoles in the White Imagination, 1865–1934*, 87 Fla. Hist. Q. 404 (2009).

12. Prior to Big Cypress, the federal government had created a number of smaller reservations for the Seminoles. *See* Seminole Tribe of Florida, *Culture and History*, *at* http://www.stofthpo.com/History-Seminole-Tribe-FL-Tribal-Historic-Preservation-Office.html ("In 1907, the Department of the Interior set aside 540 acres of land near Dania for Seminole use. In 1911, President Taft set aside lands in Martin, Broward and Hendry Counties as reservation. By 1913 there were 18 Indian reservations in Florida, ranging in size from 40 acres to 16,000 acres."). For a further discussion, see James W. Covington, *Florida Seminoles: 1900–1920*, 53 Fla. Hist. Q. 181 (1974). *See also* Harry A. Kersey Jr., *A "New Red Atlantis": John Collier's Encounter with the Florida Seminoles in 1935*, 66 Fla. Hist. Q. 131 (1987).

13. Sarah Krakoff, *Constitutional Concern, Membership, and Race*, 9 FIU L. Rev. 295, 316–21 (2014) (footnotes omitted). For a further look at the events recounted by Krakoff, see Buffalo Tiger & Harry A. Kersey Jr., Buffalo Tiger: A Life in the Everglades (2002); Harry A. Kersey Jr., An Assumption of Sovereignty: Social and Political Transformation among the Florida Seminoles, 1953–1979 (1996); and the sources cited *supra* note 2. The Miccosukees' constitution and by-laws (ratified Jan. 11, 1962) can be found at http://www.indigenouspeople.net/micconst.htm. The Seminoles' constitution and by-laws (ratified Aug. 21, 1957) can be found at https://www.loc.gov/law/help/american-indian-consts/PDF/58060124.pdf. *See also* Virginia Mitchell, Seminole Tribe of Florida: Celebrating 50 Years of the Signing of Our Constitution and Corporate Charter, 1957–2007 (2007).

A small group of Indians, known as the Independent Traditional Seminole Nation of Florida ("Traditionalists"), have resisted joining either tribe. The Traditionalists reject most modern conveniences and refuse to recognize the authority of the federal and state governments. *See* Sherman v. Red Bay Stronghold Fdn., 942 So. 2d 1033 (Fla. 4th Dist. Ct. App. 2006); *The Independent Traditional Seminole Nation: The Struggle to Maintain the Traditional Way of Life*, *at* https://www.youtube.com/watch?v=QvKLMPx4-b4; Seminole Tribe of Florida, *Government—Introduction*, *at* http://www.semtribe.com/Government/Introduction.aspx ("A few dozen Florida Indians who are not enrolled in either Tribe exist as organized 'Independent' Seminoles not formally recognized by the federal Bureau of Indian Affairs (BIA). They continue to formally protest any government intervention into their lives and maintain an open land claim for much of the state of Florida with the federal government."). In 1996, the Traditionalists sued Collier County after it attempted to apply its housing rules to their homes. *See* Billie v. Collier County, 2:96-cv-00229-EAK (M.D. Fla. filed June 21, 1996). Following intense negotiations, the county agreed to "creat[e] a special cultural land-use designation to exempt the village from county building codes." Gina Edwards, *Seminoles Win OK for Village*, Naples Daily News, Jan. 18, 1997, at D1, *available at* 1997 WLNR 7464864.

The federal land claim that eventually splintered the Seminoles took 40 years to resolve. The $48 million demand, which sought compensation for land taken from the tribe under three different treaties (Moultrie Creek (1823), Payne's Landing (1832), and Macomb (1839)) as well as the 1944 law creating Everglades National Park, was filed in 1950. Although a $16 million settlement with the United States was reached in 1976, the matter dragged on for another 14 years (thereby inflating the final payout to $50 million) because of disagreements among the Miccosukees, Seminoles, Traditionalists, and the Seminole Nation of Oklahoma over how to share the proceeds. For a further discussion, see Harry A. Kersey Jr., *The Florida Seminole Land Claims Case, 1950–1990*, 72 Fla. Hist. Q. 35 (1993). *See also* Pub. L. No. 101–277, 104 Stat. 143 (Apr. 30, 1990), *available at* https://www.gpo.gov/fdsys/pkg/STATUTE-104/pdf/STATUTE-104-Pg143.pdf (directing that 75.404% be given to the Oklahoma Indians and 24.596% to the Florida Indians, with 77.20% of the latter amount going to the Seminoles, 18.16% to the Miccosukees, and 4.63% to the Traditionalists).

14. Early in their history, cattle ranching also was important to the Seminoles but ended with the loss of their lands in the 1830s. Ranching resumed "in 1936 when the United States Government shipped 500 head of drought relief Hereford cattle from Arizona to the Seminole Indian Agency." Ed Sievers et al., *Seminole Indian Ranching in Florida*, 7 Rangelands 209, 209 (Oct. 1985). Today, the Seminole Pride Beef brand is on the verge of becoming an important contributor to the tribe's revenues, using "more than 12,000 head . . . grazing on 38,200 acres. . . ." Seminole Tribe of Florida, *Seminole Cattle History, at* http://www.stofinc.com/sempridebeef/seminole-cattle-history/.

15. *See* Harry A. Kersey Jr., *Pelts, Plumes, and Hides: White Traders Among the Seminole Indians, 1890–1930*, 51 Fla. Hist. Q. 250 (1973).

16. In addition to baskets, beaded clothing, dolls, and pottery, the tribes became famous for their colorful patchwork. *See further* Dorothy Downs, Art of the Florida Seminole and Miccosukee Indians (1995); David M. Blackard, Patchwork and Palmettos: Seminole-Miccosukee Folk Art Since 1820 (1990).

17. Paige & Van Horn, *supra* note 8, at 53–54. In a press release, the U.S. government trumpeted the opening of the Miccosukee's Tamiami rest stop:

> The Miccosukees of Florida, kin to the Seminoles and Creeks, but consistently aloof from both tribal organizations, have emerged from the Everglades after more than a century and are now going into their own tribal business. . . .
>
> The Department of the Interior reports that December 19 is set for the dedication of their first tribal enterprise—a restaurant financed in part by a $150,000 [BIA] loan. Located 40 miles west of Miami, it is expected to attract the steady stream of tourists who travel U.S. 41, the Tamiami Trail.
>
> The restaurant and an adjacent new filling station are expected to provide employment to tribal members and produce revenue for the tribal budget. The enterprise, to be maintained by Miccosukee workmen and staffed with Miccosukee waitresses, has already brought some measure of prosperity to Miccosukee families. Tribal members were among the construction workers. . . .
>
> The Miccosukees are not strangers to residents of southern Florida. Jimmy Tiger's

> Indian Village—the homestead of his family and relatives about 30 miles west of Miami on the Tamiami Trail—is open to the public; and a crafts shop markets jackets, blouses, skirts and similar clothing of Miccosukee creation and design. . . .

U.S. Department of the Interior—Bureau of Indian Affairs, *News Release*, Dec. 12, 1964, *available at* http://www.bia.gov/cs/groups/public/documents/text/idc017120.pdf.

18. *See* Moe v. Confederated Salish and Kootenai Tribes of Flathead Reservation, 425 U.S. 463 (1976).

19. Sturtevant & Cattelino, *supra* note 2, at 446.

20. Seminole Tribe of Fla. v. Butterworth, 658 F.2d 310, 311, 314–15 (5th Cir. 1981) (Unit B), *cert. denied*, 455 U.S. 1020 (1982). The district court's opinion (which the Fifth Circuit affirmed) is reported at Seminole Tribe of Fla. v. Butterworth, 491 F. Supp. 1015 (S.D. Fla. 1980).

21. 480 U.S. 202 (1987). For a detailed analysis of the case, see Ralph A. Rossum, The Supreme Court and Tribal Gaming: California v. Cabazon Band of Mission Indians (2011).

22. 25 U.S.C. §§ 2701–2721. IGRA's speedy (some would say hasty) passage, and the diverse forces that had a hand in shaping its provisions, are recounted in Steven Andrew Light & Kathryn R.L. Rand, Indian Gaming and Tribal Sovereignty: The Casino Compromise (2005). Because IGRA is limited to federally recognized tribes and authorizes gambling only on "Indian land," it has engendered a great deal of political gamesmanship. *See further* The New Politics of Indian Gaming: The Rise of Reservation Interest Groups (Kenneth N. Hansen & Tracy A. Skopek eds. 2011). *See also* Jim Rosica, *With Moves in Louisiana, Nevada, Will Poarch Give Up on Florida?*, Fla. Politics, June 30, 2016, *at* http://floridapolitics.com/archives/215078-poarch-band-florida-casino (describing the efforts of the Alabama-based Poarch Band of Creek Indians to open a casino on a one-acre piece of land outside Pensacola that it claims qualifies as Indian country).

23. Although it is beyond the scope of this chapter to thoroughly discuss IGRA, its essential features can be quickly summarized. Under the statute, Indian gambling is divided into three classes. Class I (social gambling) and Class II (bingo) do not require state authorization. In contrast, Class III ("Las Vegas-style" gambling, including craps, roulette, slots, and table games such as baccarat and blackjack) obligates the tribe to enter into a "compact," or agreement, with the state. *See further* Kathryn R.L. Rand & Steven Andrew Light, Indian Gaming Law and Policy (2d ed. 2014).

The Miccosukees have opted to limit themselves to Class II gaming and therefore have not needed Florida's permission for their gambling activities, have not had to share any of their revenues with the state, and have not had to make public any of their financial records. *See* Nick Sortal, *Miccosukees Steer Clear of Politics: Tribe Still Offers Class II Bingo-Type Slots—No Blackjack, No Taxes, No Hassle—Bingo Hall Offers Five-Figure Jackpot*, Miami Herald, Mar. 18, 2016, at 25G, *available at* 2016 WLNR 7934123. *See also* Tamiami Partners, Ltd. by and through Tamiami Dev. Corp. v. Miccosukee Tribe of Indians of Fla., 63 F.3d 1030 (11th Cir. 1995) (general description of the Miccosukees' gambling operations).

In contrast, upon the passage of IGRA the Seminoles immediately requested a compact. When Florida officials refused to discuss the matter, the tribe took them to court but had its claim thrown out because of the state's Eleventh Amendment immunity. *See* Seminole Tribe of Fla. v. Florida, 517 U.S. 44 (1996). *See also* Seminole Tribe of Fla. v. United States, Affidavit of Jim Shore (dated Sept. 14, 2007), No. 07–60317 (S.D. Fla.), *available at* 2007 WL 3282787 (recounting the tribe's efforts to gain a compact through 2007). (In 1980, Shore, who lost his sight in a 1970 automobile accident, became the first Florida Seminole to graduate from law school when he received a J.D. from Stetson University; in 1982, he was named the tribe's general counsel. *See further* R. Howard, *Jim Shore Interview*, Samuel Proctor [University of Florida] Oral History Program—Seminole Collection (June 29, 1999), *at* http://ufdc.ufl.edu/UF00008109/00001/1j; *Seminole Tribe General Counsel Jim Shore Accepts Honorary Degree from FSU*, FSU News, Dec. 12, 2005, *at* https://www.fsu.edu/news/2005/12/20/shore.degree/; Wikipedia: The Free Encyclopedia, *at* https://en.wikipedia.org/wiki/Seminole_Tribe_of_Florida (under "Notable Florida Seminole").)

Subsequently, however, a new governor (Charlie Crist, elected 2006) who did not share his predecessors' (Lawton Chiles and Jeb Bush) aversion to gambling, signed a compact with the tribe. *See* Robert M. Jarvis, *The 2007 Seminole-Florida Gambling Compact*, 12 Gaming L. Rev. 13 (2008). The Florida Legislature, incensed at being left out of the negotiations (and believing it could have struck a more lucrative deal), went to court and managed to scuttle the deal on separation-of-powers grounds. *See* Florida House of Representatives v. Crist, 999 So. 2d 601 (Fla. 2008), *cert. denied sub nom.* Seminole Tribe of Fla. v. Florida House of Representatives, 555 U.S. 1212 (2009). In 2010, the tribe and the state agreed on a new compact. In return for giving the Seminoles slots and table games (but not craps or roulette), the tribe agreed to give a portion of its revenues (approximately $200 million per year) to the state.

In 2015, the portion of the compact allowing table games expired (the remainder of the compact runs through 2030). Although the tribe and Florida's current governor (Rick Scott) reached an agreement on an expanded compact that would pay the state $300 million per year while giving the tribe craps and roulette as well as the right to open an additional casino (at Fort Pierce), the Florida Legislature failed to approve the deal during its 2016 session. *See* Dan Sweeney, *Seminoles Elect New Chairman After Ouster*, S. Fla. Sun Sentinel, Nov. 2, 2016, at 6B. In November 2016, however, the tribe's right to offer table games for the entire length of the compact was confirmed after a judge found the state had allowed various third parties to violate the tribe's exclusivity rights. *See* Seminole Tribe of Fla. v. State of Fla., 219 F. Supp. 3d 1177 (N.D. Fla. 2016).

24. *See* Donald Craig Mitchell, Wampum: How Indian Tribes, the Mafia, and an Inattentive Congress Invented Indian Gaming and Created a $28 Billion Gambling Empire (2016).

25. *See* Daniel Ducassi, *Unredacted Deposition Reveals $2.2B in Seminole Gambling Revenue Last Year*, Politico, May 13, 2016, *at* http://www.politico.com/states/florida/story/2016/05/unredacted-deposition-reveals-22b-in-seminole-gambling-revenue-last-year-101710; Nick Sortal, *Indian Gambling Revenues in Florida Rise 2.5% in 2012*, Orlando Sentinel, Mar. 27, 2014, at A12, *available at* 2014 WLNR 8265450 ("According to a worksheet that projects annual distributions from the tribe to local governments, the Hard Rock casino in Tampa was responsible for 41.5 percent of the tribe's revenues. The Hollywood Hard Rock was next at 27.3 percent, followed by Coconut Creek (14.5 percent), Hollywood Classic (7.5 percent), Immokalee (6.9 percent) and Brighton (2 percent) in 2012."). For a further look at the Seminoles' gambling operations, see Jessica R. Cattelino, High Stakes: Florida Seminole Gaming and Sovereignty (2008); Lauren Gensler, *An Alligator Wrestler, A Casino Boss and a $12 Billion Tribe*, Forbes, Nov. 8, 2016, at 104; Seminole Gaming, *Our Properties*, *at* http://www.theseminolecasinos.com/.

26. *See* Miccosukee Tribe of Indians of Florida, *Gaming*, *at* http://www.miccosukee.com/gaming/; *Miccosukees Steer Clear*, *supra* note 23.

27. The Miccosukees also have used their money to fight water pollution in the Everglades. *See* Tim Padgett, *Last Stand*, TIME, June 27, 1999, *available at* http://content.time.com/time/magazine/article/0,9171,27411,00.html ("Miccosukee chairman Billy Cypress likes to usher guests onto the [casino's] rooftop and point west to his tribe's home: the Everglades. An 18,000-sq.-mi. expanse of shimmering water, waving sawgrass and emerald tree hammocks, it is one of America's most vital but abused natural treasures. Like the endangered wood storks that glide overhead, the fewer than 500 Miccosukees rely upon this unique 'river of grass' for their survival as a tribe. And they rely on gaming profits to buy the multimillion-dollar legal and scientific clout they need to protect the Everglades. 'The money allows us to be like the cowboys,' says Cypress, 48. 'We can bring in the hired guns.'"). For a further discussion, see, e.g., Miccosukee Tribe of Indians of Fla. v. United States, 716 F.3d 535 (11th Cir. 2013); Miccosukee Tribe of Indians of Fla. v. South Fla. Water Mgmt. Dist., 48 So. 3d 811 (Fla. 2010); Miccosukee Tribe of Indians of Florida, *Environmental Issues, at* http://www.miccosukee.com/tribe/ (under "Tribe").

As has been pointed out elsewhere, the upturn in the Miccosukees' fiscal fortunes has come at a heavy cost: internal feuding, claims of mismanagement, unwanted publicity, and even an increase in obesity. *See* Chad Gillis, *Tribes in Florida's Everglades Pay Price of Prosperity*, USA Today, Mar. 24, 2014, *at* http://www.usatoday.com/story/news/nation/2014/03/24/florida-everglades-tribes-pay-price-of-prosperity/6827375/. By far, however, the most serious consequence has been the IRS's allegation that the tribe's members have failed to pay as much as $1 billion in gambling taxes. In 2016 this argument received a significant boost in United States v. Jim, 2016 WL 6995455 (S.D. Fla. 2016), the first case to reach the merits.

Each year, Sally Jim received a percentage of the tribe's gambling profits. In 2001 her share came to $272,000. Like the rest of the tribe, Jim was told that no taxes were due on this money. When the IRS discovered this fact, it took Jim to court. In a blistering opinion, U.S. District Judge Cecilia M. Altonaga sided with the government:

> Since the 1960s, the Tribe has distributed quarterly payments in the form of checks or cash, issued in equal amounts to each tribal member. While these payment amounts were originally very small—about $20–25 several times a year—around 1990, the Tribe started operating a gaming facility known as the Bingo Hall or Miccosukee Indian Bingo Gaming (hereinafter, the "Bingo Hall"), offering class II gaming, including bingo, poker, and video pull-tab machines. The Bingo Hall began generating larger amounts of income, allowing the Tribe to distribute increased quarterly assistance payments to its members. Today, the Tribe's quarterly distributions reach into the tens of thousands of dollars per tribal member.
>
> On December 8, 1994, Congress added a provision to the Internal Revenue Code[] requiring American Indian tribes to withhold federal income tax from any payment of net revenue from class II gaming. *See* 26 U.S.C. § 3402(r). In response, the Tribe enacted a "gross receipts tax" or "gross receipts license fee," which it applied to its gaming facility. This license fee is a percentage of the gross revenue of the Bingo Hall, and the Tribe places the fee into a non-taxable distributable revenue ("NTDR") account. The Tribe distributes its quarterly assistance payments to its members from this NTDR account. The Tribe argues these payments do not constitute net revenue derived from gaming so as to render the payments taxable under 26 U.S.C. section 3402(r) or under

the Indian Gaming Regulatory Act ("IGRA"), 25 U.S.C. section 2701 *et seq*. Rather, it asserts these payments are excludable from federal taxation as general welfare benefits or "income from the land."

Jim raised these same arguments when the IRS issued its tax assessment finding her indebted to the United States in the amount of $278,758.83—including taxes on the $272,000.00 in tribal distributions she received in 2001, as well as interest, penalties, and statutory additions. . . .

The vast majority, if not all, of the Tribe's distributions come from the Tribe's net gaming revenue. (*See* Tr. Ex. 46, at 3 (stating the total trust fund distributions for the year ending September 30, 2001 were $32,268,000.00), at 14 (stating the gross receipts license fee for the Bingo Hall was $32,103,681.00 and for Miccosukee Resort and Convention Center was $546,810.00 for the year ending September 30, 2001); Tr. Ex. 52, at 3, 11 (showing the Bingo Hall subsidized the Miccosukee Resort and Convention Center); Tr. Ex. 53, at 3 (showing total trust fund distributions for the year ending September 30, 2002 were $36,335,300.00), at 13 (showing the Bingo Hall paid $37,462,023.00 in gross receipts license fee for year ending September 30, 2002)). The Tribe produced no documentary evidence substantiating its claim that sources other than the Bingo Hall contributed to the NTDR account. (*See* Tr. Ex. 46, at 13–14 (not showing tribal leases and rentals paying any gross receipts license fee)). Tribal representative, Billy Cypress ("Cypress"), testified he could not suggest a percentage of the NTDR account deposits derived from non-gaming sources. . . .

From before 1995 to 2009, Cypress was chairman of the Tribe. . . . Cypress testified that although he told tribal members distributions from the Tribe were not subject to federal income tax and instructed members not to report distributions on their federal income tax returns, he also instructed members at General Council meetings not to disclose they were receiving distributions to persons outside the Tribe. Cypress also instructed members not to report distributions to credit card agencies, and not to cash their distribution checks in places where they would be reported to the IRS. . . .

During 2001, four members of Jim's household were entitled to receive distributions from the Tribe—Jim; her husband, Alex Osceola ("Alex"); her daughter, Alexis Osceola ("Alexis"); and her adopted daughter, Tamara Jim ("Tamara"). . . . The Tribe's distributions were not based on the needs of the recipient, and the only guideline to be eligible for distribution was that the recipient must be a member of the Tribe. . . . Jim testified the Tribe is a matriarchal society; thus, tribal custom establishes the mother is the head of the household. When the Tribe made quarterly distribution payments, Jim, as the head of household, generally picked up a check equal to the per capita amount of the distribution multiplied by the number of members in her household. . . .

[T]his is not a situation where Jim asserted a "sincere, albeit erroneous, belief" that her tribal distributions were not subject to federal income tax. *Jourdain v. Comm'r of Internal Revenue*, 71 T.C. 980, 991 (1979), *aff'd sub nom. Jourdain v. C. I. R.*, 617 F.2d 507 (8th Cir. 1980). To the contrary, Cypress's testimony revealed the Tribe instructed its members, including Jim, to take active measures to conceal from the IRS their distributions. . . .

Accordingly, the Court finds Jim has not established her failure to timely file her 2001 tax return is excused by reasonable cause; thus, sanctions are appropriate pursuant to 26 U.S.C. sections 6651(a)(1) and (2). Sally Jim is liable to the United States in the amount of $278,758.83, as of April 9, 2015, for unpaid federal income taxes, penalties, and interest assessed against her for the 2001 Tax Year. . . .

Id. at *1-*3, *6.

Cypress was ousted as the tribe's chairman in 2009. However, after his successor tried to work with the IRS, Cypress was returned to power:

> For decades, the Miccosukee kept their business largely private, using their sovereign status as a shield in countless civil and criminal legal cases with outsiders. But the tribe's tax troubles came to light during an internal rift when Cypress was out of power [2009–16], which led to a lawsuit accusing him of stealing $26 million from Miccosukee bank accounts, including casino profits. That dispute further sharpened the IRS' targeting of the tribe for failing to withhold taxes on gaming income doled out to members.
>
> The tribe's traditional distribution of casino income—$120,000 to $160,000 yearly for each member—has turned into a massive tax liability.
>
> Cypress took a tough stand against the IRS crackdown on the tribe's income from gaming profits in a special election [in] March [2016], after the Miccosukee General Council voted to remove Chairman Colley Billie. [Billie] had attempted to settle the tribe's dispute with the IRS and started to withhold taxes from the distributions to tribal members—a step the agency demanded.

Jay Weaver, *Miccosukee Court Loss Could Clear Way for IRS to Claim $1 Billion in Back Taxes*, Miami Herald, Aug. 23, 2016, at 6A, *available at* 2016 WLNR 25640086.

In an attempt to avoid responsibility, the tribe has blamed its lawyers—not only did it fire its longtime general counsel, see Noreen Marcus, *Bernardo Roman Out as Tribe's Chief Counsel*, Miami Daily Bus. Rev., May 11, 2015, at A1, it filed multiple lawsuits against its outside law firm (Lewis Tein PL). This proved to be an expensive mistake, as the firm was awarded $4 million in damages. *See* David Ovalle, *Miccosukees to Pay $4M to Former Lawyers Over Frivolous Lawsuits*, Miami Herald, May 20, 2016, at 4A, *available at* 2016 WLNR 15355424. In addition, the attorneys who brought the lawsuits now are under investigation by the bar. *See* Celia Ampel, *Florida Bar Files Complaints Against 2 Lawyers in Miccosukee Tribe Saga*, Miami Daily Bus. Rev., July 26, 2016, at A1.

For a further recounting of these events, see, e.g., Miccosukee Tribe of Indians of Fla. v. Cypress, 814 F.3d 1202 (11th Cir. 2015); United States v. Billie, 611 F. App'x 608 (11th Cir. 2015); Miccosukee Tribe of Indians of Fla. v. United States Dep't of Justice, 103 F. Supp. 3d 1314 (S.D. Fla. 2015); Miccosukee Tribe of Indians of Fla. v. Cypress, 2015 WL 235433 (S.D. Fla. 2015); Miccosukee Tribe of Indians of Fla. v. Lewis, 165 So. 3d 9 (Fla. 3d Dist. Ct. App. 2015).

28. *See* Jessica R. Cattelino, *"One Hamburger at a Time": Revisiting the State-Society Divide with the Seminole Tribe of Florida and Hard Rock international*, 52 Current Anthropology S137 (2011); Chabeli Herrera, *How the Seminole Tribe Came to Rock the Hard Rock Empire*, Miami Herald, May 23, 2016, at 16G, *available at* 2016 WLNR 15627754. For a look at the Miccosukees' diversification efforts, see Dennis Wiedman, *Global Marketing of Indigenous Culture: Discovering Native America with Lee Tiger and the Florida Miccosukee*, 34:3 Am. Indian Culture & Res. J. 1 (2010).

29. Jason Parker, *Dolphins Sign Naming Rights Deal for Stadium with Hard Rock*, Fansided, Aug. 16, 2016, *at* http://fansided.com/2016/08/16/dolphins-sign-naming-rights-deal-hard-rock-stadium/. The deal's terms are more thoroughly discussed in Hal Habib, *For Miami Dolphins, Reported $250M Hard Rock Deal is Smashing Success*, Palm Beach Post, Aug. 17, 2016, *available at* 2016 WLNR 25120344.

30. *See, e.g.*, Longo v. Seminole Indian Casino-Immokalee, 813 F.3d 1348 (11th Cir. 2016) (fired casino security guard could not sue tribe due to sovereign immunity); Contour Spa at the Hard Rock, Inc. v. Seminole Tribe of Fla., 692 F.3d 1200 (11th Cir. 2012), *cert. denied*, 568 U.S. 1086 (2013) (spa operator's federal claims for breach of lease dismissed due to tribe's sovereign immunity); Furry v. Miccosukee Tribe of Indians of Fla., 685 F.3d 1224 (11th Cir.), *cert. denied*, 568 U.S. 1028 (2012) (father's claim that tribe's casino had served his daughter excessive amounts of alcohol, thereby contributing to her fatal automobile accident, dismissed due to sovereign immunity); Lobo v. Miccosukee Tribe of Indians of Fla., 279 F. App'x 926 (11th Cir. 2008) (casino workers' pay lawsuit dismissed due to the tribe's sovereign immunity); Sanderlin v. Seminole Tribe of Fla., 243 F.3d 1282 (11th Cir. 2001) (police officer's disability discrimination claim dismissed because of tribe's sovereign immunity); Everglades Ecolodge at Big Cypress, LLC v. Seminole Tribe of Fla., 836 F. Supp. 2d 1296 (S.D. Fla. 2011) (developer's breach of lease lawsuit dismissed on sovereign immunity grounds); Inglish Interests, LLC v. Seminole Tribe of Fla., Inc., 2011 WL 208289 (M.D. Fla. 2011) (citrus grove operator's breach of lease claim dismissed due to tribe's sovereign immunity); Costello v. Seminole Tribe of Fla., 763 F. Supp. 2d 1295 (M.D. Fla. 2010) (casino card dealer's wage lawsuit dismissed due to tribe's sovereign immunity); Perry v. Seminole Tribe of Fla., 2009 WL 2365892 (M.D. Fla. 2009) (plaintiff's wrongful arrest claim dismissed due to the tribe's sovereign immunity); Seminole Tribe of Fla. v. Schinneller, 197 So. 3d 1216 (Fla. 4th Dist. Ct. App. 2016) (casino patron's slip-and-fall case dismissed because of tribe's sovereign immunity); MMMG, LLC v. Seminole Tribe of Fla., Inc., 196 So. 3d 438 (Fla. 4th Dist. Ct. App. 2016) (production company's suit for alleged breach of joint venture agreement dismissed due to tribe's sovereign immunity); Seminole Tribe of Fla. v. Ariz, 67 So. 3d 229 (Fla. 2d Dist. Ct. App. 2010) (wife of pedestrian killed by automobile driven by casino employee could not sue tribe due to sovereign immunity); Seminole Tribe of Fla. v. McCor, 903 So. 2d 353 (Fla. 2d Dist. Ct. App. 2005) (casino patron's injury claim dismissed due to tribe's sovereign immunity); Miccosukee Tribe of Indians v. Napoleoni, 890 So. 2d 1152 (Fla. 1st Dist. Ct. App. 2004) (injured casino's worker's claim for compensation dismissed due to tribe's sovereign immunity); Cupo v. Seminole Tribe of Fla., 860 So. 2d 1078 (Fla. 1st Dist. Ct. App. 2003), *review denied*, 870 So. 2d 821 (Fla. 2004) (same). *See also* Miccosukee Tribe of Indians of S. Fla. v. Bermudez, 145 So. 3d 157 (Fla. 3d Dist. Ct. App. 2014) (no need to consider tribe's claim of sovereign immunity in automobile collision case where other grounds existed for dismissing plaintiff's case).

31. For a listing of these courts, see National American Indian Court Judges Association, *National Directory of Tribal Justice Systems*, *at* http://www.naicja.org/our-programs/directory; Tribal Court Clearinghouse, *Tribal Courts*, *at* http://www.tribal-institute.org/lists/justice.htm.

32. As sources of law, treaties normally play a special role because they affect such matters as tribal boundaries and governmental powers. However, they are much less important when dealing with the Miccosukees and Seminoles for two reasons: 1) the tribes never signed a peace treaty with the United States; and, 2) both tribes attained federal government recognition through the application process rather than by treaty.

33. *See* Seminole Tribe of Florida, *Government: How We Operate—Tribal Court, at* http://www.semtribe.com/Government/TribalCourt/TribalCourt.aspx (under "Codes" and "Forms").

34. On the tribe's website, for example, there is only a single brief mention of the court:

> The Miccosukee Tribe now operates a Clinic; Police Department; Court System; Day Care Center; Senior Center; Community Action Agency and an Educational System ranging from the Head Start Pre-School Program through Senior High School, Adult, Vocational and Higher Education Programs and other Social Services. These programs incorporate both the traditional Miccosukee Indian ways and non-Indian ways into their system and are all located on the Tamiami Trail Reservation, where the Miccosukee community resides.

Miccosukee Tribe of Indians of Florida, *Tribe: Tribal Programs & Business, at* http://www.miccosukee.com/tribe/. For what are apparently the only two opinions that the tribe has allowed to be published, see Lovermi v. Miccosukee Tribe of Indians of Fla., 23 Indian L. Rep. 6090 (Micc. Tr. Ct. 1996) (dismissing appeal of employment firing decision because tribe had not waived sovereign immunity), and Mandel v. Miccosukee Tribal Gaming Agency, 22 Indian L. Rep. 6148 (Micc. Tr. Ct. 1994) (affirming administrative denial of bingo licenses sought by non-Indians). Notwithstanding the tribal court's order, the *Mandel* case was extensively litigated in federal court and in 2002 resulted in the confirmation of a $9.3 million arbitration award ($17 million with interest) against the tribe. *See* Tamiami Partners, Ltd. v. Miccosukee Tribe, 35 F. App'x 855 (11th Cir.), *cert. denied*, 537 U.S. 1030 (2002), *reh'g denied*, 537 U.S. 1149 (2003). *See also* Susan R. Miller, *Court Upholds Ruling that Former Casino Managers are Owed $9.3 Million*, Miami Daily Bus. Rev., Apr. 22, 2002, at 24.

35. In *Lovemi*, for example, the Miccosukee Tribal Court considered "legal precedent from sister tribal courts [to see] how other tribal judicial systems [had] dealt with [the] issue [of sovereign immunity]." 22 Indian L. Rep. at 6091.

36. *See further* Matthew L.M. Fletcher, *Toward a Theory of Intertribal and Intratribal Common Law*, 43 Hous. L. Rev. 701 (2006).

37. *See* Billie v. Stier, 141 So. 3d 584, 586 (Fla. 3d Dist. Ct. App.), *review denied*, 157 So. 3d 1041 (Fla. 2014) (tribal court order determining child custody was not entitled to recognition under the Uniform Child Custody Jurisdiction and Enforcement Act, Fla. Stat. §§ 61.501–61.542, where "although the father was allowed to attend the proceedings, he was unable to understand what was happening as the proceedings were conducted largely in the Miccosukee language and he was not given an interpreter [and] the mother testified in Miccosukee for over twenty minutes and the Tribal Court gave the father only a two-minute summary in English"). The lack of interpreters appears to be a regular problem in Miccosukee tribal court proceedings. *See Miccosukee Tribal Court a Contrast*, *supra* note 3.

38. As with the rest of the federal Bill of Rights, the Fifth Amendment does not apply to Indian nations. *See* Talton v. Mayes, 163 U.S. 376 (1896) (holding that because they were not created by the U.S. Constitution, tribal courts are not bound by its provisions). Congress, however, has imposed certain due process requirements on tribes through the Indian Civil Rights Act of 1968, 25 U.S.C. §§ 1301–1304. Even so, the doctrine rarely looks precisely the same in tribal court as in state and federal courts. In particular, it has been recognized that tribal courts may adapt due process standards to the unique needs of their cultures and com-

munities—including the exigencies of achieving justice in a small community. *See further* R. Stephen McNeill, Note, *In a Class by Themselves: A Proposal to Incorporate Tribal Courts into the Federal Court System without Compromising their Unique Status as "Domestic Dependent Nations,"* 65 Wash. & Lee L. Rev. 283 (2008) (arguing that Congress should declare that tribal courts have the same status, and are subject to the same rules, as state courts).

39. *See* Seminole Tribe of Florida, *Filing Your Case in Tribal Court: A Pro Se Guide*, at 6, *available at* http://www.semtribe.com/Government/TribalCourt/Forms/STOF%20Pro%20Se%20InstructionsREV42016.pdf.

40. *See* United States v. Bryant, 136 S. Ct. 1954, 1958–59 (2016) ("The Sixth Amendment guarantees indigent defendants, in state and federal criminal proceedings, appointed counsel in any case in which a term of imprisonment is imposed. *Scott v. Illinois*, 440 U.S. 367, 373–374, 99 S.Ct. 1158, 59 L.Ed.2d 383 (1979). But the Sixth Amendment does not apply to tribal-court proceedings. *See Plains Commerce Bank v. Long Family Land & Cattle Co.*, 554 U.S. 316, 337, 128 S.Ct. 2709, 171 L.Ed.2d 457 (2008). The Indian Civil Rights Act of 1968 (ICRA), Pub.L. 90–284, 82 Stat. 77, 25 U.S.C. § 1301 *et seq.*, which governs criminal proceedings in tribal courts, requires appointed counsel only when a sentence of more than one year's imprisonment is imposed. § 1302(c)(2).").

41. *See, e.g.*, *Stier*, 141 So. 3d at 586 (explaining that "the father's attorney was not allowed into the [Miccosukee court's] proceedings even as an observer").

42. For an example of such a triple prosecution, see United States v. Zacherle, 2008 WL 5000145 (E.D. Wash. 2008).

43. *See* Paige & Van Horn, *supra* note 8, at 62 ("[The desire to govern themselves] led to the Miccosukees negotiating a contract in 1971 with the Bureau of Indian Affairs 'that resulted in the Miccosukee Tribal Council assuming the administration of all programs previously administered by the bureau . . . [and] responsibility for hiring all . . . personnel and managing . . . funds.'") (citations omitted); Harry A. Kersey Jr., *Buffalo Tiger, Bobo Dean, and the "Young Turks": A Miccosukee Prelude to the 1975 Indian Self-Determination Act*, 29:1 Am. Indian Culture & Res. J. 1 (2005); Miccosukee Tribe of Indians of Florida, *Tribal Programs & Business*, *supra* note 34 ("On May 4, 1971, officers of the Miccosukee Corporation, acting for the Miccosukee Tribe, signed a contract with the BIA authorizing the Corporation to operate all programs and services provided for the Miccosukee Community and formerly administered by the BIA. The Tribe's intent in negotiating this matter was clear; the people wished to decide their own fate and gradually develop total independence.").

44. *See further* Fredric R. Brandfon, Comment, *Tradition and Judicial Review in the American Indian Tribal Court System*, 38 UCLA L. Rev. 991, 1006 (1991) ("The idea of separate governmental powers is a concept alien to Indian society.").

45. *See Miccosukee Constitution*, *supra* note 13, art. III, § 1 ("The Miccosukee General Council shall be composed of all adult members 18 years of age or over. Twenty-five members shall constitute a quorum, provided at least three clans are represented, and no business shall be conducted unless a quorum is present at all times."); *id.* § 3 ("The elected officers, in addition to serving the Miccosukee General Council, shall be the Miccosukee Business Council when the General Council is not in [s]ession. . . ."). The reference to "clans" in § 1 is explained *infra* note 55.

46. *See Miccosukee Tribal Court a Contrast*, *supra* note 3 ("The Miccosukee Tribal Court was established in 1981. . . . Its modern building is next to the police department by the tribe's

Tamiami Trail administration complex. . . . The inside of [its] courtroom reflects nods to both the past and present, with modern wood paneling and five big windows juxtaposed against a huge representation of the tribe's emblem: a chickee hut. . . .").

47. Robert O. Saunooke, *Tribal Justice: The Case for Strengthening Inherent Sovereignty*, 47 Judges' J. 15, 18 (Fall 2008).

48. *Miccosukee Tribal Court a Contrast*, *supra* note 3.

49. *Id.* ("There is no Miccosukee jail, although the tribe can send someone to Miami-Dade jail for up to a year. That has not happened recently, former Miccosukee officers said. 'In our customs, we don't believe in jail. But it is in our code,' [Petties Osceola Jr., the tribal customs judge,] said.").

50. *Id.* ("In October 2000, Miami-Dade prosecutors asked the tribal court for help reaching uncooperative witnesses who the tribe was shielding in the murder prosecution of Kirk Douglas Billie. He was accused of drowning his two children by rolling an SUV into a canal near the reservation. The tribal court refused to help, siding with elders who forgave Billie and declared the deaths an accident. 'They sincerely believe this matter has been dealt with and resolved according to Miccosukee customs and traditions,' the tribal court ruled. But the state didn't forgive Billie and fought to prosecute him. Miami-Dade jurors ultimately convicted him of murder."). For a further look at the state's prosecution of Billie, see Miccosukee Tribe of Indians of Fla. v. United States, 2000 WL 35623105 (S.D. Fla. 2000); Billie v. State, 963 So. 2d 837 (Fla. 3d Dist. Ct. App. 2007), *review denied*, 978 So. 2d 159 (Fla. 2008); Billie v. State, 881 So. 2d 637 (Fla. 3d Dist. Ct. App. 2004); Billie v. State, 863 So. 2d 323 (Fla. 3d Dist. Ct. App. 2003); Pearl Goldman, *Criminal Law: 2007–2010 Survey of Florida Law*, 35 Nova L. Rev. 95, 103–04 (2010).

51. *Miccosukee Tribal Court a Contrast*, *supra* note 3 ("[F]ormer Miccosukee police officer Alonzo Moncur II . . . recalled arresting a tribe member for public intoxication at the Miccosukee Resort and Gaming complex. The man choked Moncur while trying to escape, he said. Anywhere else, that would be a felony charge of battery on a law enforcement officer. Instead, the tribal court fined the man $500 and banned him from the casino for six months, Moncur said. 'This guy could have killed me and nothing would have happened to him,' Moncur said. . . . 'I don't think there is justice in these courts. The judges are often not even lawyers, and more importantly are paid by the tribe. They usually follow the tribe's position in judicial matters,' said [Washington, D.C. attorney Dennis J.] Whittlesey, who is involved with a wrongful death suit against a Miccosukee tribe member. . . . When Chairman Billy Cypress crashed his car into a non-Indian couple, almost killing them on a state road in 2006, the case went to tribal court. He was acquitted. The victims did not attend the trial because they were not allowed a lawyer, according to former Miccosukee Police Chief Dave Ward.").

52. Miccosukee Tribe of Indians of Fla. v. Kraus-Anderson Constr. Co., 607 F.3d 1268, 1270 (11th Cir.), *reh'g and reh'g en banc denied*, 408 F. App'x 345 (11th Cir. 2010), *cert. denied*, 564 U.S. 1018 (2011).

53. High Stakes, *supra* note 25, at 180 (footnotes omitted). The mention of a "2001 Miccosukee court ruling" is a reference to the Kirk Douglas Billie case discussed *supra* note 50. Likewise, "The Green Corn Dance councils" is a reference to the "court" sessions that were held during the annual summer "Green Corn" festival. During the festival, punishments would be meted out as required:

> [T]he court or fasting day [was] the most important day at the Green Corn Dance. . . . On this day there was the annual court or council meeting, to determine the punishment for serious crimes of the past year and to discuss political problems. The meetings were run by special officers: the headman . . . of the Panther, Wildcat, or Wind clan (who could be the medicine man); the moderator or peace maker . . . of the Bird clan; the councilman or enforcer of the Panther or Wind clan; and two men helpers of the same clans.
>
> The court determined by consensus punishment for crimes such as murder, personal injury, clan endogamy, adultery (by both men and women), incest, theft, breaking someone else's property, gossiping, and, before recent times, learning to speak English and talking English in the presence of other Seminoles, associating with White people, and even owning paper and pencil. Examples of punishment include killing a murderer (there was a case in 1938, known to the non-Indian authorities who did not interfere or punish the enforcer); for clan incest resulting in a birth the father was killed while the mother was scratched, her hair was cut short, the tip of her nose was cut off, and she was whipped; for adultery the perpetrator's own clan whipped and scratched the person, and cut off the tips of his or her ears; for wounding, a fine in silver, money, cows, or horses was enforced. At least in cases of murder, the clan of the one killed took the initiative in the punishment, so a murderer in the same clan as that of the one killed had a better chance of survival. . . .

Sturtevant & Cattelino, *supra* note 2, at 440.

54. Eileen Soler, *Court in Session: First Seminole Tribal Court Takes Civil Cases into Own Hands*, Seminole Trib., Feb. 27, 2015, at 1A, 5A (quoting committee member Deloris Alvarez).

55. The Seminoles are made up of eight clans, see Seminole Tribe of Florida, *Clans, at* http://www.semtribe.com/Culture/Clans.aspx ("Each Seminole Indian born of a Seminole mother is a member of her 'Clan'—a traditional extended family unit. . . . Each clan is characterized by a non-human entity with which [it] shares many traits, such as strength, courage, or endurance. There are eight Seminole clans—Panther, Bear, Deer, Wind, Bigtown, Bird, Snake, and Otter. Clan members are not supposed to marry within their clan. . . . Several historical clans, including Alligator, are now extinct. The Panther clan is the largest clan in today's Seminole Tribe of Florida."), and, as explained *supra* note 2, have six reservations. As a result, considerable effort was made to assure both familial and geographical diversity, as evidenced by the backgrounds of the eventual appointees:

> *Trial Court*
> Chief Judge Moses B. Osceola (Hollywood) (Bird Clan)
> Associate Judge Tina Marie Osceola (Immokalee) (Panther Clan)
> Associate Judge Mary Tigertail (Big Cypress) (Otter Clan)
> *Court of Appeals*
> Chief Justice Willie Johns (Brighton) (Wild Cat Clan)
> Associate Justice Moses Jumper Jr. (Big Cypress) (Snake Clan)
> Associate Justice Amy Johns (Brighton) (Wild Cat Clan)

See further Eileen Soler, *Profiles in Justice: Tribe's First Court Justices, Judges Take the Bench*, Seminole Trib., Feb. 27, 2015, at 5A.

56. *Court in Session*, *supra* note 54. The Council Oak is "a huge oak tree . . . near the corner of U.S. 441 and Stirling Road on the Hollywood Reservation" that once served as a Seminole meeting place. *See* Seminole Tribe of Florida, *The Council Oak*, *at* http://www.semtribe.com/History/TheCouncilOak.aspx. In 1957, the Seminole constitution was signed under the Council Oak, and today the tribe's two signature steakhouses (in Hollywood and Tampa) are both called Council Oak. For a further discussion of the tree's importance (both as a link to the past and as a modern-day marketing tool), see Renee Ann Cramer, *Signs at Odds? The Semiotics of Law, Legitimacy, and Authenticity in Tribal Contexts*, *in* Law, Culture and Visual Studies 471, 486 (Anne Wagner & Richard K. Sherwin eds. 2014).

57. *See* Seminole Tribe of Florida, *Seminole Tribal Court Ordinance*, *available at* http://www.semtribe.com/Government/TribalCourt/Forms/STOF%20Judicial%20Code.pdf.

58. Seminole Tribe of Florida, *Tribal Court*, *at* http://www.semtribe.com/Government/TribalCourt/TribalCourt.aspx.

59. *Profiles in Justice*, *supra* note 55.

60. *Court in Session*, *supra* note 54 ("Court offices are staffed and furnished in Hollywood and Big Cypress, but hearings can be held anywhere as needed.").

61. *See* Gallagher, *supra* note 3 (quoting Helene Buster as saying, "We will be getting signatures on a Memorandum of Understanding from all the various court systems and agencies we deal with on a regular basis. I mean, we are working with the DCF (Department of Children and Families) of the state of Florida right now, they know it is coming. They are ready to turn everything over to us."). At least one family law attorney already has updated her website to reflect her practice before the court. *See* Rebekah Brown-Wiseman, *Seminole Tribal Court Family Law*, *at* http://www.southfloridafamilylawattorney.com/Family-Law-Overview/Seminole.shtml ("Family law attorney Rebekah Brown-Wiseman is one of the initial members of the Seminole Tribe of Florida Bar Association and part of the Seminole Tribe of Florida Tribal Court. Ms. Brown-Wiseman was the first attorney to file a dissolution of marriage action with the Seminole Tribal Court. As a divorce, paternity and adoptions attorney, Ms. Brown-Wiseman exclusively practices in family law and supports the Constitution of the Seminole Tribe of Florida.").

The decision to have the court begin its work in these areas was explained by Helene Buster in a 2012 interview:

> "We have so many cases in the state court," said Buster. "It would make things so much easier, not only on our department [Family Services], but on our community, if we had our own court."
>
> A tribal court development committee was initiated five years ago and is currently in the process of selecting tribal judges and justices in accordance with the Seminole Tribe of Florida's constitution. It has also determined that the court will focus primarily on civil cases.
>
> When asked about the need for a tribal court, Buster explained that in the county or state systems there are many misunderstandings related to culture and tradition. In some cases, the outside systems have viewed what the Tribe knows to be a tradition as an act of abuse, and the Tribe has had to "battle" against that misconception. Through education, understanding has improved over the last couple of years, but in a tribal court this traditional or cultural barrier would not be an issue.

For example, in the Seminole community, scratching is used as a form of discipline, and some outside systems have considered it to be abusive. A tribal court will not only recognize this cultural practice, but will also be familiar with the custom to know if it has gone beyond a form of discipline and become a form of abuse.

Buster says that a tribal court will hold community members to task at the same level or maybe higher than an outside system. While she would rather not have situations that require court involvement, she believes that a tribal court is in the best interest of the community.

"A tribal court will strengthen the sovereignty of our tribe and make us more self-contained," said Buster.

Maggie Scott, *The Heart of the Matter*, NICWA News, Winter 2012, at 11, *available at* http://www.nicwa.org/newsletter/2012%20Winter.pdf.

62. *Court in Session*, *supra* note 54. Such an expansion is anticipated by § 3–13 of the STCO, *supra* note 57, which provides: "The Seminole Court shall exercise broad original jurisdiction consistent with Seminole customs and traditions, the Seminole Constitution, laws and ordinances and applicable laws of the United States." *See also id.* § 3–14 (granting the court personal jurisdiction over tribal members, those eligible for such membership, and persons and entities doing business within the tribe's borders).

63. *Id.* §§ 3–15 (trial court); § 3–16 (appellate court).

64. Seminole Tribe of Florida, *Judicial Advisor*, *at* http://www.semtribe.com/Government/TribalCourt/Employment.aspx.

65. *See* Seminole Tribe of Florida, *Court Administration*, *at* http://www.semtribe.com/Government/TribalCourt/CourtAdministration.aspx.

66. *Court in Session*, *supra* note 54.

67. *Id.*

68. *See* Seminole Tribe of Florida Bar Association, *Qualifications for Admission*, *available at* http://www.semtribe.com/Government/TribalCourt/Forms/Admission%20to%20Practice.pdf; STCO, *supra* note 57, at § 3–116(C) ("Any attorney wishing to practice before the Seminole Court shall submit an application, along with a filing fee as set by the Director of the Administrative Office of the Courts, to the Clerk of Court with the following information: . . . (C) Acknowledgment that the attorney is aware of and has knowledge of the Seminole Court rules of procedures and all relevant Tribal laws, customs and traditions.").

69. *Id.* § 3–117 ("Lay Advocates[:] An individual may represent a Party in an action before the Seminole Courts upon approval of the Chief Judge, or Chief Justice if representation in the Appellate Court is requested.").

70. *Id.* § 3–115. To assist such parties, the court has published a *pro se* manual. *See supra* note 39.

71. *See* Seminole Tribe of Florida Judicial Commission, *Seminole Tribal Court Code of Judicial Conduct*, *available at* http://www.semtribe.com/Government/TribalCourt/Forms/STOF%20Judicial%20Code%20of%20Ethics%20Final.pdf. The national sample code can be found at http://www.judges.org/wp-content/uploads/ntjc_samplecode.pdf.

72. *See* Seminole Tribe of Florida, *Seminole Tribal Court Judicial Commission Ordinance*, *available at* http://www.semtribe.com/Government/TribalCourt/Forms/STOF%20Judicial%20Commission%20Code.pdf.

73. *Id.* § 3.22.

74. *Id.* § 3.25.

75. *Id.* § 3.27(D).

76. *Id.* § 3.29.

77. As the Seminoles' website points out, "The Seminole Tribe of Florida currently employs more than 2,000 non-Indians and purchases more than $24 million dollars in goods and services from more than 850 Florida vendors a year. In addition, the Tribe pays $3.5 million in federal payroll taxes." Seminole Tribe of Florida, *Tourism/Enterprises*, *at* http://www.semtribe.com/TourismAndEnterprises/. These figures do not include the tribe's casinos, which employ 10,000 workers and have contributed more than $1 billion to the state's coffers since 2010. *See* Florida Legislature—Office of Economic and Demographic Research, *Gaming: Revenue Overview* 10 (Mar. 26, 2015), *available at* http://edr.state.fl.us/Content/presentations/gaming/GamingRevenueOveriew_3-26-15.pdf; Spectrum Gaming Group, *Gambling Impact Study: Part 1*, at 239 (July 1, 2013), *available at* http://www.spectrumgamingcapital.com/wp-content/uploads/2015/07/FGIS_Spectrum_28Oct2013.pdf. Although the Miccosukees do not release similar statistics, and do not share their gambling revenues with the state, see *Miccosukees Steer Clear*, *supra* note 23, one source reports that the tribe has 1,500 employees. *See* http://www.manta.com/c/mmftxwv/miccosukee-tribe-of-indians-of-florida. *See also* Dennis Zotigh, *Meet Native America: Colley Billie, Chairman of the Miccosukee Tribe of Indians of Florida*, National Museum of the American Indian Blog, Feb. 28, 2014, *at* http://blog.nmai.si.edu/main/2014/02/meet-native-america-colley-billie.html ("The Miccosukee Tribe of Indians of Florida owns several successful enterprises in South Florida, including the Miccosukee Indian Bingo, Miccosukee Resort & Gaming, Miccosukee Golf & Country Club, Miccosukee Indian Village & Airboat Rides, Miccosukee Tobacco Shop, two service plazas, a restaurant, and a general store.").

About the Contributors

James M. Denham is professor of history and director of the Lawton M. Chiles Jr. Center for Florida History at Florida Southern College in Lakeland. His previous books include *Florida Founder William P. DuVal: Frontier Bon Vivant* and *Fifty Years of Justice: A History of the U.S. District Court for the Middle District of Florida*. He holds a B.A., M.A., and Ph.D. from Florida State University.

David J.R. Frakt is former associate professor of law at Barry University in Orlando. He currently is in private practice in Orlando and also is a lieutenant colonel in the U.S. Air Force (Judge Advocate General's Corps). His scholarship has appeared in the *Duke Law Journal*, *Harvard Human Rights Journal*, and *University of Pittsburgh Law Review*. He holds a B.A. from the University of California (Irvine) and a J.D. from Harvard University.

Robert M. Jarvis is professor of law at Nova Southeastern University in Fort Lauderdale. His previous books include *Out of the Muck: A History of the Broward Sheriff's Office* and *Teaching Legal History: Comparative Perspectives*. He holds a B.A. from Northwestern University, a J.D. from the University of Pennsylvania, and an LL.M. from New York University.

Tonya Kowalski is professor of law and co-director of the International and Comparative Law Center at Washburn University in Topeka, Kansas. Her scholarship has appeared in the *Florida State University Law Review*, *Seattle University Law Review*, and *Tulsa Law Review*. She holds a B.A. from the University of Florida and a J.D. from Duke University.

Robert W. Lee is judge in the Civil Division of the Broward County Court (Seventeenth Judicial Circuit) in Fort Lauderdale. His scholarship has appeared in the *Barry Law Review*, *Nova Law Review*, and *St. Thomas Law Review*. He holds a B.A. from Jacksonville University, an M.A. from California State University (Dominguez Hills), and a J.D. from the University of Florida.

Donna Litman is professor of law at Nova Southeastern University in Fort Lauderdale. Her previous books include *Florida Wills, Trusts, and Estates: Cases and Materials* and *LexisNexis Practice Guide: Florida Estate and Probate Practice*. She holds an A.B. from the University of Miami and a J.D. from the University of Florida.

Ernesto A. Longa is professor of law librarianship at the University of New Mexico in Albuquerque. He is the author of the book *Anarchist Periodicals in English Published in the United States (1833–1955): An Annotated Guide*. He holds a B.A. from the University of Florida, an M.L.I.S. from the University of Washington, and a J.D. from St. Thomas University (Miami).

M.C. Mirow is professor of law at Florida International University in Miami. His previous books include *Latin American Constitutions: The Constitution of Cádiz and its Legacy in Spanish America* and *Florida's First Constitution: The Constitution of Cádiz*. He holds a B.A. from Boston University, a J.D. from Cornell University, a Ph.D. (law) from Cambridge University, and a Ph.D. (law) from Leiden University. A Spanish version of his chapter was presented in Berlin, Germany, at the XIX Congreso del Instituto Internacional de Historia del Derecho Indiano.

Christopher A. Vallandingham is adjunct professor of law and a law librarian at the University of Florida in Gainesville and a captain in the U.S. Army Reserve (Judge Advocate General's Corps). He is a contributor to the books *The Central Intelligence Agency: An Encyclopedia of Covert Ops, Intelligence Gathering, and Spies* and *Prestatehood Legal Materials: A Fifty-State Research Guide*. He holds a B.A. from the University of South Florida, an M.S.L.I.S. from Florida State University, and a J.D. from the University of Florida.

Index of Cases

Ainsworth v. Schoen, 140n10
American Ins. Co. v. 356 Bales of Cotton (Canter), 69n112
Anderson v. Presbytery of Central Fla., 130n59
Archdiocese of Miami, Inc. v. Miñagorri, 127n34
Austin v. Mt. Zion Primitive Baptist Church of W. Palm Beach, 138n104

Baldwin v. Mills, 126n10
Bendross v. Readon, 136n88
Bethel AME Church v. Domingo, 133n74
Billie v. Collier County, 183n13
Billie v. State (2003), 193n50
Billie v. State (2004), 193n50
Billie v. State (2007), 193n50
Billie v. Stier, 191n37
Bloch v. Bloch, 139n109
Bryan v. Itasca Cnty., 172

California v. Cabazon Band of Mission Indians, 172
Carroll v. Fellure, 135n85
Contour Spa at the Hard Rock, Inc. v. Seminole Tribe of Fla., 190n30
Cook v. Fernandez, 86n57
Costello v. Seminole Tribe of Fla., 190n30
Covington v. Bowers, 137n100
Crowder v. Southern Baptist Convention, 135n87
Cubbin-Will v. Presbytery of Tropical Fla., 130n59
Cupo v. Seminole Tribe of Fla., 190n30

Davis v. United States, 181n4

Epperson v. Myers, 137n96
Everglades Ecolodge at Big Cypress, LLC v. Seminole Tribe of Fla., 130n90
Ex parte Milligan, 103n10
Ex parte Quirin, 103n10

First Baptist Church of Cape Coral, Fla., Inc. v. Compass Constr., Inc., 126n9
First Free Will Baptist Church of Blountstown v. Franklin, 135n85
First Indep. Missionary Baptist Church of Chosen v. McMillan, 138n104
Fleischer v. Fleischer, 140n109
Florida Atl. & Gulf Central R.R. Co. v. Pensacola & Ga. R.R. Co., 86n55
Florida House of Representatives v. Crist, 186n23
Franzen v. Poulos, 133n73
Freeman v. Department of Highway Safety and Motor Vehicles, 125n9
Full Gospel Temple of Tallahassee v. Redd, 131n65
Furry v. Miccosukee Tribe of Indians of Fla., 190n30

Garcia v. Church of Scientology Flag Serv. Org., Inc., 141n117
Georgia v. McCollum, 154n1
Gibson v. Board of Pub. Instruction of Dade Cnty., 163n139
Goodman v. Temple Shir Ami, Inc., 134n83
Gray v. Gray, 104n21

Hamdan v. Rumsfeld, 103n10
Hamdi v. Rumsfeld, 103n10
Hemphill v. Zion Hope Primitive Baptist Church of Pensacola, Inc., 137n98
Hodgson v. Butts, 75n273
Hosanna-Tabor Evangelical Lutheran Church and Sch. v. Equal Emp. Opportunity Comm'n, 124n2
Hoy v. Presbytery of Tropical Fla., 130n59
Hunt v. Finegan, 86n57

Inglish Interests, LLC v. Seminole Tribe of Fla., Inc., 190n30

Jones v. Pensacola, 85n20
Jones v. Wolf (Ga. 1979), 132n67
Jones v. Wolf (U.S. 1979), 124n4
Jourdain v. C.I.R., 188n27

Kedroff v. St. Nicholas Cathedral of Russian Orthodox Church in N. Am., 124n4

Larson v. Presbytery of S. Fla., 130n59
Lewis v. Seventh Day Adventists Lake Regional Conf., 133n73
Lobo v. Miccosukee Tribe of Indians of Fla., 190n30
Longo v. Seminole Indian Casino-Immokalee, 190n30
Lovermi v. Miccosukee Tribe of Indians of Fla., 191n34

Malichi v. Archdiocese of Miami, 127n33
Malicki v. Doe, 125n8
Mandel v. Miccosukee Tribal Gaming Agency, 191n34
Mansour v. Islamic Educ. Ctr., 141n122
Maryland & Va. Eldership of Churches of God v. Church of God at Sharpsburg, Inc., 132n67
Meisels v. Uhr, 140n110
Meltzer v. Board of Pub. Instruction of Orange Cnty., Fla., 125n9
Miccosukee Tribe of Indians v. Napoleoni, 190n30
Miccosukee Tribe of Indians of Fla. v. Cypress (S.D. Fla. 2015), 189n27
Miccosukee Tribe of Indians of Fla. v. Cypress (11th Cir. 2015), 189n27
Miccosukee Tribe of Indians of Fla. v. Kraus-Anderson Constr. Co., 193n52
Miccosukee Tribe of Indians of Fla. v. Lewis, 189n27
Miccosukee Tribe of Indians of Fla. v. South Fla. Water Mgmt. Dist., 187n27
Miccosukee Tribe of Indians of Fla. v. United States (2000), 193n50
Miccosukee Tribe of Indians of Fla. v. United States (2013), 187n27
Miccosukee Tribe of Indians of Fla. v. United States Dep't of Justice, 189n27
Miccosukee Tribe of Indians of S. Fla. v. Bermudez, 190n30
Midrash Sephardi, Inc. v. Town of Surfside, 126n9
Mills v. Baldwin, 126n10
MMMG, LLC v. Seminole Tribe of Fla., Inc., 190n30
Moe v. Confederated Salish and Kootenai Tribes of Flathead Reservation, 185n18
Mudd v. White, 104n18

New Jerusalem Church of God, Inc. v. Sneads Cmty. Church, Inc., 133n74

Partin v. Tucker, 138n103
Perry v. Seminole Tribe of Fla., 190n30
Plains Commerce Bank v. Long Family Land & Cattle Co., 192n40
Presbyterian Church in the U.S. v. Mary Elizabeth Blue Hull Mem. Presbyterian Church, 138n103
Presbyterian Church (USA) by Presbytery of Central Fla. v. Herrero, 131n60

Rekas v. Polish Nat'l Catholic Church, W. Diocese, 133n75
Robbins v. Florida Conf. Ass'n of Seventh Day Adventists, 126n9
Rolle v. Judge, 138n101
Rosenberger v. Jamison, 136n90

Sanderlin v. Seminole Tribe of Fla., 190n30
Scott v. Illinois, 192n40
Seminole Tribe of Fla. v. Ariz, 190n30
Seminole Tribe of Fla. v. Butterworth, 185n20
Seminole Tribe of Fla. v. Florida, 185n23
Seminole Tribe of Fla. v. McCor, 190n30
Seminole Tribe of Fla. v. Schinneller, 190n30
Seminole Tribe of Fla. v. State of Fla., 186n23
Seminole Tribe of Fla. v. United States, 185n23
Serbian Eastern Orthodox Diocese for the U.S.A. and Canada v. Milivojevich, 125n8
Sherman v. Red Bay Stronghold Fdn., 183n13
Southeastern Conf. Ass'n of Seventh-Day Adventists, Inc. v. Dennis, 133n73
Spivey v. Teen Challenge of Fla., Inc., 141n119
St. John's Presbytery v. Central Presbyterian Church of St. Petersburg, 124n5
State v. Wilson, 156n27
Stephens v. Orman, 86n56
Stewart v. Preston, 76n293

Talton v. Mayes, 191n38
Tamiami Partners, Ltd. v. Miccosukee Tribe, 191n34
Tamiami Partners, Ltd. by and through Tamiami Dev. Corp. v. Miccosukee Tribe of Indians of Fla., 185n23
Towles v. Roundtree, 86n57
Townsend v. Teagle, 132n67
Trustees of the Internal Improvement Fund v. Bailey (1862), 86n56

Trustees of the Internal Improvement Fund v. Bailey (1863), 86n57
Turner v. Turner, 140n109

Umberger v. Johns, 138n102
United States v. Arredondo, 27n99
United States v. Billie, 189n27
United States v. Bryant, 192n40
United States v. Clarke, 27n99
United States v. Jim, 187n27
United States v. Jones, 109n58
United States v. Long, 108n57
United States v. Percheman, 27n99
United States v. Perkins, 105n31
United States v. Wheeler, 104n22
United States v. Wiggins, 27n99
United States v. Zacherle, 192n42

Walker v. Board of Pub. Instruction for Broward Cnty., Fla., 156n28
Ward v. City of Miami, 163n139
Watson v. Jones, 124n4
Wheeler v. Reynolds, 104n20
Wier v. Session, Second Presbyterian Church of Fort Lauderdale, Fla. (1998), 131n61
Wier v. Session, Second Presbyterian Church of Fort Lauderdale, Fla. (2002), 131n61
Word of Life Ministry, Inc. v. Miller, 135n84

Yulee v. Canova, 86n56

General Index

Admission to the Bar
  Armed Forces, 105n37
  Negro Municipal, 149–50
  Territorial Florida, 63
  Tribal, 175, 179–80
Alternative Dispute Resolution
  Religious Organizations, 110, 111, 113, 115, 122, 123
  Spanish Florida (Second Period), 20
  Territorial Florida, 69n112
Appeals
  Armed Forces, 100–102
  British Florida, 32–33
  Confederate Florida, 82
  Religious Organizations, 113, 115, 116
  Spanish Florida (First Period), 13
  Spanish Florida (Second Period), 20
  Territorial Florida, 55, 55–56, 57
  Tribal, 176, 178
Attorney Ethics
  Negro Municipal, 149
  Territorial Florida, 63
Attorneys General
  British Florida, 42n73

Choice of Law
  Religious Organizations (religious or secular), 123
  Territorial Florida (American or Spanish), 51, 62–63
  Tribal (common law or customary law), 174–76, 178–79
Civil Disputes
  Armed Forces, 108n37
  British Florida, 30, 32
  Confederate Florida, 81, 82–83
  Religious Organizations, 110–11, 113–14, 116–23
  Spanish Florida (First Period), 13
  Spanish Florida (Second Period), 19–20
  Territorial Florida, 50, 54, 55, 56, 61–63
  Tribal, 179, 191n34
Civil Law
  Rejected in Florida, 46
Colonial Administration
  British Florida, 28–29
  Spanish Florida, 9–11, 16–17, 21–22
  Territorial Florida, 43–45, 51–53, 63–64
  Tribal, 166–73
Common Law
  Adopted in Florida, 46
Constitutions
  Confederate, 78
  Florida (1861), 78
  Florida (1865), 84
  Florida (1868), 84
  Florida (1968), 108n54, 123, 125n9
  Religious Organizations, 114, 118
  Spanish (Cádiz), 17, 21, 65n27
  Tribal, 171, 175, 178
  United States
    Article I, section 8, clause 4 (naturalization), 69n118
    Article I, section 8, clause 14 (armed forces), 105n33
    First Amendment, 111, 114, 118–22
    Fifth Amendment, 51, 96, 191n38
    Sixth Amendment, 51
    Fourteenth Amendment, 125n8
Courthouses
  Armed Forces, 94, 108n56
  British Florida, 30
  Negro Municipal, 144, 153
  Territorial Florida, 59
  Tribal, 175, 179

Court Officials
Armed Forces, 99
British Florida, 35
Confederate Florida, 80
Negro Municipal, 146
Religious Organizations, 112
Spanish Florida (First Period), 11
Spanish Florida (Second Period), 17–18, 20
Territorial Florida, 58–59
Tribal, 178, 179
Court Records
British Florida, 28
Confederate Florida, 79
Negro Municipal, 148
Religious Organizations, 110, 116, 122
Spanish Florida (First Period), 15–16
Spanish Florida (Second Period), 16–17, 19–20
Territorial Florida, 51, 61, 62
Tribal, 173–74
Courts
Armed Forces
Article 32 Investigations, 96–99
Court of Appeals for the Armed Forces, 101–02
Court of Criminal Appeals, 101–02
Courts-Martial
Drumhead, 105n36
General, 96
Special, 95–96
State, 105n35
Summary, 95
Military Commissions, 90–92
Notable military trials in Florida, 90–94
British Florida, 29–30
Confederate Florida, 78–83
Negro Municipal, 143–44, 149–53
Religious Organizations, 111–22
Spanish Florida (First Period), 9, 11–12
Spanish Florida (Second Period), 18
Territorial Florida
Circuit Courts, 55–56
County Courts (1821–22), 49–51
County Courts (1822–45), 56–57
District Courts, 46–49
Municipal Courts, 57
Superior Courts, 54–55
Transfer of cases to state courts, 64
Tribal, 166, 173–80, 193n53
Court Sessions
Armed Forces, 94, 102
British Florida, 30, 32
Confederate Florida, 80, 81
Negro Municipal, 148
Territorial Florida, 54
Criminal Law
Armed Forces, 90–94, 99, 102, 104n21
British Florida, 30, 32, 33
Confederate Florida, 81–82
Negro Municipal, 147–49
Religious Organizations, 111
Spanish Florida (First Period), 13
Spanish Florida (Second Period), 19, 20
Territorial Florida, 50–51, 54, 55, 56–57, 59–61
Tribal, 176, 179

Evidence
Armed Forces, 94, 97, 98, 99
Confederate Florida, 82
Negro Municipal, 150
Religious Organizations, 112–13
Spanish Florida (Second Period), 18
Territorial Florida, 57, 59
Tribal, 174

Family Law
Religious Organizations, 123–24
Tribal, 179

Jails
Armed Forces, 104n21, 105n35
British Florida, 30
Negro Municipal, 147, 153
Territorial Florida, 61
Tribal, 176
Judges
Armed Forces, 99
British Florida, 33–35
Confederate Florida, 78–81
Negro Municipal, 144–47, 150–53
Religious Organizations, 112
Spanish Florida (First Period), 9–11, 12–13
Spanish Florida (Second Period), 17–19, 45–46
Territorial Florida, 46–48, 57–58
Tribal, 175, 177, 178–79
Judicial Ethics
British Florida, 33, 34, 35

Negro Municipal, 151
Spanish Florida (First Period), 13–14
Territorial Florida, 47
Tribal, 178, 180
Juries
Armed Forces, 96–97, 99–100
British Florida, 32
Confederate Florida, 82
Negro Municipal, 147
Territorial Florida, 48, 60–61
Tribal, 174

Land Claims
Florida, 20–21, 53–54
New Mexico, 28n94
Law Books
British Florida, 30
Confederate Florida, 80
Territorial Florida, 55, 64

Maritime Law
British Florida, 32–33, 35
Confederate Florida, 79, 80
Spanish Florida (First Period), 14
Territorial Florida, 49, 54, 55–56, 69n112

Precedents
Confederate Florida, 82
Religious Organizations, 116
Tribal, 174
Probate Law
Spanish Florida (First Period), 14
Spanish Florida (Second Period), 20
Territorial Florida, 48–49

Slavery
Confederate Florida, 81–82, 154n1
Spanish Florida (Second Period), 19, 20
Territorial Florida, 44, 46, 49
Sovereign Immunity
Territorial Florida, 51
Tribal, 172–73

Witnesses
Armed Forces, 97, 98
Negro Municipal, 147, 148, 150
Religious Organizations, 112
Spanish Florida (First Period), 14
Spanish Florida (Second Period), 20, 46
Territorial Florida, 50–51, 59, 60
Tribal, 174, 175

FLORIDA GOVERNMENT AND POLITICS

Series editors, David R. Colburn and Susan A. MacManus

The 57 Club: My Four Decades in Florida Politics, by Frederick B. Karl (2010)
The Political Education of Buddy MacKay, by Buddy MacKay, with Rick Edmonds (2010)
Immigrant Prince: Mel Martinez and the American Dream, by Richard E. Fogelsong (2011)
Reubin O'D. Askew and the Golden Age of Florida Politics, by Martin A. Dyckman (2011)
Red Pepper and Gorgeous George: Claude Pepper's Epic Defeat in the 1950 Democratic Primary, by James C. Clark (2011)
Inside Bush v. Gore, by Charley Wells (2013)
Conservative Hurricane: How Jeb Bush Remade Florida, Matthew T. Corrigan (2014)
The Failure of Term Limits in Florida, by Kathryn A. DePalo (2015)
Jigsaw Puzzle Politics in the Sunshine State, edited by Seth C. McKee (2015)
Making Modern Florida: How the Spirit of Reform Shaped a New State Constitution, by Mary E. Adkins (2016)
Florida's Minority Trailblazers: The Men and Women Who Changed the Face of Florida Government, by Susan A. MacManus (2016)
Florida's Other Courts: Unconventional Justice in the Sunshine State, edited by Robert M. Jarvis (2018)